THERAPEUTIC

THERAPEUTIC GROUP ANALYSIS

BY

S.H. FOULKES

KARNAC

LONDON   NEW YORK

First published in 1964 by
George Allen & Unwin Ltd.

Reprinted 1984 with permission of
the Literary Executor by
H. Karnac (Books) Ltd.
6 Pembroke Buildings
London NW10 6RE

Reprint 2002

ISBN: 0 946439 09 5

www.karnacbooks.com

Printed & Bound by Antony Rowe Ltd, Eastbourne

TO THE MEMORY OF
KILMENY FOULKES

Preface

This book is based on twenty-five years of intensive study of patients in psychotherapeutic groups. The attitude is psychoanalytic but the method and technique are new. The background of consideration is the mental matrix of the group as a whole inside which all intrapsychic processes interact. This has a profound significance for psycho-analytic concepts and the many problems connected with them in psycho-analytic practice and theory. In addition the observations now possible in this 'group-analytic situation' gave rise to new insights and theoretical concepts. The relation is a dialectic one. The new situation leads to new concepts, but the present writer was also consciously led to develop this method as a result of new insights. These concerned particularly the growing evidence that what was thought to be biological, is often cultural inheritance. The task was to find a method and theory which would do away with pseudo problems such as biological versus cultural, somatogenic versus psychogenic, individual versus group, reality versus fantasy. Instead we must endeavour to use concepts which from the beginning do justice to an integrated view.

As in the individual field, in psycho-analysis, so in this multipersonal, supraindividual, field, the study of the pathological proved most fruitful, opening the doors to dynamic unconscious forces which are otherwise closed and barred. It is not accidental therefore that observation and discovery in the therapeutic group are of special significance. Group-Analysis as here conceived, should prove a contribution to a truly social, transpersonal psychopathology and transcultural anthropology.

ACKNOWLEDGMENTS

I wish to thank the Editors of the following Journals for their kind permission to include in this book material previously published in their Journals:

Acta Psychotherapeutica: (Chapter 10)
British Journal of Medical Psychology: (Chapters 1, 3, 7, 11, 13)
Bulletin of the Menninger Clinic: (Chapter 15)
International Journal of Group Psychotherapy: (Chapters 4 and 9)
International Journal of Psycho-Analysis: (Chapters 8 and 14)
International Journal of Social Psychiatry: (Chapters 18 and 19)
I also wish to thank the Army Psychiatric Services AMD. 11, for permission to include material from a memorandum prepared for Army use in Chapter 15, and Messrs S. Karger for permission to use material published in Vol. 2 of *Topical Problems of Psychotherapy*, 1960.

These acknowledgments refer to a number of papers previously published which have been incorporated into this volume fully or in part.

A complete list of publications by the author will be found in the Appendix where references will be found to the appropriate chapters.

S. H. F.

Contents

Part I

THE EVOLUTION OF GROUP-
ANALYTIC PSYCHOTHERAPY

HISTORICAL PERSPECTIVE

Historical accounts of group psychotherapy are in abundance. Klapman made a beginning, Corsini a thorough study. Among recent books one by Kadis and others (*A Practicum of Group Psychotherapy*) and one edited by Rosenbaum and Berger contain extensive surveys, to mention but a few. There is no intention of writing another such account here. Like our history books these presentations are strongly influenced by the writers' various national and doctrinal affiliations and personal bias, prejudices and involvements.

As this book is about my own work, all I will try to do is to put this in some sort of perspective. I will focus on the situation as it existed at the time of my first publications, that is, roughly, on the first five years of development, out of the twenty-five years here reported. Before doing so I should like to make a few quite subjective and personal observations. I became a medical student knowing that I wanted to be a psychiatrist. I was greatly stimulated by the books of Jaspers, Gruhle and others, but soon found my way to the work of Freud. Since then (1919) I knew that the precise name of what I wanted to be was a psychoanalyst.

I chose to have a thorough training in Medicine, Neurology (with Kurt Goldstein) and of course Psychiatry (Kleist, Wagner-Jauregg, Pötzl). This was valuable experience, the more so as I observed wherever I was and whatever I saw with the eyes of the psychopathologist.

In the mid-'twenties I came across one or two papers by Trigant Burrow which must have made a deep impression on me. They put the idea of group analysis as a form of treatment into my mind. There were other influences in the air at that time: apart from plays like *Six Characters in Search of an Author* by Pirandello, I remember being greatly impressed by Maxim Gorki's *The Lower Depths* (*Nacht-asyl*)—quite recently revived in London. Here was a play without a hero, a leaderless group on the stage, driven by strong, anonymous forces. I pondered about the pathogenic and therapeutic power of the theatre and of everyday life.

Fifteen years elapsed between this first germinal inception

and my first actual experience with a group. This took place under quite different circumstances, early in World War II, but in private, civilian practice in Exeter. After the first session held in a waiting room at 23 Dix's Field I went home to my late wife and said to her 'a historical event has taken place in psychiatry today, but nobody knows about it'. I remembered Trigant Burrow—nobody else did at the time—but I did not know then that he had never practised group analysis as I understood it and in the light of later closer acquaintance I think somewhat overestimated the range of his work. I did know, though, that he had come to consider psychoneurosis as a faulty biological development of the human species and called his system now 'phylo-analysis'. Thus I felt free to call what I was doing 'Group Analysis', the first to have used this term since Burrow.

Of Wender's and Schilder's work in the USA I knew only from hearsay. Social psychology hardly existed, there was no work on small groups and no method of approach to them whatever, to my knowledge. Psycho-analytic contributions to cultural anthropology—with a few exceptions—fell lamentably short, partly through ignorance of the subject, more so through the onesidedness and bias, largely unconscious, of the psycho-analysts. Freud's work had always been in the centre of my interest. As a psycho-analyst I adhere to the classical line of approach. Otherwise in applying psycho-analytic knowledge to psychotherapy I keep an open mind towards all innovations and all criticism from whatever quarter they may come. My interest in work in the group situation arose from my own observations with psycho-analytic patients, and from my particular interest in theoretical problems. I am convinced that this work is the best method to make the revolutionary discoveries of psycho-analysis effective on a broader front both in therapy and in teaching. Moreover, that the study of mental processes in their interaction inside the group-analytic situation will teach us much that is new and help to solve theoretical, conceptual problems which are self perpetuating in the psycho-analytical situation. Therapeutic group analysis is the foundation upon which a new science of psychotherapy can rest. For myself I have always looked upon psycho-analysis in the light of life as a whole and not upon life from the perspective of the analytical couch.

Now to a more objective account. A word about the great pioneers of individual psychotherapy in modern times, Freud,

Jung, Adler, and the significance of their work for group psychotherapy might be indicated. About the importance of psycho-analysis this whole volume bears witness.

Freud's explicit contributions, e.g. 'Group Psychology and the Analysis of the Ego' are not really relevant. He uses the group model in order to illustrate the operation of processes as revealed in the analysis of the individual patient in isolation. *Jung*, more than Freud even, was greatly concerned with the collective and archetypical unconscious. He and those close to him appear to have disliked the idea of 'group treatment' but I have met a number of Jungians amongst the younger generation in London who showed particularly good understanding for a group dynamic analytical approach. *Adler*, it is true, stressed the community and saw the individual's relationship to it in perspective. He may well have held occasional group discussions or even therapeutic meetings with a number of mothers at child guidance clinics, as is reported, or on similar occasions. But to proclaim him posthumously as a group psychotherapist is not justified. Nowhere, to my knowledge, did he put the group, the social interactional network into the centre of either his method or theory. Had he done so, Adler could have made a great contribution at the time. As it was, he extolled the individual as the indivisible entity, as a reaction to psychoanalysis, which had taken the individual to pieces in order to look into his inner working mechanics, and correspondingly refuted Freud's interpretations and method.

Trigant Burrow did put the group into the centre of his orientation. That was and remains his great merit. He built up on Freud and Jung—so far as their work went at the time—but hardly mentions Adler, though Burrow's emphasis on the disastrous human obsession with the 'I-persona' is reminiscent of the latter's orientation.

Group psychotherapy can be practised with or without an analytic orientation. We are here only concerned with the latter. In order to make clear what had been done before the present method made its appearance the best way is to indicate shortly *what different authors actually did* in their work with groups.

Trigant Burrow lived with a number of closely connected colleagues and co-operators and they seem to have spent a number of years together, living together in the same campus in a sense analysing each other mutually and partly collectively under his guiding influence. Study of tensions which could be demonstrated in physiological, measurable, objective terms occupied more and more a central position. These are understood as an expression of a phylic aberration of the human species, as a result of which the individual is vitally ill at ease, desperately and defensively concerned with his ego identity. No therapy is possible, only the whole species could overcome its faulty development. I am not sure that this short account conveys sufficiently an orientation which has led to some profound insights and formulations. Enough has been said, however, to make it clear that we are dealing with a totally different approach from the one described in this book.

Louis Wender applied a class method, using his own psychoanalytical experience and skill, interpreting individual psychopathology and stimulating some mutual experiences and exchanges in small sub-groups. In a session which I attended, still in 1949, we were seventeen in the classroom, Wender in the position of the teacher in front.

Paul Schilder never exceeded five patients in a group and did not yet dare to mix sexes. All the patients had been intensively analysed by him individually beforehand over a number of years. Questionnaires were used, case notes presented in turns and interpretatively discussed. He found these groups useful in particular for the analysis of ideologies, on which he wrote interestingly.

S. R. Slavson became known at the time for his work in activity groups with children and adolescents. This was alive and original. His analytic approach to groups, which he cultivated later, was largely theoretical, the absence of the experience of the psychiatrist and psycho-analyst being noticeable. Slavson has considerable merit as an organizer and editor. He adheres strictly to psycho-analytical concepts. These have absolute validity, being merely modified, inevitably, by the group situation. Slavson writes precisely and tends to make dogmatic pronouncements.

Following on Schilder's and Wender's publications *Alexander*

Wolf began practising group psychotherapy of a psycho-analytic type in the US A. He published his experiences in 1949 and has since made many valuable contributions. His work has influenced many group psychotherapists in the US A. It is rather a prototype for the application of psycho-analytical principles in a group setting, as it grows from individual treatment, when the analysis of dreams, transference, resistances, etc., appears not substantially affected by the group situation. Like Schilder's, Wolf's patients joined the group after more or less intensive individual preparation, as a result of which a 'special relationship' with the therapist was established, even explicitly—e.g. patients' surnames and fees were kept confidential. Groups met three times a week, sometimes with two or three additional 'alternate' sessions—without the therapist—with a membership as large as eight to ten. Emphasis appears to be on transference in the family model and on the orthodox aspects of the therapeutic process.

Group constellations and interactions were used much in the sense of the present writer's 'mirror reaction'. A peculiar feature was the working through in different phases, e.g. dreams, transference, resistance, etc., under the therapist's directions. This is difficult to reconcile with a psycho-analytic or a group-analytic attitude as understood here, where the absence of direction and control in so far as patients' productions are concerned is essential. There is also a good deal of didactic activity on the part of the therapist apparent, although this would perhaps not be recognized as such. I have gone into this method at some length, because it is instructive by way of contrast to the group-analytic approach described in this volume (see specially Part V).

Theoretically Wolf speaks, even now, of the 'mystique of group dynamics', unaware that he is working—willy-nilly—with the psychodynamics even in his own type of group. The group-analytic point of view is the opposite: it considers that all psychodynamics are originally multipersonal, at the very least two-personal, refer ultimately to the group (tribe, family, community, species) and are thus primarily group phenomena. The difficulty here is partly semantic, in that the term group dynamics is in the US A associated with the work of K. Lewin and his followers, but more fundamentally due to our upbringing in a psychology which was based on the isolated individual. Since I have become aware of this I prefer to use the term 'group processes' or say explicitly psychodynamics, as used by Freud. The latter insight, namely that psychodynamics are not only interpersonal but transpersonal phenomena goes to the very roots of any approach to group psychology and requires a fundamental turn of mind, for which the undergoing of group-analytic treatment is perhaps the best preparation.

In England *Joshua Bierer* introduced independently a form of group psychotherapy in a mental hospital. His orientation was on Adlerian lines and had no bearing on group analysis with which it was contemporary. He preferred a more leader centred and more 'active' method. Bierer's main merits lie in his pioneering a therapeutic approach to the community of the hospital, including day hospital and therapeutic clubs and in his great flexibility in the use of 'situational' treatment.

Maxwell Jones began with didactic class and discussion methods, but became slowly, after the war, more analytic in his orientation. He devoted himself to social psychiatry and his institutional work in terms of the 'therapeutic community'—as it was now called following the 'Northfield' example—is well known. His attitude differs, however, considerably from that of Bierer.

W. R. Bion had made a mark with his leaderless selection groups. Together with Rickman he confronted a group of neurotic soldiers with their own neurotic behaviour and its consequences. In a later section it is described how these ideas came to fruition and fulfilment in the creation of a therapeutic community, for the first time really conceived as such, at Northfield during World War II. After the war Bion was put in charge of group psychotherapy at the Tavistock Clinic. Like most of his other colleagues there he qualified as a psycho-analyst after the war and was strongly influenced by Melanie Klein. This has a bearing on the type of group psychotherapy at the Tavistock Clinic.

Though this falls after the period here considered a word may be said about its development by way of comparison and contrast to group analysis. The therapist confines himself entirely to interpretations, in particular transference interpretations. These are given preferably in terms of the group. This emphasizes the therapist in relation to the group, which is perceived as if it was one patient. Thus it can be maintained that the analyst functions principally in the same way as in the two-person situation. The group analytic situation appears to have been retained as far as numbers, regular sessions, seating arrangements, etc., go. Whether the situation is as strictly defined analytically I am not so sure, e.g. as regards meetings of patients outside the session.

There was no group psychotherapy in existence on the Continent, but interest began to stir after the war, especially in Holland and France, later in Germany and Switzerland. Apart from direct contacts, the analytical approach in Great Britain reached the Continent largely via America.

In England group psychotherapy has thus been led from the beginning by a number of respectable psychoanalysts and the standard of its practice is relatively high.

Chapter I

GROUP ANALYSIS

A STUDY IN THE TREATMENT OF GROUPS ON PSYCHO-ANALYTIC LINES

(JOINTLY WITH EVE LEWIS, MA)

One of us (S.H.F.) had for many years given much thought to the inherent possibilities of collective treatment. He was, therefore, particularly glad to have the occasion to put his ideas to a practical test. It has not only fulfilled but far exceeded our expectations. While it is an economy of time for the therapist, group treatment of this type actually intensifies the effect and thus shortens the duration of treatment.

We shall report on four groups, two male and two female. Two (M.1 and W.1) were of private patients and individual treatment was combined with group treatment whereas in the Clinic Groups (M.2 and W.2) group treatment was only supplemented by occasional short personal interviews.

It is clear that the therapeutic aim under these circumstances is a more modest one than is the case where a full analysis is possible. To restore the balance of the patient's mind and to enable him to resume a satisfactory function in social, family and professional life within a reasonable period was the task for all practical purposes. This was to be achieved, in so far as possible, through a genuine change in mental economy, based therefore on a lasting foundation. This is not a small claim, but group analysis can and does meet it. Under favourable conditions the patient is enabled to work out the stimulus received, to solve his conflicts in a way better adjusted to reality than he has done hitherto and to derive benefit far beyond the immediate improvement. There are many side aspects exceeding the merely therapeutic aim into which we cannot enter here, but we would like to mention the educational value of such treatment. The concrete realization of the part which social conditions play in their troublesome problems, the social front of inner conflicts, so to speak, sets people thinking in a critical way and makes them experience the part they themselves are playing, both actively and passively, as objects as well as instruments of these conditions—an altogether desirable contribution to their education as responsible citizens, in particular of a free and democratic community.

Our observations refer to four different groups of patients, two composed of men, two of women. The numbers attending varied from five to ten people at a time, the average in individual groups being about five in one and nearer eight or ten in another. Some patients formed part of the group from the beginning; others participated for shorter periods and their places were taken by new people. The actual number of cases upon which these observations are based was about fifty. The optimum for a group would seem to be in the neighbourhood of eight, with a bias in favour of a slightly larger rather than a smaller number. A larger group can easily carry a few people who, for some reason or other, are inhibited; a smaller group is more dependent upon all the members being active. In regard to the fact that the sexes were kept separate, it can be stated that there appears to be no objection in principle to having mixed groups. We have, indeed, the impression that some people of each sex would actually benefit from a closer contact with the problems and views of the opposite sex. But so far the experiment has not been made, as the possible difficulties appeared so great that it was felt to be undesirable to add any unnecessary complicating factor. It can, however, now be stated that no difficulties have arisen which could not be dealt with inside the group itself whilst they were still germinating.

The groups met once a week for a period of an hour and a half. Most of the patients in M.1 and W.1 were also seen privately at the rate of once or twice a week. In most instances attendance at the group was in place of one hitherto private appointment. In the two Clinic groups, the group took the place of individual treatment. Patients were then seen individually in turn about once a fortnight or once in three weeks, or when they had anything very personal to discuss. In this form the group proved at the same time valuable as a kind of clearing station for revision of diagnosis and medical treatment.

Since patients were free to attend for as long as they chose and as regularly or irregularly as they wished, they arranged the period of their treatment to suit their individual needs. All of them were greatly interested, and for many it appeared to have a kind of fascination. Even after they felt no further need for attendance, they still continued to look in from time to time or returned for a short period if they had encountered some slight setback for some reason. ('Open' groups in later terminology.)

We conducted the groups principally together. This is a luxury arrangement which we can, from our experience, highly recommend where it can be had. As it happened, M.2 was for the most part conducted by S.H.F. alone during the last half year, and w.2 by Mrs Lewis alone during that period. Actually this simplified the conducting, but certain transference reactions come better into play when two analysts of different sexes are present.

TYPE OF CASE

The cases covered the whole range of the usual material of the nerve specialist. Diagnostically: all forms of psychoneuroses; psychopathies; a good proportion of mild psychoses, but also more acute psychotic conditions; and organic cases responding to psychotherapy, e.g. epilepsy, epileptiform and choreiform syndromes.

SELECTION

Neither diagnosis nor the symptom picture were considered as a selective principle. The decisive points, apart from practical considerations were (a) whether the patient's personality and condition as a whole would seem to qualify him for the group; (b) whether he had reached a stage in his personal treatment favourable to his inclusion, so that he might be expected to benefit thereby; (c) whether, from the point of view of the group, there were or were not peculiarities in his situation, person or condition which might disturb it; (d) his own reaction to the proposal, not merely his declared attitude, but also his emotional reaction, which naturally might completely change after further analysis. In the main patients had had individual analysis before being admitted to a group, but there were also interesting experiences with several who were introduced to a group without having had any previous personal treatment. It was surprising how readily people took to it, although no persuasion of any kind was used. Naturally the attachment to the analyst, the desire to extend contact with him and to meet him in a freer social situation, acted in themselves as a strong stimulus.

METHOD AND APPROACH

The explanations and instructions given to the patients best reflect our own attitude and approach. They were along the following lines: 'You have some idea now of the kind of mental conflicts and problems which cause your trouble and in which your different symptoms are rooted. You have become familiar with the existence and power of the unconscious mind and with the many ways in which it disguises itself, masquerades as apparently purely physical trouble and you have also acquired some experience with our method of approaching it (free association, interpretation, etc.). You have experienced how things can change, symptoms become modified or disappear, how you yourself have changed. While everything has its individual aspect and can be understood on personal grounds, you may find that you have much in common with other people, however different their symptoms might be from yours. In fact, we are all in the same boat. These are human problems, arising out of the clash between our fundamental impulses, anxieties, and reality: in particular the requirements of the community in which we live, the various prohibitions and restrictions which are imposed upon us from our earliest days and accompany us at every step. While you can freely discuss your own difficulties and bring forth what you like, those of other patients have not only an interest for you but often a direct bearing upon yourself. Many things can be better discussed with and explained to a number of people who can exchange their own views and experiences at the same time. We thus have occasion to touch upon many essential problems which it would take a very much longer time to come across individually. You are invited to join and speak your mind freely. You need not stick to any one point which has been brought up; it is not primarily a matter of discussion and you are not expected to make particularly informed or intelligent remarks. Just bring up anything which enters your mind, on the same lines as in the individual session.'

The emphasis was thus in favour of a kind of 'group-association' method. In spite of this the tendency in all our groups was more in the direction of a discussion circle or a Brains Trust.

When the preliminary period of treatment was short or patients were introduced to the group immediately after the first interview, merely a simple explanation was given as to what took place and how they could help themselves by taking part in it.

As to matters of technique, the basic principles of an individual psycho-analysis hold good, and it can be assumed that the experienced psycho-analyst should find no difficulty in modifying his technique according to the new situation. There are, however, decided differences also. The group reacts as a whole and not merely as the sum of its individual members. The transference reactions of the group as a whole are a different matter from the transference situations of the individuals concerned. We certainly went through periods in which the analysis of collective resistance formed the main part. Reactions between the members are complex and need careful watching. Much skill and tact is needed in interpreting them. The therapist must, of course, also observe the indirect effect which patients' attitudes and communications have upon others. Where possible the actual analysis of these reactions was left over till the personal interview. It is interesting to record that the group in most cases became the centre round which the private interview turned rather than the contrary being the case, but skilled handling soon welds the two together with the result of an intensification all round. We cannot enter here into elaborate rules of technique, details which are anyhow a matter of intuition based on experience.

The individual transference situation changed. In individual analysis, the analyst remains totally in the background as an actual person. The sense and effect of this is that the patient's unconscious phantasies of his parental images, or parts of them, can come fully into play, manifesting themselves by means of transference to the analyst. In the freer situation of the group, the analyst becomes more real as a person. This takes the edge off the transference phantasies as regards the deepest unconscious levels. For this reason, if not for many others, group treatment could not be combined, at least not at the same time, with full psycho-analytic treatment. These deep unconscious phantasies nevertheless become effective, but they cannot be expected to become fully conscious, that is, in other words, transference cannot be fully analysed in the group. Thus transference reactions are kept in more moderate proportions, nearer to the reality level which is all to the good when a comparatively more superficial readjustment is intended.

The present writers preferred to keep their own 'personalities' in the background, so as to come close to the analytic situation.

However, what is sauce for the goose is sauce for the gander: while the analyst is more exposed, he is freer to encourage here, by a nod or a smile, to quell there, bring out a theme more clearly or let another fall away. His role is somewhat similar to that of a conductor directing an orchestra. But he maintains his fundamental position as an analyst by using his power not for influencing the patient's decisions and actions in life itself but merely for the purpose of analysis.

There is no objection to the analyst behaving like any other member of the group, relating his own experiences, stating his own associations. Our experience points to caution in this. All the groups seemed to prefer to leave the analyst in a position of authority and to make him the representative of the ideals by which they wanted to be guided. Again following analytic principles, we felt that, within limits, they should be allowed to do so.

QUALIFICATIONS OF THE PSYCHOTHERAPIST

Naturally anyone who wants to conduct a group on analytic lines should himself be a well-trained psycho-analyst, as much in the interest of the group as in his own. Considerable experience in psychiatry is indispensable, a sound knowledge of medicine, biology, sexuology, sociology, folklore, etc., is highly desirable. If the therapist has formed a concise and comprehensive view of the interrelationship between 'mental' and 'physical' manifestations, so much the better, as he will be up against these questions at every step. The same is true of questions concerning religion, the spiritual and the supernatural.

Given these preconditions, the conducting of these groups is a fascinating experience. It is a source of unending information and stimulation, at the same time, a tool of great potency and very wide application. It needs very little imagination to perceive the range of such a group, especially as it is so flexible. One may safely predict that it might well become one of the indispensable institutions of the psychotherapy of the future.

The widest possible range of themes came up for discussion; not once, taking all the groups together, was there a repetition of subject. A random selection shows the following topics of discussion: fear of becoming insane, of losing control, headaches, menstruation, phobias (of spiders, insects, cattle, bats, etc.), street anxiety, birth, babies, food, education, children and parents, traumatic experiences, dreams, symbolism, relations of the sexes, marital relations, superstitions, the inter-relation of the mental and physical, revenge, compulsion, homosexuality, religion, hair and head, inner objects, hypo-chondriacal manifestations, sleep. Each of these subjects was the centre of discussion for the best part of one whole session, though many subsidiary matters were also raised. An equally varied number of topics arose from requests for information, and it is truly astonishing how great a thirst for knowledge is shown, what information is desired, and how high a level of attention the discussion, in simple terms, of abstract philosophical subjects commanded. S.H.F. was particularly struck by this fact in the group 2, composed of labourers, skilled artisans and clerks. At the same time, unconscious material, arising from so-called deep levels, made no small contribution side by side with the everyday problems which are associated with habits, attitude to work, superiors, inferiors, embarrass-ments, social inhibitions, hobbies, etc. All of these led to a lively exchange of views. Just as animated was the relating of experiences in current events—in the Army or at Dunkirk, in air raids, especially immediate reactions to the blitz upon Exeter. The analysis of ideologies from all levels is important. The whole attitude towards health and disease, towards nervous and mental afflictions in particular, was naturally under constant review, both implicitly and explicitly.

THERAPEUTIC EFFECTS

In general it can be stated that these were very good. There was scarcely a case which did not benefit, whilst in a large proportion of the patients the improvement was considerable, sometimes astonishing. Some of the most striking improvements were in the psychotic or mildly psychotic cases. Sometimes an individual would surprise us all by changing his fundamental outlook, perhaps of years or even a lifetime. Yet this reorientation was genuine and sustained. Contrary to what might have been expected, the multiplication of troubles did not have a contagious effect; instead, what may be called the therapeutic level rose steadily. There were occasional complaints in the beginning that no advice was given or that it was all very interesting but would not help immediate troubles. These objections came in particular from hypochondriacs, who insisted upon regarding their symptoms as organic. Nevertheless, they too improved after a while, often with a striking and even dramatic change of front.

The group was also found to be of great assistance to patients nearing the end of treatment or who had discontinued individual treatment altogether. In these cases it served gradually to wean the patient from transference. The type of patient to whom it was found to be especially helpful was the infantile personality who needs continuous support if he is to be able to carry on his daily life with any measure of success. For this type it afforded a permanent focus of support to which they could return more or less at will whenever a setback or other difficulty might occur.

The group sessions supplemented individual treatment by bringing up new material. Symptoms and other expressions of unconscious conflict were shown in many different aspects, as manifested in other persons (mirror reaction; personification). As this effect is a mutual one, the intensification is manifold. The individual's problems fall into perspective, the patient's weakened sense of the obligation to be fit ('defektes Gesundheits-gewissen' of Kohnstamm) may be restored.

SAMPLE OF CASES

We shall give a few sketches of such cases in whom there was a marked effect, without doubt due wholly or mainly to the group itself. There will be a few examples from each of the groups which can be said to give a fair cross-section.

Group M.2

Case 1. A young man who had been discharged from the army because of a nervous breakdown and had reason to fear trouble in connection with homosexual impulses. He had a shocking early history, also studded with mental traumata. He took part regularly for about half a year, then gradually reduced his visits to about once a month. He was in a state of depression when first seen. In the group he spoke freely about things troubling him and sometimes burst into tears. He did not personally touch on homosexual problems, but these were brought up by others once or twice and he listened with marked effect to the various attitudes of the others. He improved greatly, overcame his depression, felt more confidence in his office. His libido turned very definitely towards the other sex. He thinks of joining up again.

Case 2. A man who had been discharged from the army after a state of fugue following Dunkirk. At first scarcely able to speak articulately, reminiscent of a schizophrenic disintegration of language. Attended irregularly over some months. Took great interest and also an active part in the discussion, greatly encouraged by the good reception which his dry and humorous way of presentation found with the others. The improvement in language was striking, he also became much more stable in his mood. This patient, by the way, once recalled and worked out what had been going on during sodium amytal investigation in hospital. He dissolved an unsatisfactory engagement and became engaged again. Took better to work.

Case 3. A number of severe neurotics of the hypochondriacal type improved uniformly in the course of three or four months' treatment. They all attended regularly and had the most lively discussions which they greatly enjoyed. The worst of them, in whom the condition, as with most of the others, was a life-long one, a very intelligent man of about thirty, brought forward most of the material. He also voiced all objections and doubts possible. He was analysed in public, so to speak, in which the others shared, also bringing forward material of their own. This patient ultimately improved beyond recognition, allowed himself for the first time in his life seriously to look at his physical symptoms as mental communications, which he began to understand. He also—rather suddenly—changed his attitude towards work in a favourable sense. He realized a great deal of unconscious goings on in regard to his wife and two boys. In his wake, so to speak, the others turned out to have changed —more or less silently—in the same sense.

Case 4. A compulsion neurotic improved as to his conversion

symptoms and in general ways. His wife—a schizophrenic—
was a patient at the same time in group w.2. They were
advised to make an end to their quite impossible marriage,
which was anyhow not consummated after several years. This
was a good thing for both of them. He did not improve so far
(about three-quarters of a year) as to his obsessional character
but took up more intensive private treatment.

Group W.2

Case 5. Street fears and claustrophobia gradually becoming
more acute over three years. Never kept her away from work
for more than a few weeks at a time, but she could not leave
home even for a single night and could not go to dances, church
or cinema. Suffered from depression, extreme fatigue and
fainting attacks. Was put straight into the group with ten
minutes' preparation only. After two months, during which she
had had sixty minutes' private treatment only, has gained some
insight into the sexual fears which underlie the trouble, has
been twice to the cinema with no ill effects other than a momen-
tary panic on first going in, and has been able to take her turn
(for the past two weeks) fire watching at her place of business.
On some days now feels 'quite her old self'.

Case 6. Extreme depression; impulses to suicide and to 'taking
both children with her'. Violent and continued headaches; fear
of developing fits; extreme fatigue. Paranoid fears about
neighbours. Had been seen alone for a total of four hours
before joining the group and had already told all the above
details. Was a little better. At first group meeting told of
suicide and murder impulses, with strong emotional reaction.
The week following was 'the best she had known for over
eighteen months'. It seemed somehow to help saying these
things out loud to other people instead of fighting to keep
them out of her mind. It was also a help that they didn't think
she was terribly wicked.

Group M.1

Case 7. A young man with epileptiform attacks since schooldays.
There is no doubt an organic component, but under a year's
analytic treatment the underlying, deeply repressed emotional
factors came out more and more clearly. He had now only

occasional attacks during which articulate, if sometimes confused, expression took the place of former screaming and
shouting. There was still total amnesia, but analysis was possible on the basis of accurate reports from the mother. He was
very violent in these attacks, in particular against his mother
whom he implored at the same time to help him. He showed,
even during the attacks, very great fear of his father, when the
latter tried to come near him. There was a strong preponderance
of oral—and in particular anal—sadistic impulses and an
enormous piled-up aggression. Ambivalence towards both
parents was very pronounced, manifestly there was hero wor-
ship of the father and a very tender affection for the mother.
This patient had already very considerably changed for the
better when he first joined the group after a year's treatment.
Now he had again a violent attack in which he threw furniture
about and beat his mother, hitting her badly. He came straight
from this into the group, still slightly dazed, but in an euphoric
state of mind. The analysis of what had happened took two
group sessions almost completely. The group's attitude was
remarkable. They were extremely humane and tolerant, making
light of it without making in the least fun of it. This had a most
beneficial effect upon the patient who thereafter was one of the
most active members. He progressed further very considerably
and has not had an attack since for half a year now. It must,
however, be mentioned in this connection that since the time
of his last attack he lives away from home, a measure which
seemed desirable, in particular in view of a little sister who
lived in the house. He now takes half a grain of luminal very
occasionally when he gets in a state of depersonalization, which
used to be a foreboding of a pending attack, instead of the two
grains which he had to take originally.

Case 8. A schizophrenic who had been a Sergeant Instructor in
the Army and had been discharged because of a 'nervous
breakdown'. He also suffered from a severe stammer. He
became much more stable after some hours' treatment and could
resume his work in an office. He came only once to the group
before leaving. He spoke perfectly fluently and addressed the
group, all complete strangers to him, vividly on psychological
matters, working out for himself what had happened to him
during his private interviews. The group was greatly stimulated
by this experience.

Case 9. By contrast, a neurotic, life-long stammerer, with an unfavourable childhood history has not improved much so far, neither inside nor outside the group.

*Group W.*1

Case 10. Schizophrenic. Violent 'hysterical' attacks with crying and screaming; slashing of clothes belonging to women by whom she was sexually attracted; running away from home; self-wounding. Very inhibited, with much negativism and opposition. After a year was put into the group. By this time I (Mrs L.) was fully aware that her choice of profession (the nursing of sick children) was occasioned by an unconscious impulse to have sexual intercourse with little boys. I was also certain that she had highly sadistic phantasies about children, including killing phantasies and I had tried to elicit these, but with no success. At the first meeting another patient mentioned, by chance only, that she was 'afraid to be left alone with a child in case she should be tempted to kill or injure it'. The patient said nothing during the group but came back two hours later very excited and saying I was trying to drive her mad; that I had plotted with this patient to trap her. In this and subsequent interviews she readily told all her phantasies. There were at first a few more minor acts of destruction, but these have completely ceased for five months, though they had been going on continuously for six years. She has so much improved that she dreams directly of sexual intercourse with children and has been able to see the first phantasy—intercourse with father turned into a baby.

Case 11. Hysteric—hypochondriac—psychotic (?). Came with eczema and sciatica (both organic in origin but varying with her emotional condition). Repressed homosexual—paranoid—bursting with hatred and jealousy. Primary situation: a strong incestuous attitude to the father, completely repressed and compensated for by a strong and solicitous attitude to the mother. Jealousy of brother and sister similarly repressed and turned to devoted affection. She had been under the necessity of repressing all apparent sexuality—did not enjoy any form of beauty, music, literature, art, etc.; hated men—though a highly trained midwife, had managed to reach the age of thirty-eight apparently knowing nothing of masculine genital anatomy or how coitus took place. Treated for a year before joining the group. The immediate result was a considerable loosening in the private interview and insight into her attitude to brother and sister. At the fifth attendance the other patients began to talk about their 'feelings' about fire, water, and Walt Disney's *Fantasia*, especially with reference to the swirls of colour, and their changes in size and form. Each was expressing her own unconscious sexual difficulties. The patient 'felt terribly upset and tense' throughout, and wondered why she felt 'absolutely unable to utter a single word on such a harmless subject'. On leaving, felt 'released and rested' but could not think why. After telling all this at the next private interview, she was silent for about three minutes, then said that she felt she really must face up to the question of sex. She had always been quite certain she had no sexual feelings at all: but somehow now realized that she had: and, moreover, felt able to talk and ask about them.

Case 12. This patient was in a state of rather acute schizophrenia when first seen. Dubious whether she could be treated outside a nursing home. Improvement was very good. In the course of a few months she had changed so completely that she would hardly be diagnosed; found a new appointment in her profession where she worked very satisfactorily. The course of treatment is of special interest in itself. It rested on a very good contact which enabled her and the analyst to understand her inner problems in her own language. Success here was not due to the group, but the analyst had no doubt that it helped matters considerably when she was encouraged to join the group after a degree of improvement had been reached. Every time she enacted the same ceremony: when seeing the analyst in the morning she explained that it was not right for her to attend the group in the afternoon. All the other patients were sincere, were really suffering and wanted to be cured, while she herself was merely pretending, was a fraud. She was then encouraged and told to come in spite of it. She would then come, take an increasing part, helping others by her understanding and making her own confessions, thus benefiting considerably in spite of herself. She recognized in several of the other patients' reports stages through which she herself had passed previously. By contrast to most of the others, she was remarkably frank in acknowledging sadistic trends in herself. Although it has no bearing on our theme, there is an interesting point: she attributed her typically schizophrenic absence of feelings and emotion to having 'deadened' herself. It turned out that she used to masturbate with strongly sadistic phantasies. From a certain moment she suppressed this abruptly and completely, deliberately deadening all libidinal sensations. We could gauge her general improvement very accurately as libido, sensations and emotions returned step by step. She gradually left off treatment when she had fallen in love with a man who was clearly a substitute for the analyst. Transference had not been analysed in this case, had remained entirely behind the scenes as far as the patient was concerned. Her proposed marriage seemed, however, very well adjusted to reality circumstances and she had, moreover, no intention to proceed with it for two years. She has so far fully maintained her improvement and moved further in a desirable direction.

THERAPEUTIC FACTORS

Whereas in group therapy, as much as in any other psychotherapy, the fundamental agents are catharsis, transference and the becoming conscious of the repressed by interpretation and analysis, the factors of identification, counter-identification[1] and projection seem of particular importance.

The group has, however, *some specific therapeutic factors*. We shall mention the most important ones which we could so far discern.

(1) The patient is brought out of his isolation into a social situation in which he can feel adequate. While he can express himself freely according to his own inclination, he can feel understood as well as show understanding for others. He is a fellow being on equal terms with the others.

(2) The patient's realization that other people have similar morbid ideas, anxieties or impulses, acts as a potent therapeutic agent, in particular relieving anxiety and guilt. That other people suffer as well, or even more, acts as a relief; that others break down or show insufficient will power to tackle difficulties makes for resolution to do better. It is easier to see the other person's problems than one's own. Repression and the repressed, for instance, can be recognized when pointed out to others. This

---

[1] Counter-identification: a process by which a person models his own attitude by way of contrast to another person. The term is particularly apt to express the close relation of this process to the mental mechanism known as identification.

acts, however, at the same time as an analytic agent in one's own person. The discussion, interpretation or analysis of such material is, therefore, effective in a number of people at the same time, even if they merely listen to it. A good deal of the therapeutic effect, in particular also relief of anxiety and guilt feelings, is therefore brought about in the position of projection. Apart from counteracting narcissism, forces of identification and contrast are at work here. This whole set of factors we feel inclined to distinguish by giving them a special name, for which we propose *'mirror reaction'*.

(3) The loosening and stimulating effects in a group are in parts also of a specific nature. Many more themes are touched upon and it is easier to talk about them when they have been brought up by others. Something similar takes place on a deeper level so that even deep unconscious material is expressed more readily and more fully. It is as if the 'collective unconscious' acted as a *condenser*. This was exemplified in particular in connection with dreams and symbolism, common phobias and the like. In formations such as symbols which are productions of a collective unconscious, the pooling of associations in a group seems a particularly adequate means of throwing them into relief.

(4) Explanations and information, for which there is a great demand and surprising interest, are of course not peculiar to the group situation, but in one respect there is a significant difference: that is the element of *exchange*. This not only makes discussion more lively and full, but alters the emotional situation, just as children accept many things from each other which they would oppose if they came from their parents.

The factors we have singled out are, therefore:

(1) The group situation fosters social integration and relieves isolation.

(2) 'Mirror reaction'.

(3) Activation of the collective unconscious; condenser phenomena.

(4) Exchange.

SPHERES OF USEFULNESS

From what has been said, the use of the group method for the treatment of nervous disorders is obvious. It can, of course, be applied in hospitals. That it can be applied outside such conditions is one of the points of special interest resulting from our observations. It should be of equally great value in connection with medical cases of a functional or organic order. It might be very useful for the nursing staff of mental institutions or other hospitals as an educational factor. The same is true for medical students and in particular future psychiatrists. The group is an excellent medium for teaching purposes. From the point of view of the psychiatrist or psychologist, it is a source of information and mass observation of peculiar value. It also acts as an observation post and clearing house. Other not directly medical applications are manifold but outside the scope of this paper. Treatment and study of delinquents on these lines commends itself.

INDICATIONS AND CONTRA-INDICATIONS

Its indications are the same as and supplementary to any form of psychotherapy, with the exception of a fully fledged individual analysis. Even there it might have its useful place, but more likely after analysis than concurrently. Wherever possible it should be combined with individual analytical psychotherapy, but it can stand on its own legs, as our clinic groups prove. In many cases it is likely to prove the method of choice.

Contra-indications are few and show themselves individually if each case is considered on its own merits. Our experience so far does not enable us to draw any particular line. Paranoia or strong paranoid features are certainly not favourable and caution must be exercised. Epileptics took well to it in the individual cases which we saw, which were two. Psychoses should not be in the majority. Groups of psychotics only are a different matter. Individual psychotics inside a group of psychoneurotics did particularly well and influenced the group as a whole favourably.

RECOMMENDATIONS

No hard and fast rule can be laid down as to the optimum number of patients, but it must be stressed that it is a group and not a mass treatment. Intimate individual contact with each participant must be fully maintained, even if he is seen only in the group. Whenever possible it should be complementary to thorough individual psychotherapy. Rapid changes in the composition of the group would be contrary to its essential character, and a certain basic continuity is necessary. At the same time, a moderate flow of incoming and outgoing cases is favourable and mitigates the danger of the group becoming stagnant. Fortunately this requirement falls in readily with practical circumstances. As a matter of fact, occasional guests, so to speak, did well for themselves as well as stimulating the groups.

SUMMARY

A new method of group psychotherapy has been described.

The results were very encouraging. A high percentage of complete practical cures were achieved, almost all the others improved appreciably, only very few responded little up to the present. In no case was any lasting adverse effect noticeable.

Conditions, methods, therapeutic factors, indications, are discussed.

ANNOTATIONS TO CHAPTER I

The paper on which this chapter is based was of some historical importance and interest not only in regard to 'Group Analysis' but also to group psychotherapy in general. It is for this reason reproduced here fairly fully. It is particularly apt to serve as a first introduction in this presentation of my work, looking back now on twenty years of developments, just as it was then conceived, quite consciously as a kind of overture to the major themes lying ahead.

The article was based on two years' work with fifty patients at Exeter during the first part of World War II and was written in 1942.

In the groups described in this paper, the individual participants had all had individual psychotherapy before, which was continued at a reduced rate. A typical case would have had perhaps three weekly sessions for a year which were then reduced to one, apart from the weekly group session. In the clinic groups described, on the other hand, the patients were mostly without previous or concurrent individual treatment.

The reciprocal significance of the individual and the group situation was already discovered. The differences in the technical handling in the two situations were clearly understood. The therapist shifted slowly to the group situation as the preferred frame of reference. The specific character of the group situation was appreciated and the principle established to deal with difficulties within the group itself. These first four groups were of one sex, as were Schilder's, but it was already felt that there was no principal objection to groups of mixed sex.

The form of communication was for the first time modelled on free association (group association). Changes in the transference situation, collective resistances were noted and there is a first account of 'group specific factors'. The patients sat round a table. The attitude of the therapist was that of the psychoanalyst but in relation to the group as a whole. At this stage 'combined treatment' (concurrent individual and group psychotherapy) was considered to be the method of choice though the complications arising from this dual situation were not overlooked. Further experience has made still clearer the merits and demerits of combined treatment or group analysis by itself and our bias has on the whole been to leave the group situation uncomplicated while the patient participates in a group.

Mrs Eve Lewis, a psychologist and analytical psychotherapist, readily and with unusual understanding shared in this work and also joined me in this first publication. Cases 1, 2, 5, 6, 10 and 11 are her own observations.

Chapter II

ON GROUP-ANALYTIC
PSYCHOTHERAPY

METHOD AND DYNAMICS

It might be anticipated that different forms of group psychotherapy will be developed according to the individual school to
which the therapist belongs: Jungian, Freudian, Horneyan,
Adlerian, etc. Such a development would overlook the principal
importance of the group situation itself, that is to say that more
than one patient is taking part at one and the same time, usually
a small number between five and ten.

This group situation introduces quite new features of its own,
which are not present in the individual situation between one
therapist and one patient. This is true though the majority of
group therapists are not aware of it at the present time. Group
Analysis with the special features as presented here was first
practised by the writer in private practice and out-patient
clinics in 1940.

The name group analysis is meant to pay tribute to two
facts: first, that it has common ground with psycho-analysis in
its general clinical and theoretical orientation and, secondly,
that is has a place inside group therapy similar to that which
psycho-analysis has inside psychotherapy, from its intensity and
its intentions. There is a risk, however, that the name group
analysis may mislead some people into thinking that they have
to do with psycho-analysis in groups, a sort of substitute or
cheap edition, embarked upon perhaps to economize time or
expense. Being a psycho-analyst myself I particularly want to
emphasize that nothing like this is in my mind. The psycho-
analytical situation which is the essence of psycho-analysis as a
method can only be established between one therapist, the
psycho-analyst, and one patient, the analysand, alone. The
quintessence of psychoanalytic therapy, the analysis of the
unconscious, infantile Oedipus conflict in a transference situation does not permit anything else. Group analysis, on the

contrary, focuses on the dynamics within the group (in between all its members). Its more elaborate designation of 'group-analytic psychotherapy' does justice to both points just mentioned: it is a form of psycho-analytical psychotherapy, and its frame of reference is the group as a whole. Like all psychotherapy it puts the individual into the centre of its attention.

How does group analysis take place? A small number of patients, who are suitable for a common approach, preferably seven or eight in number, assemble regularly, as a rule once a week, at an appointed time and place. The room should be comfortable and of adequate size, seating arrangements are best left flexible, with movable chairs so that all participants can see each other and talk to each other. As a rule members sit in a circle or semicircle, perhaps round a fireplace or a table.[1] The atmosphere is informal and details are allowed to be flexible according to the prevailing circumstances. The duration of each session is approximately one and a half hours. The group may be composed of men, women or a mixture of both sexes.

As a rule there is no other contact apart from this either between patients or between any of them and the therapist. One may keep rigidly to this but experience has taught that the possibility of a personal talk with the therapist alone is better not denied. This can be done either by the therapist making himself available immediately before or after the group session or by setting a special time for this purpose perhaps on a different day. As long as this facility is used with discretion its advantages outweigh possible disadvantages. To avoid contact between patients themselves outside the group meeting entirely is almost impossible; an attempt to enforce such a rule would, in addition, introduce an unwarranted note of rigidity and artificiality into the situation. It is, however, important to avoid that these contacts of patients outside become a cause of leakage or a nucleus of sub-group formation. This can be done by appealing to the understanding of the participants and by pointing out the adverse effects of such occurrences in time. As a rule members become co-operative in abstaining from discussing topics, or individuals, connected with the group or if such discussion has taken place, in bringing the matters discussed back to the group in the presence of all.

Alternatively the group may be *combined* with individual

[1] In later development the circle has become the standard situation (1962).

treatment. This may take the form of a regular appointment once or more a week, or of occasional appointments if and when there is a special request for them.

Two forms of group have emerged and become more clearly defined: the *open* and the *closed* group. In the open group individuals join and leave on their own merits. Numbers can be slightly larger, selection more loose and there is not too much emphasis on regular attendance. The group tends to be more individual-centred and more leader-centred; the discussion perhaps less likely to reach deeper psychopathological levels.

The essence of the closed group is that its participants begin and end their treatment together as a group. Regularity of attendance is essential here. It lends itself well to more deliberate selection according to problems or syndromes. The group can become more truly group-centred, reach deeper levels. This type of group can be run over a predetermined course of time, say three months, six months, a year or more.

Midway in between these two forms of group is what may be called a 'slow-open' group. This is the form groups in practice seem to take on almost invariably when circumstances permit more intensive treatment over prolonged periods, of several years. It is for all practical purposes a closed group in the sense that the participants remain the same over prolonged periods. Individuals nevertheless join and leave in their own right and are replaced. The total duration is indeterminate. For individual patients nine months are a lower and five years an upper limit, the average duration is two to three years. There is emphasis on regular attendance and the number of participants at any one time is fixed and limited to seven or eight patients.

The keynote in group-analytic sessions is informality and spontaneity of contributions which leads to what I have described as a 'free-floating discussion'. The conductor gives a minimum of instructions and there are no set topics, no planning. While he is in the position of a leader, he is sparing with leading the group actively. He thus weans the group from wanting to be led—a desire which is all too strong—from looking upon him as an authority for guidance, for instance, as a doctor who will cure them. The group does not like this, especially a group of psychoneurotics, because it undermines one of the strongest neurotic defence positions. The more the conductor succeeds with this weaning procedure, the more he promotes the active participation on the part of the patients.

Their personalities become more actively engaged and can be observed in action in their dynamic interplay.

What is latent in one person is manifestly stressed in the other. Both symptoms and defences can be observed in action, their meaning and significance are revealed in a living situation. Different attitudes, character and symptom formations are represented by actual persons. The members of the group have to cope with these experiences. Changes are observable directly, and one is not dependent on the self-reflective report of the patient.

The need for understanding and acceptance forms an ever-present stimulus for communication. As to therapeutic factors involved, we find in the first place those that we know from individual analysis: the becoming conscious of the repressed unconscious, catharsis, insight, the analysis of defence mechanisms and—above all—'working through'. But there are also 'group-specific' factors, such as activation, exchange, mirror reaction, active participation, social interaction and communication.

One of the significant experiences a patient can make is that morbid ideas, e.g. obsessions or impulses which he thought were confined to himself, sometimes literally to himself alone in the whole world, are present in that haphazard selection of people he finds in the group.

By way of contrast he observes strange manifestations in other participants towards which his first impulse would be to point out how ridiculous or unreasonable they are, that one must pull oneself together and so forth. What other people would think if they knew about him is what he dreaded most, and most of all unconsciously. Now he is himself one of these 'other people'! In other words, the patient in a group sits on both sides of the fence of a neurotic conflict, a conflict for which his symptomatic disturbances are an uneasy compromise. He experiences either side both actively and passively. He also experiences a change of attitude as disguise becomes unmasked, distortion removed and entanglement unravelled. The patient learns that his troubles as well as those of the others, arise from conflict over basic human needs which all have in common, not only in this particular group but in the community at large. In this process he is greatly helped where other people's disguises make use of the same mechanisms, in particular defence mechanisms, as his own, but equally, where they use quite different ones. In the latter case he has less immediate understanding but is emotionally more detached. He gains a better appreciation of the dynamics of such a display from his more detached position, which in turn helps him where he is more entangled. The processes here described can be directed towards increasing transformation from autistic neurotic symptom formation to articulate formulation of problems which can be shared and faced by all in common. This is a very different proposition from what was first presented: a host of complaints for which one looked to a doctor for a 'cure'. Meanwhile isolation is replaced by social contact, communication is possible even in such matters as were previously considered particularly intimate, private and secret and charged with anxiety, apprehension and guilt; rivalry and competitiveness are replaced by co–operation, imagination about other people's minds, by genuine information based on testing in frank and mutual exploration. Individuality emerges as complementary to the group. Superstition and prejudice give way to insight and enlightenment, insight, more important, gained by one's own living experience made by one's own effort with one's own means. Thus it can never be static again, one has had to change while making these experiences.

A few words may be said here on the conductor's function, without entering into his technique. He is a participant, he observes, has his eye on the group as a whole, as well as on the individual members whom he perceives against this background.

While he allows the group to make him into what they like, typically into an omnipotent father-leader figure, he does not actively assume such a role, but uses it in the best interests of the group, as the group's most devoted servant. While the immature group needs the sanction and support of such a leader-image, that need diminishes with growing maturity and integration. The group analyst makes a significant move by encouraging the independence of the group (and its members) so that they can eventually accept him as a leader on a mature level. This process has great significance in the modification of the superego of each individual.

The conductor must see to it that this coming down to earth is a gradual process borne by the group's growing independence, and does not come as a sudden disappointing disenchantment which would produce bewilderment and shock.

The therapist has to observe and watch the balance between

analytic or disturbing processes and integrative or supporting ones. One of his tasks is to point out, to bring to light and to interpret everything which counteracts integration, as he analyses resistances and defences impeding the therapeutic process.

The group-analytic situation is characterized by the attitude of the conductor, as indicated, with its stress on active participation, unreserved discussion of interpersonal relationships, insight based on the articulation of all contributions as they arise spontaneously without direction or selection. It thus does full justice to the unconscious dynamics.

All sets of therapeutic factors seem to fall into two categories, analytic or supportive. The former are, on the whole, more of a long-range nature and more strictly responsible for lasting change. In their immediate effect they are rather more upsetting and disturbing to the patient. The supportive factors are of more immediate help, relieving, stabilizing, and encouraging. As has been pointed out, both these sets of factors work hand in hand, their favourable blending being one of the important things the conductor must watch and direct. They must be seen as they affect (*a*) any one individual, and (*b*) the group as a whole. They can be set in motion in any one of the following ways, separately or in combination; by action or words directed:

(1) By the conductor towards the group as a whole.

(2) By the conductor towards any one individual.

(3) By any member towards the group as a whole.

(4) By any member towards any other individual or individuals.

(5) By the group as a whole towards any individual member.

The above scheme should be kept in mind for everything happening in group therapy. It refers to effects upon patients and leaves out of account the effects upon the conductor, who is after all an individual member of the group and subject to the same influences. He is the only member of the group who has to observe these processes, including how they affect himself and his own position. For this reason he cannot be fully submerged in the group but has to retain a certain detachment.

The indications for group therapy include all forms of psychoneuroses, such psychotic patients as are approachable, psychosomatic disorders, psychopathies, delinquencies. Its indications are, in a sense, as wide as those of psychotherapy altogether, but in addition group therapy may be said to make a category of patients amenable to treatment who would not respond to individual psychotherapy. As an example of this one might think, for instance, of the favourable effect of the group approach on psychotics, even in deteriorated conditions which has been reported. Indications for group treatment should not be seen as alternative to individual treatment, but rather as supplementary and complementary to it. Inevitably practical considerations also play their part.

In saying a few words on indication and proper selection I shall confine myself to group analysis and to the type of patient for whom it would appear the optimum form of treatment, the treatment of choice. Through inevitable overlap this will include such patients as might equally well respond to other intensive forms of psychotherapy or to psycho-analysis. It must be kept in mind that group analysis is an intensive, deep-going form of psychotherapy. It makes high claims regarding the qualities and training of the group analyst as well as his current resources. I, for one, would not undertake to conduct more than four different groups of patients at the same period of time and prefer not more than one on any day. If one conceives in the future of specialists who will concentrate almost entirely on this work, this programme might be doubled, but I do not think they could do more than about eight groups without losing a desirable standard of work, their freshness, interest and spontaneity. I mention this because indication and selection of patients should be looked upon rather in the light of whether they qualify for and merit such treatment than merely whether they might benefit by it. With this in mind, we might give special consideration to the following conditions:

GENERAL

1. Degree of co-operation; genuine preparedness to take stock and to change (not superficial keenness).

2. Relative, at least potential, stability in character and potential social integrity.

3. Capacity to learn and to gain insight; intelligence not below average, preferably high.

4. Potential social value of individual.

MORE SPECIFIC

More favourable: character disturbances, social difficulties, lack of success in life, inhibitions of all sorts, recurrent neurotic conflict situations ('fate neurosis'), anxiety states, phobias, certain psychotic or psychosis-near states with well-preserved personality (e.g. depersonalizations and some forms of schizophrenia), psychosomatic conditions.

Less favourable: obsessionals, predominantly conversional hysterics, epileptics, perversions, manifest sex disturbances (for instance, vaginism, frigidity, impotence), addictions, deep hypochondriacal syndromes. (All of these can, however, benefit considerably and some of these types can be expected to do very well in specially selected groups.)

Unfavourable: paranoia or pronounced paranoid states, depressions.

A list is, of course, wholesale and too static. The best test for any individual is often the group itself. Much depends on the particular group and the conductor.

This list also envisages out-patient conditions. Inside a suitable setting, corresponding to in-patient conditions, selected groups of psychopaths, delinquents, addicts, can do very well, as experiences in the USA and those of Dr J. C. Mackwood with groups inside prisons, seem to show.

In conclusion of this short survey of group analysis as a therapy, I want to stress that its aims and effects are not those of a symptomatic treatment, relying on relief, reassurance, encouragement, etc., but a laying open and dealing with the very basis of neurotic conflicts and suffering. It mobilizes the 'character basis' (W. Reich) itself and can lead to radical changes of personality or to a considerable modification of it. In this respect it can only be compared to psycho-analysis or similar deep-going psychotherapeutic procedures.

For practical purposes, however, and for a fair assessment of its results, it must be kept in mind that it is very much more economical in time and expense than these long methods. This can be made clear easily if we compare the following: supposing we take two years of psychoanalysis, comprising, say, 400 sessions, as a standard figure, which is certainly not too high, and we assume that the same patient would have two years of combined group-analytic psychotherapy at the rate of one weekly group session and one weekly individual session. This would consume 200 hours during the same time, taking the group session as one and a half hours. As regards the therapist's time, however, 120 of these hours would be shared between eight patients. Thus to treat eight patients at that rate by daily psycho-analytic treatment over two years would take 3,200 hours; by combined group-analytic treatment, which is a very intensive form of treatment, it would take 760 hours. In my experience, by and large, the therapeutic achievement—and I mean genuine and lasting results—in relation to the time spent is incomparably greater in group-analytic treatment. Important as this economy in time undoubtedly is, in view of the vast problem of neurotic and other mental suffering, I want to emphasize once more that this is not, in my opinion, the essential merit of group analysis. The really essential contribution which group therapy, in particular group analysis, makes to psychotherapy is that it adds another dimension to it, thus bringing for the first time the basic social context of human psychology and psychopathology into full view and living perspective.

Chapter III

GROUP THERAPY

SURVEY, ORIENTATION, CLASSIFICATION

Conditions under which modern man lives force him to cope with mass and group problems to an extent hitherto unknown. The totalitarian states themselves make vast-scale experiments in solving these problems. If we want to escape these nightmare conditions, the urgency of scientific studies of the group and of developing techniques to deal with it needs no stressing. Such studies and techniques can be said to constitute for the freer countries of the west the counterpart of the mass techniques of the totalitarian states.

In the meantime the problems themselves are pressing, groups and individuals run into difficulties, they suffer and need treatment. In the psychiatric field, the advent of group therapy reflects this state of affairs and mediates against the price that must be paid by individuals as well as by groups for the greater responsibility which is a condition of greater freedom from state or mass control.

In what follows, I shall try to give an orientation and can do no more than mention a few of the methods used by way of illustration. In so doing I shall speak, for convenience of presentation, about the individual and the group, although I believe that in practice these two can never be separated and should not be considered even theoretically in isolation.

We can broadly classify three more or less distinct categories of group therapy.

(1) Group activities of all sorts, such as arise in life spontaneously or in organized forms. To this category belong religious movements, such as the Oxford Group, physical culture movements, recreational and educational activities, discussion groups and so on. These group activities may have considerable incidental or accidental therapeutic effects which may or may not be used. They are not in themselves group therapy. Some of the earliest work inside psychiatry, such as Pratt's

Thought Control Clinic in Boston, or Marsh's work (see Klapman, 1946), are related as regards the mechanisms involved.

(2) Group activities deliberately arranged with therapeutical intent. Almost anything can be the centre of these activities: music, dancing, puppet shows, dramatic performances, films, art clubs, games, brains trusts, discussion groups, reading classes, and the like. These are occupational therapies in groups. A simple term might help us to decide here when these activities are group therapy. Let us call the group's manifest activity the *occupation*. The group's manifest occupation may be distinct from its hidden or latent occupation or, if you like, its pre-occupation. If the occupation is considered essential, we are dealing with occupational therapy in groups. If, on the contrary, the group situation is considered essential, its occupation incidental, we have to do with group therapy. This distinction must also be borne in mind when we discuss group psychotherapy proper.

It is a factor of considerable importance that the dynamics of all the above-mentioned groups are essentially related to the more strictly psychotherapeutic or analytic groups. If our concepts are correct, they must be able to describe and define the dynamics of these groups as well. *Vice versa*, valid general dynamic formulations should enable us to define accurately the characteristics of the particular group in the therapeutic situation which concerns us.

(3) Group psychotherapy. For group therapy to be group psychotherapy three conditions must be fulfilled:

(*a*) That verbal communication and formulation are the principal occupation of the group.

(*b*) That such treatment does full justice to the individual members and their interaction.

(*c*) That the therapist who has a group before him wants to avail himself particularly of the forces which present themselves in that situation.

I believe that the group-analytic method observes these principles in a particularly pure form, and it incidentally was historically the first to establish them.

Without wanting to give an exact definition, let us bear in mind that in this context we mean by group a smallish number of people in a degree of relationship to each other. This relationship is not too highly organized, but at the same time is not completely unstructured.

All observers agree that such relationships develop, but there are those who think they consist merely in a complex summary of all the reactions which each individual member brings with him into the group. Far from wanting to redefine individual reactions from the group context, they want on the contrary to explain the dynamics of the group on the basis of the well-known and well-worn concepts of individual psychopathology, in particular psycho-analysis. Slavson in his theoretical approach is a good example of this category of observers.

Other observers go a step farther and recognize that the interaction pattern or interrelationship between people is a new phenomenon in its own right. However, if A and B are two persons between whom this interaction takes place, it would appear to me that the presence of a third person C is required if this interrelationship is to be seen in perspective. This third person can compare his view of A with B's view of A; he can see A through B, or B through A, and most important, he can focus on the interrelationship between A and B from outside, which neither A nor B can do by themselves. This model, which one might call the *model of three*, is to my mind the simplest elementary model for the understanding of interpersonal relationships. C represents that new third dimension group observation introduces.

A third group of observers to which I belong feel that they want to focus on the group itself as a common matrix inside which all other relationships develop. Here a distinction must be made between the group that has a group objective and is seen with reference to an outside factor and the *ad hoc* group existing solely to resolve the problems of its individual members, which is looked at in terms of its own changing experience from within.

This view holds it axiomatic that everything happening in a group involves *the group as a whole* as well as each individual member. In what precise way it involves any of them, or even which aspects of each are actually mobilized, is a matter of paramount interest. An unending variety of configurations, including the conductor in his particular position, can be observed. To this category of concepts belongs for instance the idea of a *location of a disturbance* in a therapeutic group.

It is sometimes felt that in talking about a group situation in such a way, one is referring to something mythical or to something which exists only in phantasy. The reverse is the case, for group dynamics lend themselves to exact treatment of a quasi-mathematical kind.

Views that do justice to the fact that the group permeates the individual, has conditioned and is going on to condition the same individual down to the least detail, might be called truly group-oriented views. This social influence is not added to the individual in a superficial or secondary way, but thrusts down to his roots. It being so, a small therapeutic group is obviously a good medium in which to observe and possibly change the reactions of those composing it.

From the very beginning my own orientation was contained in the situation which I established and later on called the *'group-analytic situation'*. This operation is now almost taken for granted. Its principal elements are as simple as they are essential:

(1) The group is literally a face-to-face group. Its arrangement is informal and no procedure of any kind is prescribed.

(2) There is no programme or plan of any kind as to matters discussed. These are allowed to arise spontaneously. The group's occupation is to tell about anything its members wish.

(3) The members are encouraged to voice their thoughts freely. Every contribution is admitted at any time, whether or not it appears to have any bearing on current discussion. They are also given to understand that remarks about each other and about the conductor are free from the usual social censorship.

(4) The conductor's attitude, as distinct from his technique which should arise from his attitude, is an essential part of his approach.

A conductor makes the members of the group participate actively in the therapeutic process. The integration which develops is offset by the impact of new material as deeper levels are reached. This integration is an important and sustaining therapeutic agency. It is, however, important to realize that such integration is not the essential objective of this group. The conductor sometimes, by no means always, allows the group to cast him in the role of leader. In my opinion his position should be variable, so that the group is better able to interpret him as the members wish. Perhaps I can best illustrate this point by recalling that one of my group patients called me 'Puck', although later his vision of me changed and I became the sinister Dr Mabuse. I find that this technique is preferable both from the therapeutic and scientific points of view. These interpretations by the patients have of course no bearing on the true function and objectives of the therapist. The conductor's attitude of dynamic neutrality allows certain basic processes to occur at a primary level, processes seldom if ever voiced in the group, which bear on the superego structure in the psychoanalytic sense. On this level the therapist inevitably takes up the position of a leader or father image, an archetype, to use Sir James Frazer's term. In this deep sense, and only in this sense, I would agree that the psychotherapeutic group corresponds to a family group. If we apply this too regularly to the manifest level, we oversimplify the issue.

It is clear that the analysis of the relationship of any individual to any other, of any individual to the group, or the group to any individual forms an integral part of the group-analytic approach. Furthermore, the immediate present situation is the context in which this happens. The group therapeutic situation itself emphasizes this. I see, however, no reason at all why this occupation should claim a monopoly. If the group focuses too much upon its own processes, this disturbs and distorts those very processes. It then becomes like the centipede which could not move once it thought about how to do it, or like the man with the beard who, when asked what he did with his long beard during sleep, developed insomnia. I believe that the group should have an occupation other than that of self-observation and self-reflection. Immediate engagement is necessary, but detachment also, and even defences must have their play. In the group-analytic group it can be clearly seen that the occupation of the group can oppose the process by which personalities become engaged and revealed. The occupation, even if it is 'discussing one's problems', can be used as a screen behind which to hide problems of more central significance.

That is why the group-analytic group is left to devise its own occupation. The screen is kept transparent as it were and arises as an *ad hoc* response to the latent preoccupation of the group.

Most of the relevant therapeutic and diagnostic factors operating can be looked on as centring in the need for verbal communication. We might describe the route taken from the autistic nature of the symptom to the more and more articulate recognition and formulation of the problem underlying that symptom as an important landmark of the therapeutic process itself. In a sense this is the same as the making conscious of the unconscious; but the group-analytic situation, while dealing intensively with the unconscious in the Freudian sense, brings into operation and perspective a totally different area of which the individual is equally unaware. Moreover, the individual is as much compelled and modelled by these colossal forces as by his own *id* and defends himself as strongly against their recognition without being aware of it, but in quite different ways and modes. One might speak of a social or interpersonal unconscious. Some of these dynamics can be observed under extremely specialized conditions, such as the analytical transference situation.

Analytic orientation means that therapy aims at basic change, change of personality, and not merely symptomatic alleviation. The group analyst does not consider improvement based on support or on the release of guilt and anxiety through sharing and encouragement to be of equal value as these basic changes which can be accomplished. In terms of psycho-analysis the aims are lasting changes in the function of the ego, superego and the distribution of libido; or, as I should prefer to put it, group analysis offers many opportunities and facilities for such changes to occur.

In its pure form this method presupposes a considerable degree of experience and training on the part of the therapist. Its essential principles can, however, be applied to such discussion groups as might be called ancillary group therapy. I have in mind, for instance, such groups as the mothers of children in child guidance clinics or the parents of schizo-phrenic children at the Bellevue Hospital, New York.

I hope I have given some idea of the great range and variety of work which can be done in this field. Psychiatrists have an important contribution to make both from a practical and theoretical point of view. I have also tried to give an outline of some more specialized methods of approach and to apply some perspective to their relative positions.

I would like to conclude this survey by stating that group therapy or group psychotherapy respectively of the kind outlined here can be applied principally to three areas:

(1) To treat particular groups with regard to their specific group problems.

(2) To treat individual problems in their native setting, for

instance, a family group. This is an important area where little work has been done.[1] This would constitute group psycho- therapy in native or original groups. It can be done in the life situation itself, what Moreno calls *in situ*, or in the consulting room.

(3) To treat groups of patients formed for the specific purpose of treatment of individual's problems. This *ad hoc* group is what is usually meant by a psychotherapeutic group. Such a group is transitory in character; it disbands when it has served its purpose. It serves that slow process which has taken many centuries to mature and is comparatively recent in man's history, the emergence of the individual from the common matrix of the group. One can assert at the same time, without contradiction, that group psychotherapy helps to reconcile the individual to the group and to strengthen his roots in it, roots which are often disrupted by the complexities of modern living.

There is an area which throws into clear relief the essential unity between individual and group, an area, to use more conventional phraseology, in which group and individual coalesce and from which they must be dynamically defined. Events in this area cannot be fully understood, unless they are described both from the individual and the group perspective. Group analysis, as I see it, highlights this important area for the purpose of therapeutic operation and scientific investigation.

---

[1] Since then this field has been developed and a number of valuable con- tributions have appeared, e.g. M. Grotjahn. *Psychoanalysis and the Family Neurosis,* New York: Norton, 1960.

Chapter IV

CONCERNING LEADERSHIP IN GROUP-ANALYTIC PSYCHOTHERAPY

This chapter is based on a paper read in January 1949 to the American Group Psychotherapy Association in New York who had invited me to talk on leadership. What they had in mind was really a paper on the therapist's technique in group analysis. For this the term 'leader' seemed to me unsuitable since the therapist does not act as a leader of a group in the usual sense. In addition the term had a political flavour at the time (Mussolini, Hitler). 'Director' would be misleading since in a technical sense he is 'non-directive'. I had already, in group-analytic usage, introduced the term 'conductor'. This allows one to express more specifically when the group analyst acts as a leader and when he does not.

The term 'leader' is used here in the ordinary sense of one who wishes to lead a group to a certain goal, in some respects the opposite of what a good therapist does who sets out to wean the group from its wish to be led. The group analyst does not often function as a leader in the ordinary sense. In thus refraining from leading he shows up, 'by default' as it were, what the group wants and expects from a 'leader'. I used this type of observation from group-analytic experience to throw some light on the idea of leadership. This is here explained as it was not apparently appreciated by part of the New York audience at the time. The paper, nevertheless, deals explicitly with what the therapist-conductor does or does not do in group analysis.

The group-analytic situation has peculiar features which have developed from its therapeutic intentions. Such a group is composed of members who are particularly disturbed in their relationship to other people. When they meet they have no other object beyond that of dealing with their disturbances. They are not given any aim or object, no set topics or programme for discussion. Instructions are kept to the bare minimum. The discussion is completely loose and undisciplined, a free association of ideas which can best be described as a 'free-floating discussion'. Ordinary politeness in social inter-course goes by the board and frank disclosure of mutual feeling, reaction and attitude is encouraged.

The therapist, the natural leader of this group, does not assume active leadership. Moreover, he is not primarily con-cerned with the formation of its members into a good and efficient group. If he were so concerned, he would do the exact opposite of all this: he would give the group a concrete aim, a strong lead, and see to it that the members are well predisposed to social co-operation, and have a high degree of individual and social integration.

This is a peculiar group then to take as a basis when talking of group formation and leadership. Nevertheless, what this group with its very specific features can teach us is valid in other types of group, both from a scientific and a practical point of view. This group throws light on the processes of group formation by emphasizing the disturbances of these processes and on the function of the leader, by default. Let us now say something about aspects which qualify it positively as an instrument of research.

(1) It is a face-to-face group comprising seven or eight patients and the therapist. This proves large enough to observe psychological reactions in their social context. The group is also large enough to be representative of its community. Yet it is intimate enough to trace the ramifications of these reactions in the individual member and to explore their roots inside the individual.

(2) The personalities come to the fore in the light of their mutual interactions. The lid is lifted, as it were, and one gets a full view of that which is usually concealed.

(3) The fact that the group is composed of psychoneurotic and, occasionally, slightly psychotic patients, and that it is concerned with therapy puts emphasis on unconscious aspects and primitive reactions. What is normally latent becomes manifest in this group.

(4) The leader—as will be seen presently—is in a favourable position as a participant observer.

Things are multidimensional in such a group: we can describe them on many different levels or cross-sections. We will select two such levels which form opposite poles of a sliding scale. We will call them the manifest and the latent or primary level.

The manifest level comprises what actually manifestly goes on in this group between the patients themselves and their doctor. It is concerned with adult, contemporary reality. The primary level refers to processes and mechanisms which are predominently unconscious; to primitive, infantile and primordial behaviour. Roughly, these two levels correspond to the secondary and primary processes of the dream.

For the sake of presentation and to introduce some simplifications, we will consider the leader and the group separately, although they are in a state of continuous mutual interaction and conditioning and cannot really be isolated from each other. It might also prove helpful to contrast analytic and integrative processes, although these, in turn, inevitably go hand in hand. Analytic processes have, more immediately, a disruptive and disturbing effect, whereas integrative ones are constructive and supporting.

We shall first consider what happens on each of these two levels, the manifest and the latent or primary one, apart and later take into consideration what bearing they have on each other. Suppose we listen on the radio on two different wavelengths not to two different concerts but to one and the same. Let us assume that we are interested in analysing the symphony—the parts the strings and wind instruments play. We would have arranged our reception in such a way that on one wavelength we hear the string instruments, whereas the wind instruments are only faintly indicated, and on the other wavelength it would be the other way round. We would then first listen in on the one wavelength, then on the other, and, finally on both of them together. This is an analogy of the way in which I propose to proceed.

As far as the group is concerned the two levels we are about to consider also correspond to two basic problems. Basic problem number one, on the manifest level, concerns the relationship to other people in adult life and contemporary reality. Basic problem number two concerns the relationship to parental authority, as represented in the primordial image of the leader, and corresponds to past, infantile and primordial reality.

We have said that, on the manifest level, the therapist does not lead. This is, however, a negative definition. One cannot simply 'not lead'. One must do something. The quality of 'not leading' follows rather by implication from what the therapist does, from the interpretation he gives to his role. What he does and does not do is more in the nature of directing or conducting. In order to differentiate this from a leader role, we shall refer to him on this manifest level as a 'conductor'.

In this way we can say that, while the therapist does not assume active leadership of the group, he conducts it continuously. We shall not enlarge upon the ways in which he does this because this would comprise in detail the whole technique of the group analyst. We can only mention here a few points which are particularly relevant for our present purpose. The conductor keeps in the background as to his person. He follows the lead of the group and makes himself an instrument of the group. Whereas the group is leader-centred, he puts, from the very beginning, the group as a whole into the centre and submits his own function completely to the interests of the group. He sees to it that his function can, in time, be understood to be in the service of the group. He is a member of the group, making his particular contribution. Whenever possible he lets the group speak, brings out agreements and disagreements, repressed tendencies and reactions against them. He thus activates and mobilizes what is latent and helps in the analysis and interpretation of content and interpersonal relationships. He encourages the active participation of the group and uses the contributions of its members by preference to his own. On the analytic side, the conductor's function can thus be compared with that of a catalytic agent.

He treats the group as adults on an equal level to his own and exerts an important influence by his own example. He sets a pattern of desirable behaviour rather than having to preach to the group. He puts emphasis on the 'here and now' and promotes tolerance and appreciation of individual differences. The conductor represents and promotes reality, reason, tolerance, understanding, insight, catharsis, independence, frankness, and an open mind for new experiences. This happens by way of a living, corrective emotional experience.

It can be seen that the conductor thus activates both analytic and integrative processes. Disturbance and bewilderment caused by the uncovering of alarming, new, hitherto unconscious material is counterbalanced by the increased strength of the group as a result of its growing integration. In fact, the energies set free through the analytic process are being used in the service of this integration. We must, therefore, modify our previous statement that the group analyst is not concerned with the formation and integration of the group. While it is true that he is not primarily concerned with it, it is nevertheless of the greatest importance that the group can balance the impact of ever new sources of disturbances through an increased level of tolerance, based on its own growing strength. This is quite apart from the importance of a better integration in its own rights. It is for this reason that the conductor addresses the group, on this manifest level, as if they were mature adults and as if they were, or were to become, an integrated whole.

Besides, in the absence of an aim at integration, the dynamic, group-disruptive, socially disturbing aspects of symptoms could not be brought out. One could say that the conductor aims at a 'tolerable imbalance' between constructive and disruptive tendencies, or upsetting and supporting influences, and that he has continuously to assess their proportion. In other words, he must judge how much new ground can be broken, and on what level, in view of the tolerance attained. This refers both to the individual members as well as to the group as a whole.

It can be seen that this interpretation of the conductor's role puts him into a particularly favourable position as an 'observer' of the group, including himself. He is aware that he could not, in any case, observe a living process without entering into it and exerting influence and change. By being inside the group as well as outside of it at the same time, he can, however, particularly well observe the dynamics of the group including those concerning his own influence.

As far as the group is concerned, each individual member is actively brought up against what I have called for our purposes the first basic problem of social life: his relationship to other people and to the group as a whole. He has to solve this actively. The clash between his own egotistic needs and impulses and the restrictions imposed by the group, as expressed in the formula 'the individual and the group', is replaced by the co-operative formula 'the individual in the group'. More explicitly, the individual learns that he needs the group's authority for his own security and for his protection against the encroachment of the other fellow's impulses. He has, therefore, to create and maintain this group's authority himself accepting willingly necessary modification of his own instinctual impulses. He learns also that, in return for this sacrifice in unbounded activity, he receives the support of the group for his own particular individuality. He is a participant in a double process, dwelling in both camps of this conflict: he must tolerate the wishes and desires of others if his own claims are to be tolerated and he must restrict in himself what he feels he cannot tolerate in others.

This attitude is acquired inevitably, as a result of emotional and psychological processes in interaction, but it can be raised also to the level of an intellectual conviction. This necessary adaptation to reality and the rules of social intercourse is the more acceptable as the analytic process at the same time frees the patient from the anachronistic fear of, and dependence upon, primordial authoritarian images.

That this happens on a manifest level is only possible because the conductor does not play the part of a leader.

In summing up what happens on this manifest level in artificial isolation, we may say: analytic and integrative processes in their interplay bring about a growing-up (maturation) on the part of the group. The conductor makes the group active participants; acting preferably through the group, he mainly contributes as a catalyst and observer; activating analytic and integrative processes, he makes the group stronger. While there is a decrescendo of his own active participation, there is a crescendo move towards integration and self-reliance on the part of the group.

We will now switch over on our wavelength and listen in to the other level.

This is, of course, under usual circumstances, unconscious. It can be made conscious to a degree in group analysis but this will usually happen only in a group who go through rather prolonged and extensive treatment. The correct handling on this level is of greater importance than the degree to which the group can be made conscious of it. The interpretation rests on what is known from psycho-analytic investigations and, in particular, from Freud's *Group Psychology and the Analysis of the Ego*.

In the unconscious phantasy of the group, the therapist is put in the position of a primordial leader image; he is omniscient and omnipotent and the group expects magical help from him. He can actually be said to be a father figure and it is all too easy to interpret his position really as that of a father or mother and see the group as representing a family. This is not my impression. Whereas family transference reactions between the members of the group and the leader can occasionally be seen, the configuration as a whole does not, by any means, necessarily shape according to the family pattern. It is true that the family is a group but not that the group is a family. Group psychology must develop its own concepts in its own rights and not borrow them from individual psychology. The group is older than the individual.

On re-reading recently Freud's book I found, to my surprise and satisfaction, Freud himself as an ally in this. I will quote: 'We must conclude that the psychology of the group is the oldest human psychology; what we have isolated as individual psychology, by neglecting all traces of the group, has only since come into prominence out of the old group psychology by a gradual process which may still, perhaps, be described as incomplete'.

Later on, when Freud talks of the relationship of a single member of the primal horde to the primal father he mentions 'his archaic inheritance which has also made him compliant towards his parents and which had experienced an individual reanimation in his relation to his father'. We can see from this that the group can reanimate this archaic inheritance directly.

However this may be, the group on this level shows a need and craving for a leader in the image of an omnipotent, godlike father figure. We can add now an important feature to our picture of the group-analytic situation: the therapist is placed by the group into the position of an absolute leader—a position which he cannot lose, although one may say he can spoil it. We shall, later on, see that this condition is essential for the meaning and weight of his actions on the manifest level, as a conductor.

The group needs the leader's authority on this immature level. Apart from the fact that individual members can, in this way, approach their individual conflicts with authoritative figures, the group as a whole can thus effect its 'second basic experience', namely the adjustment of the relationship between the leader and the group.

What does the leader in group analysis do on this level? Briefly, he accepts his position in order to use it in the best interests of the group and, eventually, to wean the group from this need for authoritative guidance. What does this imply? First of all, that he must recognize the situation for what it is.

Again, in his position as observer, he is very well placed to study the dynamic deployment of this relationship.

Secondly, he must be free from the tempation to play this godlike role, to exploit it for his own needs, or to take it in any sense personally. This presupposes that he himself does not unconsciously share in this phantasy and need. If he did he would be afraid of accepting it, a not infrequent reason why therapists are afraid of taking on groups. They are really afraid of having to live up to their own unconscious phantasy of a leader which, of course, they could not do. If a leader is fixed by his own character to any part or aspect of this primitive role, he may be quite a good leader in relationship to any group who are in need of just the 'leader type' that he personifies. The situation then becomes fixed in that relationship and cannot move out of it. We then get the different types of relationship which have been so well described by Fritz Redl. In the group-analytic situation we see these types of group-leader relationships as passing episodes in a continuous flow.

The group analyst accepts whatever position the group chooses to confer on him. This means that he does not ever actively assume such a position, or act upon it, nor on the other hand, deny it by word or deed. He behaves in this respect very much in the same way as the psycho-analyst does in the transference situation. He does so mainly for two reasons. Firstly, he must be in a position to give the group the security and immunity emanating from his authority as a leader as long as the group is in need of them. Secondly, he must accept this position as a leader in order to be able to liquidate it later on. He could not wean the group from something which had not been previously established. The conductor, however, is prepared for and, in fact, invites a decrescendo move from his authoritarian pedestal. Here again he behaves passively, he lets it happen. He does not step down but lets the group, in steps and stages, bring him down to earth. The change which takes place is that from a leader of the group to a leader in the group. The group, in its turn, replaces the leader's authority by that of the group.

In summing up as to what happens on this primary level one can say that there is an important move on the part of the group in the sense of its being weaned from the infantile need for authoritative guidance. This is the result of an all-important decrescendo move as regards authority on the part of the leader.

We shall now briefly consider how these two levels interact upon each other.

How does the manifest level influence the primary one? The first point to consider is that most of what happens on the primary level does so by implication from the manifest level. There are two moves through which the manifest level acts upon the primary one, one on the part of the leader, the other on the part of the group.

As to the leader, we see now the full implication of his refraining from active leadership on the manifest level. Only this enables him to preserve his neutrality, as it were, on the primary level. If he were to take an active leading part as a conductor, the group would be bound to interpret the position he takes up as that of a primary leader and confuse him in these two roles. On the part of the group, as we have seen before, there is a growing maturation on the manifest level as a result of analytic and integrative processes. The conductor, by inaugurating and consistently supporting these processes, digs his own grave as a leader, as it were. This growth in maturity and strength on the manifest level brings about the all-important decrescendo move as regards dependence upon, and authority of, the primary leader.

It is more difficult to state how the primary level influences the manifest one. The primary level is entirely latent but, without it as a background, much of what happens manifestly would lose all its weight and meaning. Without having this basic authority at the back of him, the conductor might simply lose all prestige by behaving as he does. The group might be bewildered and anxious, succumb to a hopeless feeling of frustration and interpret the conductor's reluctance simply as weakness and incompetence. In its despair it would look for another leader; not necessarily for another therapist, but worse still would elevate somebody sufficiently vociferous out of its own ranks into the position of leader. He, particularly if neurotic, could be expected to abuse this position and certainly not to use it in the ways here described for the benefit of the group.

The group, to begin with, without the sanction of the leader would not have the courage to inaugurate the analytic process, to break new ground, to test values and accepted codes of behaviour. The conductor's own contribution, explanations, interpretations, questioning of standards, judgments and values would not have the necessary weight; nor would his own example have the necessary significance to modify behaviour. In the clash of personalities under high emotional tension, the members of the group need the immanent presence and protection of a father figure in whose impartiality and justice they have confidence. Nor could the frank disclosures of these interpersonal relationships, often of a highly aggressive kind, come about without the validity of his sanction.

In listening on our two wavelengths together we find that the two levels have a dynamic, reciprocal relationship toward each other: a crescendo move in the maturity of the group and a decrescendo move in the authority of the leader. The crescendo move of the group on the manifest level inaugurates and maintains the decrescendo move of the leader on the latent, primary level. Dependence upon authority is replaced by reliance on the strength of the group itself. The leader furthers the analytic process throughout. This analysis of intrapersonal and interpersonal difficulties liberates energies and promotes integration.

As to integration, the position is rather different. The group borrows, at first, strength from the leader's authority and tends to integrate through him. This preliminary integration rests on immature, infantile grounds and, to a certain extent, counteracts the integration on a mature level, a group-centred integration. In his role as conductor, the therapist supports this group-centred integration directly. Gradually as the group becomes stronger and can integrate better on its own, it is less and less in need of borrowing strength. Once the decrescendo move in the authority of the leader has set in, the weaning from the leader's authority lends indirect support to the positive integration of the group. The conductor while observing this process on both levels, has to direct it in the sense here described, watching the appropriate balance between upsetting factors and the tolerance of the group to cope with them. He thus exerts an activating influence on both analytic and supportive processes.

The group itself provides two significant experiences that correspond to the two levels outlined and which, in turn, interact and mutually support each other. One is adjustment to fellow beings (social adjustment) and to present-day reality, occurring predominantly on the manifest level. The other is the correction of dependence upon authority—in particular anachronistic authority—which is predominantly on the infantile, primary plane.

The group-analytic situation is a valuable tool for psychotherapy and for the scientific study of human beings in a social setting.

It seems of particular importance that the observer avoid the fallacy of transferring the concepts gained from the psychology of the isolated individual, in particular psycho-analytic concepts, too readily to this new field of observation. If he thinks, for instance, in terms of transference of the family group containing father, mother and siblings, of projection, identification, repression, resistance, reaction formation, fixation, and so on, merely in the way they appear in the individual situation, he will find all these, to be sure, in operation; but he will not learn much that is new. If he thinks, however, of the group situation which he has in front of him, he will find a wealth of new observations as regards the dynamics of the group and, indeed, new light will be thrown upon the mechanisms operating in individual psycho-analysis.

The paramount need here is to create a scientific view of group psychodynamics and such concepts that will enable us to understand and exchange each other's experiences and problems by expressing them in a language that is commonly understood. In this way the problems and observations of the group therapist and group analyst become available as immediate contributions to the study of the group elsewhere and *vice versa*. With this orientation in the mind of the conductor, the group-analytic situation becomes the natural meeting ground of the biologist, anthropologist, sociologist and psycho-analyst. In fact it displays the living process as what it really is—a co-ordinated and concerted whole.

The second impression I hope to have conveyed is this: that the spirit in which these groups are conducted and the qualities required on the part of the conductor have an essential affinity to education according to the concepts of a democratic way of life and for good world citizenship.

We have mentioned what are the essential preconditions in the therapist and shown that his qualifications correspond to a desirable type of leader in a democratic community. He must be reasonably secure and reality-prone in his own person. He must have outgrown and be immune against the temptation, however strong, to play God and to use his group for his own satisfaction—that is, he must have solved his own Oedipus conflict satisfactorily. He loves and respects the group and his aim is to make its members self-responsible individuals. He wants to replace submission by co-operation on equal terms between equals. In spite of his emotional sensitivity, he has self-confidence, which comes from modesty, and the courage to lead, which springs from his social responsibility.

When all is said, there will remain a nucleus, not at present further reducible by science, more nearly expressed perhaps by art and religion, bound up with his own personality, a primary rapport (charisma Max Weber called it) based on love, respect and faith. Without these, he cannot awaken nor bind the spell of what the poet called 'the old enchantment'.

Chapter V

OUTLINE AND DEVELOPMENT OF
GROUP ANALYSIS

The following is a summary account of Group-Analytic Psychotherapy emphasizing method as it had developed by 1955.

One might say that group psychotherapy begins when there are more than two persons in the room for purposes of psychological treatment. Three persons may be used as a model for the new dimension thus introduced (the writer's 'model of three') but in practice our group-analytic groups begin to function properly only with a minimum number of five participants and a maximum of eight, the therapist not included. Below five there is not enough elbow-room for group dynamics to develop and above eight there is not sufficient intimacy to do justice to the individual members. At the basis of group psychotherapy lies the conviction that neuroses and other mental disturbances are in truth multipersonal phenomena. This multipersonal network of communication and disturbance is in fact the object of treatment. In group psychotherapy the group of people who are assembled and participate form also the agency of treatment.

On this occasion I propose to work our way up, so to speak, to the group-analytic group in the strict sense. In doing so, we shall compare and contrast three types of group. These three types are all objects—or can be—of a psychotherapeutic approach, and indeed of a group-analytic approach. While they are of interest for their own sake, they throw at the same time light on the third type, namely the group-analytic group itself. Moreover, we shall be able to show that all three types of group can best be understood in their dynamic properties with the help of concepts which have emerged from the study of the group-analytic group. Thus we shall get to know these concepts and their operation and at the same time have an illustration of the general validity of group-analytic observations. We shall therefore first describe these three types of group, shall then mention the relevant concepts, and apply them to the analysis of these three groups and thus arrive at a meaningful presentation of the essential features of the group-analytic group itself.

The three types of group are the following:

(1) *The Functional Group* (The group which has a function to perform). In ordinary life this is a working group, a group of workers with a definite object they wish to achieve, or a team.

(2) *The Life Group* (primary group, root group, miniature community). The simplest type of this group would be the family. However, the group as meant here would comprise people in close relationship with each other beyond family ties, such as friends, teachers, workmates, etc., all of whom are vitally interdependent. If we look at this group from the point of view of an individual patient, it would roughly correspond to Moreno's concept of the social atom, or rather, if we may make a step further in this type of concept, to a social molecule.

(3) *The Group-Analytic Group* (as a model of a psychotherapeutic group). This is a group of independent patients, ideally seven or eight, and a group analyst, who come together only for the purpose of treatment and are otherwise complete strangers.

The first of these three groups, the work group, can be met with in life, be treated on the spot (*in situ*) or be reconstructed in the studio or consulting room. An instance of this latter group is the occupational group in a hospital, engaged in pursuits such as carpentry or painting.

In the second type of group, the life group, we have two alternatives: (1) to treat it in its natural setting (*in situ*); in the case of a family for instance, that would mean at home—as the G P may find himself doing. (2) that we call the participants in person to our consulting room (a variant of this is exemplified in Moreno's psycho-drama, where only one or two of the central figures attend in person, the others being replaced by substitute actors, so called 'auxiliary egos').

The third group can by its very nature only exist in the treatment room, as out-patients in private practice, in psychiatric or other hospitals, and with certain modifications also under in-patient conditions.

We will now shortly mention the concepts which we use and which we find helpful in order to characterize the different group situations and group propositions from a dynamic and therapeutic point of view.

I. THE NATURE OF MEMBERS' RELATIONSHIP

Members in our group type two are, for example, vitally and closely related, often indeed members of the same family; in type one they are more or less closely related in only one particular setting or aspect of their lives; in type three they are totally unrelated except for their meeting in the treatment room.

This refers to pre-existing relationships. The relationships, as they develop in the process of psychotherapy, are also highly characteristic and significantly influenced by the particular treatment ('T') situation which is established.

II. OCCUPATION

This is an important concept. We shall presently see that these groups lie on a scale ranging from their occupation being really or apparently the main point of the group's existence, to the total absence of occupation in the group-analytic group, and we shall consider the consequences arising out of this. Suffice it here to say that the intensity of occupation is in inverse ratio to the concealment or the disclosure, respectively, of the personalities involved and of their relationship with each other. In other words, the presence of an occupation serves as a screen behind which to hide the more intimate and often unconscious feelings of participants towards each other.

III. COMMUNICATION

Group-analytic theory and practice has almost from its beginnings paid special attention to the communication process and has considered it of central importance. The theory of communication has since been furthered by the work of Ruesch and Bateson and the more recent work of Ruesch, Masserman and others. Communication can be verbal and non-verbal, conscious and unconscious. The latter is, of course, of particular interest to us. The present writer has earlier on stressed the process of translation, that is the raising of communication from the inarticulate and autistic expression by the symptom to the recognition of underlying conflict and problems which can be conveyed, shared and discussed in everyday language. In his present view, more is involved than that. The process of increasing the range of communication goes in two directions, both upwards and downwards as it were. There is also an increased understanding on the part of the group and its individual members for the more primitive, symbolic, unconscious meaning of communications. The group recaptures what Erich Fromm calls 'the forgotten language'. Thus the area of what the group can share, have in common, communicate, is enlarged in the on-going process of psychotherapy. Principally everything happening is considered in its communicational aspect. More will be said about this latter in connection with the group-analytic group.

By contrast, communication in our 'working group' will mostly be concerned with the object in view and will be taken at face value. It will be confined to ordinary language or otherwise agreed special symbols. The unofficial communication between members and that of a non-verbal nature will remain largely unacknowledged and unobserved consciously.

IV. LEADERSHIP

In the functional group, leadership is positive and direct. The psychiatrist called in to help such a group will also approach in his actions the functions of a good leader, unless indeed his approach be an analytic one. We will come back to this point later. By contrast, good direction, or guidance, of the group-analytic group differs markedly from good leadership in the direct sense. This is in line with the fact that no object is to be achieved and that good functioning of the group in view of any particular aim or goal is not his objective in such a group. One may say that the more achievement and good functioning of the group is important, the more is the psychiatrist's function in line with good leadership as generally understood; the more, on the other hand, analysis is important, the less is this the case.

V. ACTIVITY

Activity may be the main purpose of the group or the main agency of treatment. On the other hand, in the analytic group such activity is suspended. It should be noted that suspended action, which is so characteristic of an analytic approach, be it psycho-analytic or group analytic, is of great therapeutic moment. It is exactly by the suspension of action that the analysis of the here and now becomes possible and the chance of that specific mode of change which is so characteristic of analytic methods. It does, however, appear (see Ruesch) that we have to become more selective in deciding for what type of personality and disturbances such analytic treatment is particularly suitable and for what other types action methods, one of which is exemplified by psycho-dramatic methods, are the best.

VI. THE CONCEPT OF THE GROUP AS A WHOLE

This concept, which is particularly characteristic of the group-analytic approach, seems difficult to grasp and people seem reluctant to use it operationally. What we have in mind is not limited to individuals interacting in a group. What we have in mind is a psychological entity, a psyche group, to use Helen Jennings' term. In this context we speak of a matrix, of a communicational network. This network is not merely inter-personal but could rightly be described as transpersonal and suprapersonal. Like neurons in the network of the nervous system, so the individuals in such a network are merely nodal points inside the structural entity.

In applying this concept to characterize the different models of groups here described, we have to consider the following questions:

(a) Is the group treated as a group or is it being treated as a meeting of individuals?

(b) Is the group treated for the group's sake or for the individual's sake?

(c) Is the group treated by the group or by the therapist leader?

(d) If by the leader, is he working predominantly through the group?

Having passed in review these concepts, we shall now define in their light our three types of groups.

(1) *The Functional or Work Group*

This group as it occurs in life is of less concern to us here. It is obvious that its members meet only in one particular function and are otherwise belonging to different life groups. We have spoken about their relationships remaining latent, their occupation being in evidence, their communication being taken at face value, leadership being of the conventional kind, and their activities being confined to their occupational aim. This group, if it becomes the object of psychological advice or treatment within its function, is the purest example of a group which would be treated wholly for the group's sake. This group, if reconstructed for reasons of treatment, e.g. inside a hospital, as an activity—project—or occupational group, operates therapeutically almost entirely through the agencies of successful participation and socialization. These are indeed mighty factors, which we might call ego-strengthening or supportive, reconditioning, encouraging or what you will. At Northfield we were probably the first to discover and be fully aware of this socio-therapeutic aspect of this type of group, which hitherto had seemed more incidental to its occupational activity. We were impressed by the importance of interpersonal relationships in this type of group, and saw in them the very essence of the therapeutic value of such groups. We considered their occupations and projects as merely a means to an end, namely go encourage human contacts and relationships together with their therapeutic effects and also as a means for observation. Going one step further, it was shown that these groups in their turn could be used for an analytic approach in which genuine corrective re-experience and insight could be obtained. Examples of this will be given in chapters 14 and 16. For instance, the co-ordination group, which became the unofficial nerve centre of the whole hospital life, or the band group. There I described how these soldier patients, who had formed the band of the hospital, a small group with changing membership, found themselves disturbed in their function; but one rainy Sunday morning, through the intervention of the psychiatrist, the rift between them disclosed the human tragedy in action, laid it bare and open to heal. It was described how the restoration of the group's function went hand in hand with the resolution of their deep human problem.

At this point I would like to remark that in all these groups there is the supportive, socializing element as well as the analytic opportunity. When, therefore, I state that even in the pure analytic group there are supportive factors at work besides the analytic ones, I do mean this as a statement of fact not as a statement of deliberate conduct, as Kelnar and Sutherland seem to think, of these groups. In the purely analytic group my own attitude is purely analytic. Analytic in a group is the equivalent of psycho-analytic in the individual situation, but not identical with it. I would maintain that in the psycho-analytic situation, too, supportive factors play a considerable part. This does not mean that the psycho-analyst or group analyst deliberately cultivates these factors. In the group under discussion this sliding scale from the socializing supportive effect to the analytic one has, I hope, become particularly clear.

(2) *The Life Group*

In this type of group the members are vitally interrelated. It has no single occupation as a group but its members are interdependent as to the basic ingredients of life. This natural network, e.g. family or extended family is an important field for group-analytic therapy and research. In my own experience we have only been able to submit small particles of such a network to simultaneous treatment, such as married couples or mother, father and daughter. These experiences have, however, been most instructive.

In this type of group all forms of human reactions may be expected to be encountered, normal or abnormal, physical or mental, psychoneurotic or psychopathic, psychotic or psychosomatic conditions. Hitherto all these disturbances have been investigated largely from the endopsychic point of view. Here they will be seen as facets of the multipersonal network of interaction in which the individual's disturbances are played out. It will be noted if and how each change in each member of the network reacts on all the other members of the network. It is believed that even part reactions, e.g. symptoms, are interdependent. Hence it may also be expected that light can be thrown on the dynamics of individual psychopathology in the course of such an approach.

The problem of transference between members so closely connected, and between them and the therapist, is a very intricate one.

(3) *The Group-Analytic Group*

We come now to the group-analytic group in the narrower sense, the group we have usually in mind when talking of group-analytic treatment. We see here that the members have no previous relationship with each other. They are total strangers and should have as little contact outside the treatment situation as possible. They have no purpose for meeting other than treatment, no occupation, no programme of procedure. This, as we have seen, has the effect of bringing the personalities and their interrelationship into the open, the screen of an occupation is removed and the way is open for an analytic approach. Of particular significance is the nature of communication and the use made of communication and relationship. On the basis of frank disclosure, these are the main objects of study and interpretation and the main levers of therapy. The manifest communication in so far as it is verbal is relieved as far as possible from censorship and this becomes the equivalent of free association in psycho-analysis (free group association). Years of study and observation have taught me that it is necessary for the conductor to treat the production of the group as interconnected communications, which they always are, if they are to operate as free associations in the group. If we define the main conditions and parameters of a group along such lines as we are just pursuing, we can say that we have determined its particular 'situation'. I have been able to observe that there is an exact relationship between the total group situation and the approximation or otherwise of communication to the character of a free association. A strictly functioning work group, as described under (1) or a very conventional social gathering will strongly repress and disguise underlying latent feeling, phantasy and impulse, but a group under relaxed conditions, as for instance on a long railway journey or sea voyage, will disclose much more of this, though largely debarred from conscious recognition on the part of the participants. On a journey through Spain in a small group of travellers by bus, joined for the journey, with no occupation but that of sightseeing, for instance, I could observe that conversation was very disclosing as to the personalities, their relationships, interaction and the little group as a whole, references being always tangential, and I think for the most part unconscious. Be that as it may, in the group-analytic group the emergence of a more primary type of communication is particularly favoured by prevailing conditions. In this group all involuntary and voluntary non-verbal communications are of equal importance and so are the signs and reactions voiced of the feelings arising between members. Communication is a prerequisite for the analytic process. The work towards communication goes parallel with the process of analysis. Neurotic and psychotic disturbances are always linked with blockage in the system of communication, socialization, of the patient and the aim of analysis is precisely to translate the autistic symptom into a problem which can be verbalized. The benefit which each individual derives from working towards a free expression of his conflict in a group is intimately linked with the levels of communication which such a group can grasp. Commonly understanding ranges from symbolic and dream level to the conscious manifest meaning, but this common ground may be continuously enlarged. Group analysis shows people not only how much they have—often quite unexpectedly —in common with other people, but also how they differ as individual personalities. In this respect the process is similar to an educational experience of a very deep and fundamental nature.

The group-analytic group is essentially a transference group. Members can transfer, corresponding to their own unconscious phantasies, not only to the therapist but to each other. In this connection, it will be helpful to remember that the term transference is today essentially used in two different meanings. The more specific one corresponds to the classical concept of Transference. In the other it is used for all relationships in the therapeutic situation. It may help if we differentiate between the two by spelling the specific one with a capital 'T' and the more general one with a small 't'. I personally believe that not all relationships in a therapeutic situation should be called transference and prefer therefore to refer to the total situation with its specific characteristics as a therapeutic or 'T' situation instead of 'transference' situation. The essence of such a 'T' situation lies in the fact that old experiences and attitudes are free to be re-established in a situation where tolerance, acceptance, relative freedom are self-understood. No valuations are applied, any reaction by the patient is accepted, the relationship between members is developed in a privileged atmosphere where realistic consequences of behaviour do not arise. Thus old and neurotic reactions can be corrected in a mutual process. The manner in which communications, both verbal and non-verbal, are treated arises as a concomitant of these characteristics of the therapeutic situation ('T' Situation).

There are, many significant levels of communication. The

transference level is one of them. Another one is an autistic level in which the group as a whole, or members, can stand for inner images which are projected. Thus the group on some level can be a mother: the body other than oneself who is the first recipient of one's talk. The body image itself extends on such a level into the group. Another level again is the realistic one, that of current reality, in which the therapist is the physician, the fellow patient Mr N.M., who lives in Y Street and works as an engineer. On this level relationships can be realistic, conventional, habitual, anxious, etc., according to character. These considerations are only indicated at this point to show the complex range and significance of relationships and communication which group analysis faces.

As to the activities of the conductor, I have already said that he is only exceptionally a leader in the sense of the functional group. I must refer to a paper (see Chapter 4) in which I have said more about the way in which the manifest analytic attitude of the conductor serves at the same time for the correction of certain primordial attitudes towards a leader figure (Authority, primal father, God). Suffice it to say that the group-analyst's behaviour corresponds to that of the psycho-analyst. The differences, in my opinion, between the two techniques lie not in the fact that the group analyst is in any way less 'analytic' than the psycho-analyst but that his role and the means at his disposal are changed by the fact that he finds himself inside a group situation. The proper conduct of these groups results in the group becoming more and more a self-propelling instrument of therapy, taking their problems into their own hands. Activity, as has been said above, is suspended in the sense of acting out. The tendency to action is, as it were, frozen in midstream and used for consideration. This suspension of activity does not contradict my saying that in many ways group-analytic therapy is 'ego training in action'. What is meant in this sense by 'action' is the inner psychic action of the ego in the analytic sense. The group situation, with its ever-changing situational demands, exercises the participating individuals in having to take up some attitude towards these ever-changing situations, so that the ego can be observed and analysed in the process of operation.

As to the group as a whole, it has been from its inception a characteristic of group analysis to understand all events in the group as being meaningful in the light of the total group matrix. Thus these individuals of our group-analytic group, remaining strangers in real life, merge at the same time into a unified structure, the psyche group.

All interpretations of events are made in view of the group as a whole, the psyche group. The conductor has a different function from the ordinary leader. He is a member with special functions who participates, but not in his own private person. All the principal arrangements of the group-analytic group, which we cannot detail here, make it into a truly therapeutic 'T' situation. In such a situation old existing attitudes, in which the individual has become fixed, are allowed to be repeated and re-lived and their unconscious conflicting aspects to become manifest and conscious. This is a truly emotional experience, and by working through correction becomes possible and the way is open for creative and new solutions. As a result of the conductor's handling the group participates actively and uses the 'T' situation genuinely for therapeutic change and insight.

THE THERAPEUTIC IMPACT

The therapeutic impact is quite considerable, intensive and immediate in operation. By and large, the group situation would appear to be the most powerful therapeutic agency known to us. I imagine it will become more and more the usual psychotherapeutic approach out of which individual treatment emerges for special conditions, personalities or aims. Psycho-analysis, for instance, will always remain the method of choice for the intimate and detailed working through of the infantile neurosis, of the personal Transference neurosis under conditions of regression. On the other hand, group analysis is not less intensive than psycho-analysis, given comparable circumstances, but in certain respects is more intensive.

THERAPEUTIC FACTORS

We discern here specific (group specific) and non-specific factors. If analytic means are not specifically used, the sup-portive, socializing factors are predominant in operation, as I have, I hope, made clear. The group-analytic approach itself operates at the opposite end of the scale. The analysis within the 'T' situation, the transference situation, naturally in its immediate presentation, the 'here and now', plays a central part. It should perhaps be said that the here and now is itself unconscious.

Amongst the specific factors the most important belong to the family of 'mirror reactions', role playing and dramatization. The concept of personification (impersonation), which belongs to the mirror reactions, refers to the significance of the fact that in a group quite different personalities meet in the flesh. Thus a member may meet a manifest but unrecognized part of himself in others, or a repressed aspect strongly contrasting with himself, and he may also find new aspects of his own self in the way others react to him.

DIAGNOSTICS: THE INTRODUCTORY GROUP

Needless to say, observation in a group is of great dynamic diagnostic value. A good example of this is my Introductory Group at the Maudsley Hospital. Four or five patients are seen by me in the presence of the doctors to the Unit. Nobody has met anybody else before. We spend an hour together and there is no question that we know a good deal about the patients by the end of it; the way in which they react to each other and their attitude towards their disturbances and treatment, quite apart from all the relative factual information. After the initial slight shock reaction, during which period we put people at their ease, they begin to participate actively in cross talk. Sometimes this short session ends in quite a lively exchange between these people who had not met before and who had been somewhat bewildered and disturbed by being put together at all. Quite often a considerable therapeutic effect is noticeable, which was not one's main purpose, and this is confirmed later on. This group forms a good introduction, and is used as such, to the idea of the group situation and group treatment, and many people who would be reluctant to join groups are willing and even eager to do so after the session. Very often visitors of considerable international experience who have observed these groups have spontaneously expressed their astonishment at how much more one sees in such a session compared with an individual interview.

Method and Technique

The standard situation comprises five to eight patients, the optimum being seven, excluding the therapist. They sit, with the conductor, in a circle, preferably on identical, comfortable chairs. The session lasts for one and a quarter to one and a half hours, usually held once a week.

The combination of group psychotherapy with concurrent individual psychotherapy leads to difficulties, and the present writer now prefers to avoid this, unless it can be applied to all members of the group. Group psychotherapy may, however, with advantage either precede or follow individual treatment.

Groups may be either 'open' or 'closed'. An open group may carry on for a very long period, the members leaving for reasons based entirely on their individual case, and new members filling the vacancies created. A closed group starts and finishes treatment as a body, and is often arranged to run for a predetermined course of time. Such a group is particularly suitable for a more intensive approach for carefully selected and matched patients and for the study of special problems. Nine months has been found to be a desirable minimum period, and is a good time unit for planning (nine months, eighteen months, etc.).

The open and closed groups have quite different functions and characteristics. These differences are reflected in all technical aspects, such as the selection of patients, the 'matching' of patients for a particular group, the group dynamics, the problems brought up by the members, the beginning and ending of a group. In practice groups are rarely such pure types. The one most frequently adopted is a combination of the open and closed group, though nearer to a closed group, which renews its membership slowly. We have called this tentatively a 'slow-open' group.

The patients may be predominantly psychoneurotic, psychotic or of the psychosomatic reaction type. Psychopathies and perversions are also good subjects for group-analytic psychotherapy, provided they are in specially selected groups. The contact between members should as far as possible be confined to the group sessions, if dealing with out-patient groups.

The manifest activity of the group is verbal communication in the form of free, unselected discussion which we may call group association. Free association belongs to psycho-analysis, and cannot be applied in a group; no one could surely free-associate uninfluenced by the group situation. What happens in the group is an equivalent. In fact it is only occasionally that this group association occurs in pure form. On the other hand it occurs to some extent in any human group even, say, among travellers in a railway compartment.

The therapist, whom we have called a conductor rather than a leader, is a participant member of the group. He is non-directive, but this does not mean that he is inactive. His main function is that of analyst, catalyst and interpreter. As a group analyst, he focuses on the group context as a whole. He must be continuously aware of the fact that he is dealing with a group, and not with a number of individuals.

The present is brought to the foreground by the group situation itself. The phrase 'here and now' is often used to emphasize this aspect of group psychotherapy. Special importance attaches to what happens, and why, in the particular context of a particular group at a particular time.

Teaching and Training

A number of psychiatrists have been and are being currently introduced to this method, both at the Maudsley Hospital and through the Group-Analytic Society (London). The latter body considers the undergoing of a training analysis in groups as essential, even for candidates who have already undergone a thorough individual analysis.

The experience of taking part in an introductory group as described is of great value for teaching, especially as doctors and consultant meet to discuss the matter afterwards. The doctors exchange observations and discuss their meaning as to the group and the individuals concerned. This meeting is a good example of the group as a teaching medium.

Another good illustration of this is my supervisory seminar at the Maudsley Hospital. This takes place weekly and two or three groups are reported on by the various doctors. Everybody participates, learning, comparing and bringing examples from his own experience. In the course of years, in great variety and detail, psychopathological, psychodynamic and therapeutic problems are passed in view.

This group also has a therapeutic function of considerable importance. It takes into full account the counter-transference aspect in the therapists. We find this very significant, and this group highlights the depth of the influence which goes usually unobserved and unconscious from the conductor to the group and *vice versa*. Here again the fact that this is discussed in a group situation where all participate is relevant. It contrasts favourably with the situation as it arises in individual supervision, in which the following up of counter-transference does lead to a considerable degree of much more personal involvement. The presence, by the way, of observers as well as conductors who participate in this supervisory group is an interesting feature.

In this connection an interesting experience might be reported which occurred recently when a rather anxious doctor reported that she felt that while conducting a group she was being constantly observed. It turned out that this phenomenon is more general and that there is a superego watching inside the therapists—linked for obvious reasons with myself. This doctor had asked to have an actual observer in her group and had been told that she should give it a little more time, as she was new to conducting groups. However, to have an observer in the shape of a doctor was less anxiety producing than the 'ghost' or psychological observer, personified by myself.

Theory

Group analysis has an important contribution to make to the study of group dynamics in general, as well as individual dynamics. As to the theory of therapy: whereas psycho-analysis studies why and how people have become as they are, our main interest is concentrated on the question of how do people change. The genetic aspect of personality appears in the group situation as an individual 'vertical' dimension as it were. We rather ask what makes people change, what can we do to promote such change if desirable? The answer to this is sought in the here and now situation, in the 'horizontal' dimension of the group.

It is important to form concepts based on the group situation, and not to borrow those from the individual therapeutic situation. Such group-specific factors are in their very essence group borne, and can best be studied in the group context. The process of *communication* has impressed the present writer more and more as basic for the understanding of group dynamics. Communication here obviously includes unconscious communications. Our theory envisages a whole scale of communication in which everything finds a place, including for instance gestures and smells, and is not confined merely to such distinctions as 'verbal' and 'non-verbal' communications.

Another group-analytical concept which has proved valuable is that of *location*. This describes how any event in the group involves the total network of interrelations and intercommunications. What manifestly occurs is the 'figure', the rest the 'ground' of the configuration (Gestalt) in the group. The process of location corresponds, roughly, to the work which brings this configuration in the group to light.

It is important to observe both the manifest and the latent *occupation* of the group. In an ordinary life-group—let us say a bridge club—the manifest occupation of the group is to play bridge. This provides the excuse for all sorts of interactions between people which remain more or less hidden or latent, and those interactions most interesting from our point of view may remain completely unconscious.

In the analytic group the process is reversed. What is otherwise in the background is brought into the open. This is done by removing the manifest occupation of the group, by leaving it without any prescribed occupation. It could be said, of course, that 'talking' is the group's occupation, but the therapist does not ask the members to 'come along and talk'. A human group turns to talking as the obvious means of communication. If a therapeutic group talks for talking's sake, this must be seen as springing from motives of defence and resistance. An important therapeutic factor is what we have called *mirror reaction*. This can be dissected into a number of psycho-analytic concepts, e.g. projection, identification, etc., but there are good grounds for putting these together and giving them a collective name, emphasizing the 'mirror' aspect.

The patient sees himself, or part of himself, in particular a repressed part of himself in the other members. He can observe from the outside another member reacting in the way he himself reacts, can for instance see how conflicts and problems are translated into neurotic behaviour.

The spontaneous work towards communication, sharing of experiences, enforces a move from the less articulate forms of expression—as, e.g., in a conversional symptom—to the more articulate ones culminating in such communication as can be put into words. This whole process, which leads to better understanding and insight, is by itself therapeutic and has been called *translation*. It is the group equivalent of 'making the unconscious conscious'.

It is important to keep in mind how far such concepts are

identical with, or differ from, concepts known from the individual therapeutic situation or in how far they overlap.

In group analysis one has to do with an ego in action. Group-analytic therapy could be described essentially as an ego training in action. 'Action' here does not mean doing or, literally, acting or role playing; nor is it the equivalent of 'acting out' in psycho-analysis. The group provides a stage for actions, reactions and interactions within the therapeutic situation, which are denied to the psycho-analytic patient on the couch. However, the ego to which we refer is the ego in the psycho-analytic sense, the inner ego as a metapsychological concept, which is activated and reformed.

Part II

PSYCHO-ANALYSIS AND
GROUP ANALYSIS

INTRODUCTION

The relationship of Group Analysis to Psycho-analysis is an important one. In my capacity as a psycho-analyst and the initiator of Group Analysis in the sense of 'Group-Analytic Psychotherapy' (G.A.P.) I have made my own attitude repeatedly clear. The salient points are briefly:

(1) G.A.P. has common ground with Psycho-analysis in its clinical and theoretical orientation. The attitude of the therapist is essentially the same in both therapeutic situations ('analytic attitude').

(2) Psycho-analysis as a method takes place in the psycho-analytic situation which is a situation of two persons, the analyst and the patient (analysand). The essence of psycho-analysis is the analysis of the infantile neurosis in a transference situation.

(3) Group Analysis, by contrast, takes place in a group situation with specific properties, the 'group-analytic situation'. Its focus is on the psychodynamics within the matrix of the group, though it is undertaken for the sake of therapeutic analysis of each individual member. The operative processes in their inter- and suprapersonal aspects can best be observed in this group situation with its particular properties.

(4) G.A.P. is a form of group psychotherapy. It differs from other forms of group psychotherapy in the same way as psycho-analytic psychotherapy does from other two person (individual) psychotherapies.

I have therefore refrained from calling this method 'group psycho-analysis' as other authors (so far only in the USA) have done, though it has always been clear that this method (G.A.P.) is based on psycho-analysis (Freud). Besides these authors are not, as a rule, qualified psycho-analysts, i.e. not members of the International Psycho-Analytical Association. Even if they are, they might have quite divergent views inside psycho-analysis itself, including basic orientations as to concepts and method.

These considerations should be kept in mind in connection with this present part, which deals in detail with the relationship between psycho-analysis and group analysis and psycho-analytic psychotherapy and G.A.P. and examines many relevant aspects with benefit to both disciplines, it is hoped.

There has been no basic change in attitude but considerable development. Experience has shown that it is possible to conduct more intensive psychotherapy inside the group situation than I first thought, e.g. as regards Transference phenomena, though it is still true that the individual 'Transference neurosis' can develop and be analysed more fully only in the psychoanalytic situation. Remaining equally interested in individual psycho-analysis and psychotherapy I have also tried to specify the indications for these methods more precisely. On the theoretical side the search for a better understanding of the respective mode of operation of any psychotherapeutic situation has led me to the concept of a 'T' situation, the aim being to express in a precise formula the basic ingredients which *any* psychotherapeutic situation worthy of its name must have. The characteristic features of any particular method, including psycho-analysis and group analysis, can then be defined by the way in which these basic ingredients are represented and operate in each. This has been touched upon in the last chapter of the first part and the reader will find more in the following parts of the book.

Chapter VI

GROUP PSYCHOTHERAPY IN THE LIGHT OF PSYCHO-ANALYSIS[1]

The present historical situation shows clearly that human problems cannot be solved in isolation but only through a concerted effort of the whole of humanity. The future of the human species may well be made or marred according to whether or not it is able to grasp this fact and act upon it while there is still time. Anything we can learn as to the relationships of persons towards each other, and of groups towards each other, is, therefore, of great therapeutic significance.

Human people live always in a social setting, from the cradle to the grave. A neurotic patient asks for help because he cannot live satisfactorily in his community, or because his community cannot carry on with him. Because the forces by which he is run are anachronistic, according to an infantile and primitive pattern, he cannot adjust to his social group, and because he is not aware of the source of these forces within himself, he cannot have insight.

The main aim of a true therapy is, therefore, to develop insight and adjustment, vital inner adjustment establishing harmony between the individual and his world—*not* conformity. There is a relationship between the two: insight promotes adjustment, adjustment facilitates insight. Insight without adjustment does not go very far; adjustment without insight is incomplete but it can work. Adjustment seems the more fundamental from a therapeutic, insight from a scientific, point of view. Both meet on the testing ground of control of behaviour, when one is confronted with things and persons. If conflict involves predominantly early and primitive levels, control over present behaviour is lacking, individual analysis is the method of choice. Solution must then be sought in revision of the past, buried alive in the unconscious mind, or adjustment remains superficial, insight impotent. The group situation is the best

[1] Read to the first post-war Congress of European Psychoanalysts held at Amsterdam in 1947.

medium when sufficient inner mobility is left to make control over present behaviour possible. Insight and adjustment can now be achieved in the face of the present task and the present group.

The neurotic, this exaggeration and caricature of the norm, defends himself against the therapeutic experience principally in two ways:

(1) He persists in being run by primitive forces.

(2) He repeats his basic conflict.

This is where the therapist comes in. In individual analysis the therapist counteracts:

(1) By making unconscious content and defensive reaction conscious, enlarging the range of secondary process and of the ego, by means of the psycho-analytic procedure.

(2) By accepting himself as a substitute for all the figures of the childhood and the primordial family group, the analyst allows the patient to re-establish his basic conflict in the analytic situation. This is what is known as transference neurosis. By keeping still and passive as a person, he enables the patient to experience his own inner impulses as the source and dynamic motor of his conflicts, and thus eventually to correct them. This is known as transference analysis.

It will be noted that even in this relationship between two people the group is represented, albeit in the background, as it arises from the patient's inner mind and phantasy.

Group treatment is the resolve to take a larger part of the external world, and of a person's associates, into the field of direct observation, than is the case in individual treatment. They can now face their problems as a group, including their reactions towards each other. One could say, too, that group treatment means applying 'common sense'—the sense of the community—to a problem by letting all those openly participate in its attempted solution who are in fact involved in it.

The therapist who inaugurates this process will help the group as best he can to articulate their procedure and to face their task. He can be said to be its leader, but, in another sense, he is the first servant of the group. While sharing the concerns of the group like any other of its members, he is in the position of setting an example by his sincerity, frankness and tolerance, and by subordinating his personal interests at all stages to the interests of the group. It is his obligation to lead the group actively when his function demands it of him, and only then. If we have a group of patients only, we bring them together so that each can be observed and face himself in a group setting. Instead of two people grappling with a problem, the one in the role of patient, the other of therapist, we have now a number of people confronted with the problem, as well as with the task of its solution.

It is possible to conduct group discussions in such a way as to leave the patients full liberty and spontaneity as to content and procedure. The group equivalent of 'free association' is thus 'free floating' or spontaneous discussion. This creates a new situation without precedent. In such a situation the group cannot avoid accepting responsibility and must rely more and more upon its own resources, instead of turning to a leader or other authority for guidance.

The collective situation reduces the severity of censorship inside the individual, and the Id becomes liberated. At the same time the group sets up its own boundaries under its own weighty authority, which is a good match for the ancient Superego. In other words, the boundaries of the Ego, both towards the Id and the Superego, are under revision and the result is in favour of a more free and a stronger Ego structure. The working through of the transference situation in individual analysis has an equivalent in the group, namely the observation and interpretation of individual members' reactions towards each other, towards the group, and towards the leader.

The individuals in a group are in conflict between two antagonistic sets of forces:

(1) To repeat the old pattern, create the old deadlock, which is characteristic of our two basic ingredients of neurotic behaviour as outlined above. This acts as a group disruptive tendency (repetition compulsion).

(2) To overcome this private and egocentric isolationist attitude, to accept others, to combine and co-operate with them. This acts as a group constructive tendency. The particular form which the neurotic position assumes is in its very nature highly individualistic. It is group disruptive in essence because it is genetically the result of an incompatibility between the individual and his original group. It is at the same time an expression of aggressive and destructive tendencies. This disruptive, anti-social, destructive aspect of neurotic behaviour is forced to come out into the open and does not receive the sanction of the group. The individual in his healthy, socially adjusted aspect is supported and allowed to develop and flourish in this group. For this reason, by inevitable selection, the individual in his neurotic aspect is set upon by the others, a process in which he participates actively in his turn, when he attacks the other man's neurotic defences, and thus, by the way, his own. The group destructive energies can thus be used for the undermining of each other's neurotic position, whereas constructive forces combine and support each other. In a word, one could say that disruptive forces are consumed in mutual analysis, constructive ones utilized for the synthesis of the individual and the integration of the group as a whole. I do not want to give the impression that this process takes place automatically, without the guidance of the conductor. It is one of the most important functions of the leader to use this tendency for the progressive integration of the group. He thus allows aggressive energies to be set free in order to serve constructive ends. The most important point, however, remains that group constructive tendencies are of necessity conducive to the norm because, being compatible with the particular group in hand, they must be compatible with social life in general, and, even more specifically, with the mode of life of the particular community to which this group belongs. Therefore, essentially, adjustment in a therapeutic group means social adjustment. This seems to me a cardinal reason why the group has an inherent pull towards the socially and biologically established norm, that is why it lends itself as an instrument of therapy.

The conductor's main art is to watch and direct this process wisely and, above all, not to hinder its development. In so doing he uses the dynamic forces produced by the group itself and such a treatment deserves the name of a 'group-dynamic therapy'.

The group situation's overall function appears to be that of an activator, activating the patients' disturbances as well as the means to overcome them. Thus it lends itself to every degree of admixture with individual treatment. Individual treatment can be complementary to the group or *vice versa*. Group treatment can be used as a preparation for individual treatment or as a form of after-care. The group is an excellent forum for diagnosis and prognosis in a dynamic sense. Observation in a group setting is very useful for the assessment of the need for and actual nature of any other form of therapeutic approach.

Against the normal background represented by the group, it throws into relief social disturbances as well as the individual deflections of its members. It allows for what might be called 'the location of a disturbance'.

Like analysis, such a group-dynamic form of therapy approaches problems of neurosis and normal mental life in a basic way, operating on adjustment and insight. Its emphasis is slightly more on adjustment, more on the present and immediate, the 'here and now', more on direct observation and action than on verbal communication. The intimate revision of the personal development, Oedipus situation, pregenital sexuality, remain the domain of psycho-analysis. Group therapy, on the other hand, has a more immediate impact upon the solution of the patient's present, vital tasks. It is progressively orientated and follows up regressions only in so far as they register as disturbances in the present group. At the same time, the observation in a therapeutic group shows up very clearly in how far a patient's disturbance calls for approach on a more intimate, personal level, inside or outside the group, or should altogether be dealt with in extensive individual analysis.

It has been shown that group analysis, like psycho-analysis, is:

(1) A special method of approach.

(2) A mode of therapy.

(3) An instrument of scientific investigation.

It is the instrument of choice for the study of the dynamics of the group, a new science in which psychology and sociology meet. In view of the importance of good relations between groups of all kinds, including whole nations, the relevance of such studies need hardly be stressed at the present time.

Once again it may be the privilege of psychopathology, through the analysis of disturbances in interpersonal relationships, to throw decisive light on the social life of man in all its manifestations.

ANNOTATIONS

This was a presentation of 'group psychotherapy' to a conference of leading European psycho-analysts soon after the end of the Second World War. Neurosis and its cure are seen as problems of the community (compare Chapter 11, 'Psychotherapy in the 'Sixties', written fourteen years later). Present and past are confronted and the degree of regression is seen as a criterion for the indication of psycho-analytic or group-analytic treatment respectively (a view further substantiated in Chapter 8).

The emphasis on (insight and) adjustment needs some clarification. The latter should *not* be understood in the sense of conformity, toeing the line. It was meant in a deep sense: all values have in the last resort to pass the test of acceptance or rejection by other people, the community. This decides success or failure in enterprise, the worth of an artist and his work, even if recognition is delayed for very long periods, it decides ultimately what is a symptom, what is insanity. Adjustment is a process and is mutual. It was not a well-chosen term for this profound problem: the compatibility of the individual's 'private' world and the world of his fellow beings, which, if not achieved, always means severe disturbance.

The principle is valid, however: adjustment inside the therapeutic group means better adjustment in the country to which the group belongs, i.e. equals 'improvement'. In terms of communication, this is expressed thus: the process of communication goes hand in hand with the therapeutic process; and in my Introductory Book (1948) is a phrase, often quoted with approval and disapproval: 'collectively they (the patients) constitute the very norm from which, individually, they deviate'. To spell it out: mentally disturbed patients have as one of their common features that they deviate from the 'norm'. What is this norm? Biologically it is an abstract ideal (e.g. the anatomical norm); culturally it depends on the valuation of the particular community (tribe, nation, period). As members of their community patients subscribe to these valuations (ego, superego) and therefore agree upon them implicitly. The individual deviation is in conflict with these values and causes psychoneurotic illness and neurotic inner conflict. This conflict is re-established in our groups and thus amenable to revision. For this reason I called my condensed statement above a basic law of group dynamics. We can put it in the form of a question: how far do patients who individually deviate (say delinquents, or sexual deviants) in their heart of hearts respect—sometimes exaggeratedly—the 'norm' against which they rebel? The answer to this question represents an important criterion for a dynamic form of diagnosis. On it depends the possibility of a cure by psychological approach.

Chapter VII

SIMILARITIES AND DIFFERENCES BETWEEN PSYCHO-ANALYTIC PRINCIPLES AND GROUP-ANALYTIC PRINCIPLES

The term *group analysis* as a form of psychotherapy inevitably suggests a relationship to psycho-analysis. This is quite particularly true if used, as in my own case, by someone who is a professional Freudian psycho-analyst. This term was meant to express this inner affinity in orientation, and also to acknowledge what group analysis owes to the experiences of psycho-analysis. However it was clear to me from the very beginning that group analysis is a totally different approach to psychology and to psychotherapy than is psycho-analysis. The differences are perhaps more important to stress than the similarities, as they are not as well understood. Indeed, the term group analysis has since been adopted by some workers in the US A who see in this method scarcely more than an application of psycho-analysis. These differences are essentially due to the differences between an individual situation—a situation between two—and a group situation—a situation between a number of people. I will choose only two such situations, the psycho-analytic situation and the group-analytic situation, for the purpose of comparison.

The psycho-analytic situation I may consider as known. As for group analysis, I will use the conditions of my own group-analytic work—termed by me the group-analytic situation—as a basis. This method of group analysis is called 'group-analytic psychotherapy' in order to express clearly that it is a form of psychotherapy, but not a form of psycho-analysis, and that it is group-analytic and not psycho-analytic (i.e. individual) in orientation.

A small number, say five to ten, of more or less selected patients meet, together with the doctor, for the purpose of treatment. The situation is quite informal. The group preferably sits round in a circle or semicircle. These patients are not given any particular prescriptions as to how to behave, or what to discuss, or what to do with their time. This is an essential point, the therapeutic effects of such treatment depend to a large extent upon the active, self-responsible participation of the group's members. Of course, having problems to discuss, having complaints to make, having sufferings to report, they will for various reasons have to use words—that is to say they will use verbal communication as their chief occupation. All they are given to understand, either explicitly or implicitly, as soon as possible, is that they are to allow these contributions free and spontaneous expression as the occasion arises. They also learn that the usual social censorship is removed, or at least reduced. The group itself—including of course its conductor—sets every time afresh its own frame of reference.

It is therefore right to say that such a group uses a form of spontaneous, shifting, undisciplined discussion as its medium of communication, and that it soon understands that feelings and attitudes towards other members of the group, criticisms, emotional upsets, hatreds, likings, etc., are permissible and should be voiced. Such a group and its members very soon— and remarkably well—understand that such utterances are there for consideration, for learning something about oneself and the other person. With my own technique such a group session will take one and a half hours' time, and is held at a fixed time and place. The group will, as a rule, meet once weekly. It is this group-analytic situation, just outlined, that I will compare and contrast with the psycho-analytic situation.

In my own view, of course, these two situations are not seen as contrasting, but as complementary and mutually illuminating. But as concepts are often uncritically transferred from one to the other to the confusion of both, I shall present them here in terms of comparison and contrast.

SIMILARITIES

I shall very quickly go over some of the similarities, as they are better known and more easily understood. They are similarities in basic orientation. Group-analytic psychotherapy, like psycho-analysis, aims at basic change and not at symptomatic relief. It recognizes basic psycho-analytical concepts such as those of an unconscious mind, of defence mechanisms, of all the individual dynamics known to us from psycho-analysis; it retains the use made of interpretation, the thinking in terms of mental structure, of an ego, id, superego. There is the general attitude of the therapist—that is to say as a transference figure, not one who responds and reacts in his own person but is receptive, passive, modifiable in this respect. In short, none of these individual mechanisms and observations, the general orientation and the theoretical framework which we as psycho-analysts recognize and know from the individual psycho-analytic situation—none of these are lost or devalued because people sit round in a circle. All these basic ingredients are merely modified by their operation in a group situation.

DIFFERENCES

Now as to differences. I will, for reasons of clarity, present them under three headings: (1) method and technique, (2) therapy and its dynamics, (3) theory.

(1) *Method and Technique*

As to the first, method and technique, we have already mentioned that in the group situation both members and therapist are more active, more concerned with the *here and now*, with the presenting situation, with interaction, relationships, than would be the case in the individual situation on the couch. One might even say that this group situation has socio-dramatic and psycho-dramatic qualities and has certain affinities to the technique elaborated by Moreno (1946). Such a group, indeed, participates actively in a mutual, sometimes highly dramatic process. The group situation is a social situation, and the medium of contact lies in the interaction of its members; its dynamics operate within the common matrix of this interpersonal situation. This network of multipersonal relationships, of great complexity, must not be identified with the transference situation which forms its counterpart in the psycho-analytic situation.

The psycho-analytic situation favours regressive transference; and transference in its true sense is always a regressive phenomenon.[1] The group situation does not favour transference in this sense, and, indeed, is tending to lead away from it towards the present situation and a progressive development. The

---

[1] Later I propose to express this 'true sense' by spelling the word Transference with a capital 'T' and thus differentiate it from transference in a more diffuse sense.

psycho-analytic situation is not a group of two people. The psycho-analytic situation is a special situation, under very specific conditions, and has no similarity, or almost none, to any ordinary social situation. The group-analytic situation is also a special situation, with its specific mode of action and conditions. Yet, it is a half-way house to a social situation and shows basic processes which can be seen and observed afterwards in real life. This is of very great importance to the therapy itself, as we shall see later on.

The main differences thus lie in the character of the group-analytic situation itself, and in the handling of this situation by the conductor.

I cannot say much here about the special role and technique of the conductor. It stands to reason, in such a situation, that he will be comparatively reserved with interference; will not lay down the law. He will not give many rules of conduct, nor offer advice. He will follow the psycho-analyst in allowing the group to define his own position, the light in which he appears to them, according to their changing will, mood and needs. The conductor therefore follows similar principles as the psycho-analyst does. Yet he will avail himself of the special and new features which such a group situation introduces, and make use of the new therapeutic weapons which it offers.

Interpretations, for instance, in the group are not individually based, but group based. They take regard of, and are directed towards, the group, even if addressed to an individual, and, like any other communication, they are of a multidimensional and multipersonal effect.

(2) *Therapy and its Dynamics*

Now I come to point (2) of the differences: those regarding therapy and its dynamics. The theory of psycho-analytical therapy is not yet settled. But there will be general agreement that, to bring about its effects, the concerted action of a number of factors is essential, and that each analysis varies in the importance of one or other set of these factors. Within recent years there is a general tendency, shared by divergent quarters as far as I can see, to emphasize even more the importance attached to the working through and the analysis of the transference situation or transference neurosis respectively.

As I have said from the beginning, the *individual* transference neurosis and transference situation cannot be analysed so well in groups as they can in an individual situation for the reason that they do not, and even should not, develop to the same extent. This point is of considerable importance for the differential indication of these two techniques.

All dynamics observed and known to us from psychoanalysis can be observed in operation inside the group situation. The degree of remodulation which they hereby suffer is of high theoretical and practical interest. But in addition to this, there are the group specific factors. An important set of these factors are comprised under the heading 'mirror reaction'.

I believe that the *process of communication* is of central importance and occupies a key position in the dynamics of a therapeutic group. As I see it, pressure of symptoms and suffering reinforce the urge to communicate, to relate to each other, which is basic to human beings. This urge is one of the strongest forces in bringing and holding together the members of a group such as this. I think what Slavson calls 'social hunger' and Bion (1950) called *valency* are a closely related or even identical concept. These forces act in the direction of integration, and it may well be noted here that social and individual integration go hand in hand.

There is, in addition, relief through sharing and understanding, as well as being understood which acts as a premium (reward) for successful communication. One could say that all that acts towards better communication acts *ipso facto* towards better social integration and therefore towards mental health— or cure; all that counteracts communication, and is in the nature of a resistance, is also on the side of pathogenesis. The task which arises is to express eventually in articulate negotiable language what is to begin with unconsciously and autistically expressed in the symptom. This is an important part of the therapeutic process itself. It opens the way for all other therapeutic agencies to operate. While this work is in itself a salutary mental exercise of no mean order, it establishes at the same time a progressively more flexible, subtle and adequate network of communicational channels. Thus the group's therapeutic power grows and it can live up to the increasing claims on its tolerance, as more primitive and more elementary sources of disturbance are being reached.

This process, as indicated, penetrates the individual, goes right through him, produces changes in him which outlast the context of this particular group.

TMKF - G

Meantime, a change of equal importance takes place through the emotional experience and analysis of interpersonal relationships which reflect the inner object world, mental reality, the relationships between ego, superego and id.

'Inner' (mental) and 'outer' reality merge inside the common matrix of interpersonal social reality, out of which they originally differentiated. Analytic, uncovering, destructive energies correlate in inevitable mutual interdependence with sustaining, integrative, constructive forces, and these processes must be carefully watched and balanced.

A further word as to therapy and its dynamics may be added concerning the whole problem of dissolution of transference. This is a cardinal problem in all individual psychotherapy: how what happens in the treatment situation is translated into life— first while contact with the therapist is still maintained, later when such contact has to be given up and should, indeed, be no longer required. In the group setting, one cannot, as I say, in detail and in depth and in regressive levels analyse and work through transference reactions as one can in the individual setting. This is where it falls short. It has, on the other hand, many obvious advantages in this respect. The most obvious and the most important of these advantages is perhaps just that very fact that the group situation itself is nearer life: it is not based on a group transference or group relationships only. It is not based to anything like the same extent on an emotional dependency on the individual therapist or psycho-analyst. Not only that, but there are many connections between the therapy group and the outside world; the membrane separating the two is at least, as I put it, semi-permeable. Anything happening or changing inside a person inside such a group setting, inside such a therapeutic group, almost immediately tells in life.

Furthermore, as to the weaning process: if transference does not develop to the same extent, there is obviously not the same problem of its dissolution. The emotional bond between the members is less on regressive infantile levels and, having become progressively more adult through the group therapeutic process itself, carries over more easily into life. Newly acquired antennae, newly acquired capacity for contact, for interpersonal reaction can be extended to life situations generally.

(3) Theory

Now for a few words as to theory. Perhaps the most important contribution which this technique will make is to a social psychopathology. Every individual symptom, process, syndrome, even diagnostic category, is tested afresh in the light of the social situation. This social psychopathology which the group promotes—or in fact really is—will help us very greatly to know better what we already know, as well as to make quite new observations of equal importance. These contributions to theory will of course be both on group psychology and on individual psychology, but quite particularly on processes which can be seen, and must be seen, from both the individual's and the group's point of view, in order to be adequately described.

We may study what is the configuration of situations of tension and stress in the group; what conditions in the group and the individuals—two aspects always interrelated—precipitate crises in the particular way in which they do. That and why, for instance, a disturbance focuses on a particular individual. When we see the full story in terms of the group as well as the individual it may dawn on us how often, with our individual centred upbringing, we have known only half of the story in the past when studying the breakdown of an individual and often enough the less important half at that. Presumably as good clinicians we have known that already; still, here it happens under our own eyes inside the therapeutic field itself, and under our controlling influence.

I can only mention what this means with reference to treatment, both practical and theoretical, of neurotic, psychotic or psychosomatic disturbances in terms of life groups as, for instance, the family. The individual who has broken down and comes for treatment is often only the weakest link in a chain, or the focus of intolerable group stresses. Only a group approach will enable us to study and treat—if the two can be separated at all—this sort of proposition satisfactorily.

Group psychotherapy, and especially group-analytic therapy, is a difficult discipline from the point of view of the therapist. Thorough experience in individual psychotherapy, preferably psycho-analysis, is indispensable, but it is not enough. Those not gifted for it should better leave it alone. Those with special gifts need years of hard study, penetrating experience, before they may qualify and provided also they have proved to possess a sufficient degree of personal integration to stand up to the emotional storms and havocs they have to live through.

CONCLUSION

I want to conclude with a word of warning: the terms 'group therapy' and 'group psychotherapy' perhaps inevitably raise ideas of a kind of mass technique, or uniformity, of saving time. I hope that even this short paper has given those who may think so, or who are afraid of such a development, reassurance that this is very far from true. Indeed, I believe that only in a group situation can one do full justice to each individual.

In this connection I often thought of an experience I had as a child when we were given what were called, I think, Japanese flowers. These were very condensed little paper specks, colourful things, scarcely recognizable. In order to make them show what they were, in order to develop them one had to throw them into water, when they would spread out and develop into beautiful flowers, leaves and stems. This fascinated me as a child, and I have often thought back on it by way of comparison. The individual out of a group, in isolation, is almost like such a Japanese flower before it is in water. Only in the group situation can he spread himself out, show himself as what he is, what his symptoms mean; what he can do and what one can do for him.

I have come to the conclusion that in the future psychiatry and psychotherapy and psychopathology should be first of all based on social grounds, as observable in a group situation. Such group studies as these here described in this intimate, intense, small psychotherapeutic group may serve as a basic unit of observation. From these one might move further centrally, as it were, to the individual core and, if and where necessary, to individual methods; or further outwards, peripherally, into life itself, into social therapy on a larger scale; mental health, mental hygiene, politics, if you like.

I do hope that you will, with me, conceive such a group-analytic treatment situation as a very delicate, subtle, intense, highly individualized affair. It is the opposite of a crude mass treatment, out for quick results; it has nothing to do with this. It is in itself a most valuable way of studying while helping individuals and groups. Moreover, while introducing the principle of active participation, important for each member's own sake, group analysis uses this very factor of active participation simultaneously for the benefit of the other members of such a group, and not least, the conductor himself.

Chapter VIII

GROUP-ANALYTIC OBSERVATIONS AND THE INDICATION FOR PSYCHO-ANALYTIC TREATMENT

Before we can decide on the appropriate use of a method, we should have a clear idea of its mode of operation. An investigation into the essential factors which operate in psycho-analytic treatment was the theme of a symposium at the International Congress of Psycho-Analysis held at Marienbad in 1936. The views presented then were divergent ones, even in respect of some elementary principles. In the intervening years matters have become more complex. No longer can we assume with any degree of certainty that any two psycho-analysts share their ideas of the basic characteristics of the situation in which they operate—the psycho-analytic situation—of the role they are playing in this process, or the precise nature of their technical interventions. Even basic concepts such as transference or counter-transference vary widely in their connotation. Psycho-analysts differ in the importance they attach to interpretations, and the nature and significance they ascribe to them. Whether all this is a good or bad sign it is certain that it does not bring us nearer to a scientific approach, so that we cannot easily refute investigations from other quarters claiming to show that differences which may be found in therapeutic results are due not to the therapist's adherence to any particular school (Freudian, Jungian, etc.) but rather to the personality and the experience of the therapist concerned. Under these circumstances we cannot wonder that so little is known about the more precise indication position for psycho-analytic treatment.

The question of which factors are *specific* for an indication for psycho-analytic therapy, singly or in composition, and for what persons and conditions psycho-analytic treatment is the method of choice has long exercised my mind, both for its theoretical and practical importance. For the present purpose I shall proceed on the basis of my conviction that psycho-analytic treatment has a specific function, that the operative factors can be identified, that they act in a characteristic combination which varies from case to case and phase to phase, and that their temporal sequence is of significance. I shall furthermore use terms such as transference in their specific classical meaning and not follow a tendency towards their expansion and inflation which renders these terms almost meaningless.

The psycho-analyst is not well placed to compare his own method with that of others in its efficiency. To form an opinion on a point such as this a comparative basis of observation is necessary. Experiences with small groups of patients, conducted on the basis of specific principles which I have called 'group-analytic', establish a field for such comparative observations.

One of the features of such a group is that the dynamic interplay of pathogenic and therapeutic mechanisms takes place in a process of interaction in which we partake and which we witness. Here is displayed for us, at one and the same time, the differential reaction of individuals to the same common stimulus of material and situation. Thus I have learnt afresh, in a new light, to appreciate the difference between a transference neurosis and other neurotic disturbances, a difference which Freud discovered so long ago. It is true that our ideas about so-called actual neuroses and psychotic, narcissistic disturbances have developed much since the early days. This development has led to more precise formulations concerning the ego, the importance of object-relationships, inner and outer, the body image.

These can be observed in the group-analytic setting. Disturbances which involve the genetic structure of the ego itself, as for instance character problems or narcissistic formations, on the whole respond well to group analysis. The group situation on the other hand shows that and why, by preference, transference neuroses should be treated by individual psychoanalysis. Group analysis demonstrates in action the meaning of a transference neurosis, its regressive nature, its oedipal significance, its compelling character, as a consequence of which the patient tends to demand the therapeutic re-establishment of a situation as close as possible to the original family constellation.

If I state that the essence of psycho-analytic therapy is a genetic revision of the patient's infantile neurosis, and that its main instrument is the working through of the patient's latest edition of his neurosis in the transference situation—the transference neurosis—I am not likely to be refuted by any psychoanalyst. This is exactly what such patients' behaviour in a group calls for, implicitly or explicitly.

The opinion, which I have expressed from the first, that the group situation is not the situation of choice for the working through of the individual transference situation has been confirmed by practical observations. I will now illustrate this by one case which shows the relevant points clearly enough. I have, moreover, chosen this case because we have a triple observation by three independent observers.

The patient was first treated in a group situation, participating in two therapeutic groups with the same conductor (Dr A), and afterwards had individual treatment on psychoanalytical lines, carried out by a psycho-analyst (Dr B). I myself saw this patient only once, in consultation, but I had access to the material as seen through the eyes of both the therapists concerned.

The temporal sequence of events was that the patient had had group treatment when she saw me, and started her individual treatment after seeing me. But in presentation I shall to some extent neglect this temporal, historical account in favour of a stereoscopic view.

The patient, a married woman of thirty-nine, was sent to me by an experienced group psychotherapist (Dr A) with the special request to arrange for individual treatment for her. He reported: she attended sixty sessions over a period of eighteen months in one group. At first she had been co-operative and active, but became resistant later on. After a group discussion of incestuous problems she developed more acute panic states. After the end of this course she had three months at home, when it became evident that she needed further treatment. She joined another group, again mixed in sex, and with the same therapist; but soon, after four months, she discontinued because this group had too upsetting an effect on her. She asked to be taken on individually.

When she came to see me she said that she felt worse in that impulses to harm (strangle) her son, aged seven, were now troubling her even in the son's absence. Her present complaints began after the birth of this child, and she believed them to be due to weakness caused by his birth. She herself was born as the third of eight children, and her twin died at birth.

Her present symptoms began with irritability, fear of fainting, insomnia, back pains, indifference to sexual intercourse, and fears of crowds which, by the way, she had since childhood. During treatment she developed obsessional interest in cleaning her son's genital and anal region. Her fear of going out alone had also increased.

Her husband stated that at the time of their marriage, seventeen years previously, she had had fears of bus rides, of heights, and of collapse.

As to group treatment, her own account is this: the first group helped her a great deal during the first nine to twelve months. The group consisted of four men and four women. After eighteen months, the group ended and she began to feel worse again. The second group, in which she participated for four months, consisted of five men and five women: 'It felt like a crowd.' This remark is relevant in view of her fear of crowds. She could get no help from this group, nor give any. There were, in particular, two men in this group in front of whom she felt very small. This is repeated later on with Dr B, the individual therapist, when she felt very small in front of him. This was the expression of an identification of herself with her own son, who in turn is identified with her own father. At the same period of time when she asked for personal interview her son also had to have private lessons because he was backward at school.

One of the two men in the group for whom she felt great sympathy was lame from infantile paralysis. The other, who was quite young, about thirty, had, 'it is ridiculous to say', some attraction for her which made her feel very uncomfortable. The patient was not at this stage conscious of any connection in this with two rather remarkable facts: first, that her own son also had suffered from infantile paralysis, and secondly that her husband had an accident after five months of marriage, so that he was thought to be dying, was paralysed, and is still more or less lame on one foot.

She stated that she had not told the group therapist these facts at the time, although according to Dr A's notes they were discussed in the group. Later on, in individual treatment, she added that she had once or twice walked home with this young man and that it was this circumstance which made her want to leave the group. It is relevant that walking here stands for having intercourse, with her son that is. This was also expressed in an individual transference dream in relation to her therapist in which she was walking with him alongside tennis courts. It is important to note that she made an incestuous transference to a man in the group. She acted out her incestuous wishes, symbolically in the case of the young man in the group by feeling attracted to him and walking with him, and concretely in the increased interest in the genital and anal region of her actual son. At the same time she developed increased panics in relation to compulsive ideas of doing harm to her son.

The group therapist noted that her getting more panicky was in relation to incestuous problems having been touched upon in the group.

We will now further supplement our information by some observations which Dr B made. He saw the patient once weekly, for a total of thirty-one sessions. He stated: 'At first she tried to make me into the ideal father; however, she simultaneously became physically attracted to me and split off the father component by developing a correspondence course with a faith healer. This was all interpreted to her. Gradually I then became the cruel, rejecting father, and finally the father to whom she is very ambivalent, but trying hard to maintain a kind of relationship.

'In the course of treatment her feelings about her son became clearer. They included (1) aggression towards him, because he is responsible for her grey hairs, taking away her youth and sexual attractiveness, and because he stands for her hated younger brother. (2) Her guilt towards him because she had him for the wrong reasons, namely to mend her broken marriage; because he was born as the result of sexual intercourse and is therefore dirty; and because she has made him into a love object on whom she works out her conflict with her own father.'

Now from the information given here in very condensed form we can reconstruct sufficiently clearly for our purpose the particular transference situation at the time when she left the second group. The therapist, Dr A, was a rejecting and punishing father; the two men were split incestuous images (husband, son: father, brother) and objects of her acting out incestuous impulses. The maimed man represented at the same time her husband and her son, as he had been harmed and castrated by her. The young man represents the sexually attractive aspect of her son. She flees from the situation and at the same time asks for individual treatment. In the same way she acts out later with the faith healer *versus* the analyst. At the same time she identifies with her son, and parallel with him, asks for individual 'private lessons'. It is clear that the Oedipus situation has here become activated, in particular that the incest theme is active and represented in the two versions which I have described.

The group therapist, interestingly enough, acted exactly in the role of the patient's phantasy, namely as a reprimanding father. He saw her at this time in an individual interview and told her particularly to bring these facts and complaints forth in the group situation. Thus a patient may contrive to make the therapist act in a certain role, the deeper meaning of which is unconscious to both.

When making my observations on this particular case I was already familiar with this type of occurrence. The regression from the actual conflict to the infantile conflict can here be seen inside the group. It is a way of preserving her neurotic conflict from the impact of the group, a defensive move. Such patients cannot share the therapist with the group. They run away from a significant person. It is particularly transference neuroses who show this in a group-analytic situation, but not all of them do so. If and when they do there is a clear indication for an individual and, if possible, an individual psycho-analytic situation. For this indication to be recognized it is however necessary to differentiate between a transference relationship and other relationships. Observation in a group demonstrates this difference for all to see.

We know of course that psycho-analysis is indicated in the case of a transference neurosis. What is new is that we can arrive at the same conclusion from group-analytic observation which, moreover, adds those essential dynamic characteristics which determine our indication in the individual case.

This particular example was chosen just because it is non-controversial. But it may strengthen our trust in more surprising indications which might and indeed do appear to emerge. Observations such as this also add precision to the assessment of quantitative and qualitative factors. This is important for practical reasons. But even more important is the gain for the theoretical understanding of their essential significance. *Vice versa*, these observations throw into relief what characteristics of the psycho-analytic situation do make it a method of choice for the analysis of a transference neurosis. Here belong such features as the analyst's benevolent neutrality and non-inter- fering attitude, and the relative detachment of his personal life and values, and many traditional arrangements of the psycho- analytic technique which are sometimes not fully appreciated in their deeper significance.

In the *New Introductory Lectures* Freud repeats his old indications, unmitigatedly: 'You know already', he says, 'that the field in which analytical therapy can be applied is that of the transference-neuroses, phobias, hysterias, obsessional neuroses and, besides these, such abnormalities of character as have been developed instead of these diseases. Everything other than these, such as narcissistic or psychotic conditions, is more or less unsuitable.'

Freud, in speaking of analytical therapy, has in mind the classical situation which is in accordance with my usage in this chapter. We have since made the experience that other neurotic conditions—those then summarily called actual neuroses— states of depersonalization, certain psychotic conditions and psychosomatic conditions, do respond to psycho-analytic treat- ment; but, significantly, the situation, technique and the therapist's role deviate more or less from the classical ones. The point of importance in the present context is that the psychopathology of these conditions is different from that of the transference neuroses, and that this can be particularly well observed in a group situation.

Group-analytic psychotherapy seems particularly valuable in the treatment and study of the conditions which Freud here designates as less suitable or unsuitable for psycho-analytic treatment.

Now Freud, at the same place, mentions the test for witch- finding according to Victor Hugo: a Scottish king declared that he had an infallible method of detecting witches. He put them to simmer in a cauldron of boiling water and then tasted the soup. According to the taste he could say 'that was a witch' or 'that was not a witch'. This story is taken by Freud as a simile to illustrate the mode of selection for psycho-analytic treatment. It is certainly desirable—and perhaps possible—to progress from this 'witches' test to a more scientific way of approaching this important problem.

Chapter IX

PSYCHODYNAMIC PROCESSES IN THE LIGHT OF PSYCHO-ANALYSIS AND GROUP ANALYSIS

Group analysis is concerned with the total field of mental dynamics, whether these be better studied in an individual or group situation. In this chapter a selection will be made and particular attention paid to psycho-analytic equivalents.

Freud's contribution to group psychology was based on the findings of individual psychology, although he occasionally showed surprising insight in favour of the reverse procedure. In his book on the subject, he studied groups of an entirely different nature from those investigated by the present writer. He used two large, highly organized groups—the army and the Catholic church—as models from which to illustrate such concepts as for instance the ego ideal and identification. He did not attempt to explain the dynamic processes taking place in these groups as germane to them, but rather to show how the internal forces characteristic of individual life sought their expression through the group medium.

Classical psycho-analytic concepts can be used with advantage in a group setting but the operative processes are not identical with those observed in the individual psycho-analytic situation. The wholesale transfer of psycho-analytic concepts to a new field is particularly inadvisable when they have lost their original precision and are exciting controversy in their own field of origin. Even such concepts as transference and identification are in the process of revision, or tending to become confused.

Our psychotherapeutic groups are in principle transference groups, in the sense that members can use each other and the therapist as transference figures, as it occurs in psycho-analysis between patient and analyst. However, the pattern of relationships develops with much more complexity in the group situation and cannot be explained by applying to it the term transference. On the contrary, the observation of classical transference processes within the group setting throws new light upon them as seen in the individual setting. In psychoanalytic literature the term transference is increasingly used to cover all interactions between therapist and patient. This development applies equally well to the corresponding concept of counter-transference. The group-analytic situation could of course be termed a transference situation in this wider sense, but it is better to speak of a therapeutic, or 't'-relationship, -situation, etc., and reserve the term Transference situation for its more specific and legitimate application.

Similar considerations obtain in the case of other terms, such as identification. Here again the group reaction seen as a whole cannot be understood simply on the basis of the psychoanalytic concept, whereas the understanding of the dynamics of identifications in an interpersonal situation helps us to discern new aspects of the process which escape observation in the psycho-analytic situation.

Group analysis views man's social nature as basic to him and individuals emerge as the result of developments in the community, just as in psycho-analysis individual personality is viewed as emerging from and formed by his family. Conceiving the social nature of man as basic does not deny or reduce the importance of the sexual instinct in the sense of psychoanalysis, nor of the aggressive instinct. The infant-mother relationship is the first social relationship in the same sense as it is the first sexual and love relationship. Man's social nature is an irreducible basic fact. The group is not the result of the interactions of individuals. We conceive all illness as occurring within a complex network of interpersonal relationships. Group psychotherapy is an attempt to treat the total network of disturbance either at the point of origin in the root—or primary—group, or, through placing the disturbed individual, under conditions of transference, in a group of strangers or proxy group.

When people are brought together in a psychotherapeutic group conflicting tendencies arise, but in spite of impulses to withdraw, the need of the individual to be understood by and related to the group prevails. This fundamental need to *relate* is shown with particular clarity even in our groups. (I add 'even' because our artificial groups are in fact conglomerations of isolated individuals.) The social basis at once asserts itself.

The idea of the group as the mental matrix, the common ground of operational relationships, comprising all the inter-actions of individual group members, is central for the theory and process of therapy. Within this frame of reference all communications take place. A fund of unconscious understanding, wherein occur reactions and communications of great complexity, is always present.

A principle which can be illustrated and supported by observation in therapeutic groups is that every event, even though apparently confined to one or two participants, in fact involves the group as a whole. Such events are part of a *gestalt*, configuration, of which they constitute the 'figures' (foreground), whereas the ground (background) is manifested in the rest of the group. We have described as *location* the process which brings to life this concealed configuration; it is, however, not always a simple matter to locate this pattern of the group's reactions. Other important concepts for understanding the group-analytic process are those termed *mirror reaction, occupation* and *translation*.

Mirror reactions are characteristically brought out when a number of persons meet and interact. A person sees himself, or part of himself—often a repressed part of himself—reflected in the interactions of other group members. He sees them reacting in the way he does himself, or in contrast to his own behaviour. He also gets to know himself—and this is a fundamental process in ego development—by the effect he has upon others and the picture they form of him.

By *occupation* is meant that which is the group's reason for coming together. In everyday life this may be for the purpose of study or work, to play bridge or golf. Such a declared, manifest occupation is deliberately absent from a group-analytic group. In this it differs from a 'free discussion' group. Observation of the group-analytic group makes it clear that such an 'occupation' acts as a defensive screen to keep at bay intimate interpersonal reactions, thoughts and phantasies. This defensive or screen function makes the concept of 'occupation' important for the understanding of the dynamics both of the group-analytic group and, by implication, of any type of group. There is a tendency for analytic groups to behave as if they had an appointed *occupation* such as 'discussing our problems'. An occupation can also be latent and the group may not be conscious of it. This might be called its *preoccupation*.

Translation is the equivalent of the making conscious of the repressed unconscious in psycho-analysis. Interpretation refers to a special contribution on the part of the psycho-analyst to this translation. The whole group participates in this process, which ranges from inarticulate symptom to verbal expression, understanding and insight, from primary process to secondary process, from primitive to logical, rational expression.

Group-analytic theory recognizes this translation as part of the process of *communication*. In a group-analytic group, all observable data are held to be relevant communications, whether they take the form of conscious or unconscious, verbal or non-verbal communications.

Characteristic non-verbal communications are those made in the form of behaviour, either on the part of individual members or by the group as a whole. Appearance and dress may be communications; an exuberant tie or conspicuous shoes, provocative disorder or meticulous neatness may excite comment and lead to insight in the same way as verbal exchange. One person will press for more light to be put on in the room where the group meets, while another will prefer to sit in near darkness, or mislay his spectacles in order not to see. The group as a whole may communicate tension in the shape of silences, or fitful, disjointed conversation. It may express a cheerful mood of relief, or group gloom in which everyone sits and glowers darkly, some on the point of tears.

At one end of the scale is the inarticulate symptom: it may be nail biting, excessive blushing, palpitation of the heart, or migraine headache; at the other lies its representation in verbal imagery. Between these two must be cut an intricate sequence of steps leading to verbalization. Many complex processes have to play their part before the mute symptom of a fellow member can attain linguistic expression and its meaning be grasped by the others.

It is the *process of communication* rather than the information it conveys which is important to us. In a group-analytic group, communication moves from remote and primitive levels to articulate modes of conscious expression and is closely bound up with the therapeutic process. The therapeutic group establishes a common zone in which all members can participate and learn to understand one another. Within this process members of the group begin to understand the language of the symptom, symbols and dreams as well as verbal communications. They have to learn this through experience in order for it to be meaningful and therefore therapeutically efficient. The conductor strives to broaden and deepen the expressive range of all members, while at the same time increasing their understanding of the deeper, unconscious levels. The zone of communication must include the experience of every member in such a way that it can be shared and understood by the others, on whatever level it is first conveyed. This process of communication has much in common with making the unconscious conscious and altogether with the concepts of unconscious, preconscious and conscious in their topographical and dynamic sense. We will discuss these later.

EGO, ID AND SUPEREGO IN THE GROUP MODEL

Here we may pause to glance for a moment at the group-analytic group as a model of the mental apparatus. In what way do the psychoanalytic concepts of ego, id and superego reflect in the group? The group is like a model of the mental apparatus in which its dynamics are personified and dramatized. A process analogous to this may be seen in the theatre where the characters not only represent themselves but also stand proxy for the audience both in their individual and community reactions. A very good illustration of the way in which this happens can be found in Friedman's and Gassel's study of the Sophoclean tragedy Oedipus Tyrannus. Their paper is of no less interest to us because it was not concerned with the dynamics of the group in relation to group psychotherapy.

Oedipus, having committed patricide and incest, had to be punished in order to assuage the guilt feelings aroused in the audience by the activating of their forbidden wishes. The tragedy is played out between Oedipus, representing one wish, and the Chorus representing the other. The authors write: 'The chorus by remaining detached absolves itself from responsibility . . . actually the chorus maintains a driving demand on the hero to fulfill what the community expects . . . Oedipus accepts fully the responsibility which the community is so eager for him to assume . . . the chorus is not unlike a helpless community in the habit of throwing responsibility to the leader.' The hero, Oedipus, here represents the id, in that he stands for wishes and impulses inherent in everybody. He also embodies a kind of collective ego for the community (see

Rank's description of the heroes of mythology as embodying
'collective egos' who reflect the forces at work within the
society which creates and projects them). Furthermore he has
to be punished for the crime he has committed in the name of
the community and is thus in some sense a scapegoat. The
conflict within the audience, within any given human being, is
given expression by the conflict between Oedipus and the
Chorus. The Chorus, which in present terms could delineate
our group, plays the part of the superego; it remains detached
and objective, but exerts a driving pressure on the hero to
fulfill his destiny.

In another paper by the same authors, also of interest to us,
on the Orestes drama, the Chorus incites and drives Orestes to
murder his mother. Orestes is tried and acquitted by a jury
which gives its verdict equally for and against him, thus
expressing the ambivalence of the community towards its wish
to be rid of the maternal tie through matricide.

We find similar configurations in our own groups, though
more often the leader or conductor is felt to be in the role of
the superego. Group members may also play the part of the
superego, ego and id in relation to each other. A good example
of the latter role occurred in one of my groups, when an older,
married woman registered considerable apprehension of a
younger, single woman in the same group. Later it transpired
that this younger member symbolized the maturer woman's
fears of loss of control and impulses of an erotic nature. In
other words, here was an incarnation of her own *id* functioning
independently of her control and hence provoking anxiety. The
group also manifests something in the nature of a collective ego.

I have repeatedly observed members functioning as scapegoats in place of the conductor. The group, angry with him but
not daring to attack him directly or to show open hostility, will
relieve and displace its emotion and fury on to one of themselves,
usually a weak or absent member. The scapegoat thus chosen
bears the brunt of a vicarious attack on the conductor. It therefore very often proves correct for the conductor to look for
latent and repressed hostility directed against his own person
under the guise of the scapegoat. Here is an interesting
example of one variation of this process. One of my groups at
various times repeatedly accused me of bias against a certain
member. In such a case, I assume in principle that the group
must have its reasons, however dormant my own awareness. I

did not succeed in this instance in finding evidence of any bias either in my behaviour or attitude. At a later stage, I had to defend the same patient against strong hostility on the part of the group. This made what had happened clear to me. The group, unconsciously wanting to make a scapegoat of the member in question, defended themselves against this tendency by first projecting it on to me and then accusing me of bias. These brief illustrations of clinical observations show how personalization, displacement and location take place in our groups.

MULTIPLE DIMENSIONS IN THE GROUP

The group operates in many dimensions. How can we orient ourselves, bring some semblance of order into this chaos? In this connection I would like to draw attention to some old and very interesting concepts of Wernicke. He thought the most important spheres in which psychosis could be placed were: (1) The external world, or allopsyche; (2) the Körperlichkeit, corporality or somatopsyche; and (3) the Persönlichkeit, or autopsyche.

A recent classification on developmental grounds is that used by Erikson. He envisages three stages of childhood development which persist in some degree in adult life. These can be looked upon as corresponding at least roughly to Wernicke's spheres as indicated by me in brackets. The first he called the 'autocosmos' wherein the world is experienced and reacted to exclusively in terms of the child's own body (somatopsyche). This stage is replaced by the 'microsphere'. Here object relations are formed, but the child endows the object with his own feelings and wishes, as for instance when the sofa becomes a boat, or the doll an angry mother (autopsyche). Eventually the stage of the 'macrosphere' is arrived at, object relations being now experienced in a world genuinely shared with others (allopsyche).

Among levels leading from surface to deeper and hidden aspects, four can be discerned in the group:

1. *The Current Level.* This is analogous to Erikson's 'macrosphere', and Wernicke's 'allopsyche'. Here the group is experienced as representing the community, public opinion, etc., and the conductor as a leader or authority.

2. *The Transference Level.* This second level corresponds to

mature object relations experienced in the 'macrosphere'. It is the level most often envisaged by group psychotherapists of analytic orientation, for whom the group represents the family, the conductor father or mother and the other members siblings.

3. *The Level of Bodily and Mental Images (Projective Level).* This level corresponds to primitive, narcissistic 'inner' object relations in psycho-analysis. Here other members reflect unconscious elements of the individual self. The group represents as outer what are in truth inner object relations. The closest analogy here is with the concept of play analysis and its resultant psychopathology much associated with the name Melanie Klein. This is the level of the 'microsphere' and also corresponds to Wernicke's autopsyche. Not only may individuals embody a part of the self, but the group as a whole may do so. The group often represents the mother image. The body image is reflected and represented in the group and its members. This phenomenon would correspond with Wernicke's somatopsyche, although the concept of a body image, owed in the main to Schilder, was in no way thought of or familiar to Wernicke's generation.

4. *The Primordial Level.* This fourth level is the one in which primordial images occur according to the concepts of Freud and those particularly formulated by Jung concerning the existence of a collective unconscious.

Further illustrations of the functioning of all these levels is provided in the following table:

LEVELS AND SPHERES IN THE GROUP-ANALYTIC GROUP

(1) Current Level
Macrosphere { Group=community, society, public opinion, etc.
(2) Transference Level
Mature object relations. Group=family, father, mother, siblings.

(3) Projective Level
Microsphere { Primitive, narcissistic, 'inner' object [Allopsyche] relations
Other members personify:
(a) part(s) of self [Autopsyche]
(b) part(s) of body (-image) [Somatopsyche]
Autocosmos { (4) Primordial Level
Collective images

The conclusions arrived at by Schilder as to the close inter-relationship between ego and outside world, the social nature of consciousness, and the relation between outer world and self as a fundamental human fact, come very close to our own. Schilder writes: 'It is our contention that every experience not only refers to these fundamental spheres of self and world, but also to the spheres of the body. Human existence consists in living at once in these three spheres which form an inseparable unit. We may call the fact that experiences are experiences in the outside world, the body and the self, an *a priori* insight. I would prefer the more modest expression that here we deal simply with an experience which so far has been proved correct.'

Arriving now at even closer equivalents of psycho-analytic concepts in the group than those already shown, we will first of all examine the unconscious, conscious and preconscious in a group setting.

UNCONSCIOUS, PRECONSCIOUS AND CONSCIOUS

We have already spoken of the systematic unconscious as used in psycho-analysis. This primary language in symbolic or symptomatic form, the language of the dream, operates in the group context. We do not merely see the distinction between primary and secondary processes as in psycho-analysis, but also many transition stages, and our process of communication and translation is closely linked with the construction of an ever widening zone of mutual understanding within the group. The concept of unconscious understanding, familiar in psycho-analysis, is one on which we build continuously. Every communication is understood unconsciously on some level and has to negotiate many levels before it can be grasped and shared in its full meaning.

Group Consciousness. Group equivalents of the *topographical* idea of conscious, unconscious and preconscious, can also be clearly shown. To demonstrate this, we must recall Freud's metapsychological hypothesis that the process of becoming conscious is closely allied to or essentially characterized by the cathexis of word representation. This Freudian concept is of great importance for understanding the metapsychology of hysteria, schizophrenia and various neuroses. The group equivalent of consciousness in terms of the group entity thus consists in any one member's *saying* something in so many words. If the group is ready and able to understand and assimilate what he says, the particular matter at issue can be said to be fully in its consciousness. The verbal cathexis assumed by Freud is here represented in the act of verbal expression on the part of any one individual.

The *preconscious* could be defined as something that remains unspoken, but potentially anyone could give utterance to this particular matter. The dynamic resistance between preconscious and conscious is perhaps well represented by the feeling that 'certain thoughts are better not mentioned'. Following these lines it is easy to construe the group equivalent of the dynamic *unconscious* or *repressed*, but for this to be of use clinical illustrations would have to go into considerable detail.

FREE GROUP ASSOCIATION

An equivalent of prime importance is that which corresponds to free association in individual psycho-analysis. 'Free group association' evolved through my own approach and is significant for 'group-analytic psychotherapy'. An analytic approach to groups was made by Schilder and Wender, but my own differed from theirs in proceeding straight away to a spontaneous handling of the group situation. I instructed the patients who in the beginning had had previous psycho-analysis to 'free associate' in the same way as in the individual situation. As expected, the associations which patients were able to produce were modified by the group situation. I then waited and observed developments over a number of years, eliciting the process to which I later gave the name of 'free-floating discussion'. Then I became aware that it was possible to consider the group's productions as the equivalent of the individual's free association on the part of the group as a whole. Only at a much later date consequent on my studies in analytic groups did it become clear to me that the conversation of *any* group could be considered in its unconscious aspects as the equivalent of free association.

Today I am beginning to fathom what elements in the situation of any given group of people approximate their conversation to free group association. Naturally the group-analytic situation itself is devised to encourage an optimum degree of freedom from censorship. The group association here is therefore the nearest equivalent to free association in psycho-

analysis and plays a similar part. More concisely this can be
expressed as follows. The more the 'occupation' of the group
comes to the fore, the less freely can group association emerge;
if the occupation is a pretext, or can be completely scrapped as
in our own technique, group association can emerge freely.
Social groups can stand farther from or nearer to one or the
other of these extremes. For example in a casually thrown
together social group, such as is seen in a railway carriage, or
on a conducted motor tour, though there is nobody to interpret,
the ongoing conversation approximates to 'free group association', the unconscious meaning readily shows itself to my own
observation in such contexts.

In the group-analytic group, the manifest content of communication, broadly speaking, relates to the latent meaning of
this communication in a similar way as the manifest dream
relates to the latent dream thoughts. This matter is so important
and so bound up with our concept of a *group matrix* that I shall
once more take occasion to stress the group matrix as the
operational basis of all relationships and communications. Inside
this network the individual is conceived as a nodal point. The
individual in other words is not conceived as a closed but as an
open system. An analogy can be made with the neuron in
anatomy and physiology, the neuron being the nodal point in
the total network of the nervous system which always reacts
and responds as a whole (Goldstein). As in the case of the
neuron in the nervous system, so is the individual suspended
in the group matrix.

Looked at in this way it becomes easier to understand our
claim that the group associates, responds and reacts as a whole.
The group as it were avails itself now of one speaker, now of
another, but it is always the transpersonal network which is
sensitized and gives utterance, or responds. In this sense we
can postulate the existence of a group 'mind' in the same way
as we postulate the existence of an individual 'mind'. Whereas
it is difficult for us to abstract from the concept of an individual
in a physical, bodily way, it should not be so difficult to do so
in the mental field, and to perceive that the matrix of response
is indeed an interconnected whole. In the mental matrix
individuals also emerge, but the boundaries of these (perhaps
they should be called by some other name such as 'psyche-
individuals') do not run parallel with the boundaries of their
physical person.

EQUIVALENTS OF MENTAL MECHANISMS

We have already exemplified *displacement* in a group. Suffice it to add here that the group equivalent is seen when repressed tendencies in individuals emerge in the roles of others. The process of displacement should be strictly viewed in this context as occurring between individuals inside the group, not simply as a function of the individual mind.

Isolation occurs when an individual within the group is assigned tendencies, forces or characteristics which are shunned in a phobic way by others. Isolation in the group is also manifest by punctuating silences, or by its abruptly turning from one theme to another at a certain point.

Splitting is another process clearly shown in the group. It takes the form in this context of sub-groups, splitting into pairs, etc.

These few illustrations are given to underline the fact that even the processes akin to psycho-analytic ones should be seen as configurations in the group context. Clearly the processes of *personification* or *impersonation* and *dramatization* are particularly stressed in the group and play a much bigger part than in individual psycho-analysis. All the models of processes described in this chapter incorporate this particular group feature, namely dramatization and personification, in this as in other instances reminiscent of the dream process itself.

In conclusion, I would like to stress the difference in emphasis between psycho-analysis and group-analytic psychotherapy. Psycho-analysis, at any rate in its historical aspect, has laid great emphasis on the psychogenesis of illness. In group analysis we are more concerned with the outlook for change and the direction and means whereby to ensure it. We therefore work with operational concepts, formulated and applied in the therapeutic process itself and derived from immediate clinical observations. In our view a dynamic science is needed which will incorporate and turn to good account the revolutionary idea that therapy is research and research in this field is therapy.

Group analysis as a method will then automatically fall into correct perspective as a powerful therapy, a stimulating theory and a fertile source of information and discovery in the psycho-social field.

Chapter X

PSYCHO-ANALYSIS, GROUP PSYCHO-
THERAPY, GROUP ANALYSIS

A PERSONAL VIEW OF PRESENT TRENDS

Freud's own work in its totality has so decisively influenced the psychological climate of our time that nobody coming after him could—if he would—ignore him. This is certainly true for psychotherapy as soon as it is analytic in orientation, whether this psychotherapy takes place in the individual (two-person) situation or in the multipersonal or group situation. Yet— Freud's own contribution to group psychology notwithstanding—the idea of a psychology or psychotherapy based fundamentally upon the group is anathema to the psycho-analysts. There are a few exceptions, I am glad to say, but they are still very few, and they have made fundamental contributions. Interest is slowly growing, but the vast majority of psycho-analysts today ignore or belittle group psychotherapy.

Someone familiar with the situation both from inside and outside, with its deeper meaning and complexity, as well as its all too human practical aspects, cannot expect this to be otherwise. If I allow myself a little prophecy: I would say that this opposition of the psycho-analysts to the group movement will come into the open during the next ten years.[1] It will take practical form, too, as it will become increasingly impossible to ignore this unwelcome new arrival and an attempt at wholesale incorporation will only lead to indigestion. It will take another ten or twenty years after that until the inevitable and constructive integration has been achieved. Nor will this integration be a matter between psycho-analysts and group analysts alone. Leaving the realms of prophecy, what can we do in this situation, we who already now have arrived at, or are on the way to, such an integrated view?

As a psycho-analyst I would myself object at this stage to

[1] Written in 1957.

extending the term 'psycho-analysis' to a multi-personal situation. It is doubtful whether psycho-analysis could ever be practised in a group without a severe distortion of its essence, as I hope to show presently. For theory, too, it is better to steer clear of concepts borrowed from psycho-analysis—however useful and meaningful they may sound—if these terms have become an inflated currency: they become confused and meaningless. Keep free to develop such concepts as are born out of the group situation and relevant to it! You may say that I advocate my own approach. But what else can I do? If I did not think it the right one, I would not adopt it. Before I can proceed to say in what sense I do believe that psycho-analytic principles can be applied to groups, it is necessary to consider present trends in psycho-analysis and to outline my own position as a psycho-analyst.

Those of us who responded to the impact of Freud's early work and who lived through its later developments in current experience, eventually to become active participants in it, find ourselves in a peculiar situation. We had to find our way to this work, fighting against a sea of resistances outside, and indeed within ourselves. Accepting, under much personal sacrifice, the hazards of a very insecure and uncertain future, we had to resist at every corner the temptation of short cuts or other deviations promising a much more comfortable existence, psychological and otherwise. Now we have to defend this work, to preserve it against some of its own adherents. The many deviant schools outside psycho-analysis set us no new problems, especially as they are often honest enough not to claim any more to be forms of psycho-analysis. One may say that between them they make all the mistakes which Freud's genius has led him and us to avoid. To some extent they are legitimate elaborations and corrections, stimulated by part aspects of psycho-analysis, erring only in mistaking a part for the whole. Sometimes such a part aspect is so much made the central core that one cannot help looking at these systems as quasi-pathological formations, as if they were fixations on certain levels which psycho-analysis had passed in its course, or regressions to them when further developments were too dangerous, or reaction formations against some intolerable psycho-analytic concepts, e.g. that of castration or the Oedipus complex. What we are more concerned with are cells, cultures and schools within the psycho-analytic movement itself, pulling in different directions. These schools of thought usually attack one or more of the foundations upon which psycho-analysis rests: not by any means the same ones, however. On the contrary, with a beautiful division of labour, each one attacks one of the fundaments which the other has left standing or even proclaimed the most essential. One will declare that psycho-analysis is first and last an instinctual theory, that infantile sexuality and libido theory are the very foundations; the other that the assumption of instincts in man in the psycho-analytic way is erroneous and untenable, or that the libido theory is redundant and should be replaced by an object-relation theory (of which there are many brands)—and so forth. These differences inevitably involve all concepts and terms used, and also technical procedure, of special importance in our present context. Some see all relationships in the therapeutic situation as transference and interpret this from the beginning, or even exclusively. Others are impressed by the specific nature of Transference, by contrast with other phenomena, and concentrate on the analysis of the Transference neurosis in a relatively well-defined phase of the psycho-analytic process. Some start from the surface, as Freud did, others dive into so-called deeper interpretations. Free associations seems still basic to many, not so much to others. Therefore what goes under the name of psycho-analysis today includes considerable and often mutually incompatible variations. Enough has been said, I hope, for it to be clear that if someone else says he applied psycho-analysis to groups, this means absolutely nothing, unless one knows him, his background and his training very well. Above all, if somebody else says the same, the odds are that he applies something quite different from the first, and if twenty-five psychotherapists say that they apply psycho-analysis to groups, they are as likely as not to apply twenty-five different sets of concepts and procedures.

All these new developments make positive contributions and offer sometimes valid criticisms of psycho-analytic theory and practice. Nobody can predict what will eventually emerge from the concert of all these activities, what they will contribute to the edifice of a future psychotherapy. But it seems certain that they will never become integrated into a harmonious scientific psycho-analytical discipline consistent with Freud's work and its spirit.

With all that I do not wish to give you the wrong impression that psycho-analysis consists of nothing but contradictions. There is quite a solid centre core. Psycho-analysts still speak on the whole a common language and share certain basic convictions. They have, moreover, at least a degree of uniformity in their standards of training, qualification, practice and ethics. If and when they turn to group psychotherapy, all these are valuable assets, and even indispensable, if they are to become group analysts. But just as knowing psycho-analytic literature and having been psycho-analysed does not make anyone into a psychoanalyst, so being a psycho-analyst does not qualify anyone as a group analyst. In our experience in the Group-Analytic Society in London, the intensive participation as an analysand in a group-analytic group is of the greatest importance for all who wish to qualify as group analysts, not least for those who have often had intensive individual psycho-analytic experience over a number of years with one or more psychoanalysts.

It will have become clear that as a psychoanalyst, I adhere to the classical line of development from Freud's work, which in itself is not a solid structure but a dynamic organism, for ever on the move. This work, like everything else, is bound up with its time and it is possible that nothing in it can remain unaltered in the course of time, neither its theory nor its practice, nor its metapsychology. Future generations may have to translate psycho-analytic concepts into their own language, may have to rediscover them. Those who wish to understand the original will have to study Freud's work in historical perspective, with a gift for the flavour of its time and the man and his language, if they are to rediscover its true meaning. Psycho-analysis as a method of treatment may in time lose its importance and in its pure form become restricted in application to very special circumstances.

From this central position which I thus maintain inside psycho-analysis, it follows that I use psycho-analytic concepts in their classical, in a sense their only correct, significance. In their pure form these phenomena can only be observed in the classical psycho-analytic situation, which in turn is strictly applicable only in the treatment of a 'Transference neurosis', i.e. a patient suffering from hysteric, phobic or obsessional manifestations. The extension of psycho-analytic treatment to other forms of neuroses or psychoses necessitates already considerable modifications. The position of the psycho-analyst behind the couch, maintaining his well-known attitude of

accepting the patient's transference, confining himself to interpretations, that of the patient lying on the couch, given to free
association, are essential features. The situation still bears the
imprint of the hypnotic-cathartic one from which it has developed. It encourages the development of a regressive Transference reaction with its early primitive and psychotic character,
which is so essential for the elucidation of the patient's early
conflict situations. The psycho-analyst's use of this situation, in
which the long past and the present are as one in the consulting
room, is quite specific for psycho-analysis. Deliberate manipula-
tions, influencing, role playing are not psycho-analytic. It is
understood that I am speaking of a model in a standard situation.
The experienced and gifted psycho-analyst learns to apply these
principles with a great degree of elasticity and flexibility, but
he will always remain on psycho-analytic grounds and know
when he has abandoned them and reverted to some other form
of psychotherapy.

This psycho-analytic situation has developed over half a
century of trial and error, as if guided by one aim, the essential
aim of psycho-analytic procedure: the uncovering of the original, usually early and very early, primitive conflict situations.
So emphatic is the historical, genetic orientation in psycho-
analysis that it unhesitatingly evokes hypotheses of prehistorical
events, concerning race and species, where individual, ontogenetic sources fail to give an account. It is therefore incorrect
to equate an experimental 'a-historic' situation with the psycho-
analytical situation more nearly could it be considered as an
existential-analytic one. Psycho-analysis may lead to the radical
cure of symptoms and modify neurotic developments, but its
greater contribution is the exploration of the development and
functioning of the human mind in its normal as well as abnormal
aspects. It is based on the individual in Cartesian isolation: one
body, one brain, one mind. The world is built up from bodily
needs and sensations, although an outside reality, impersonal
and objective, is recognized. Social relationships are secondary,
the primary relationship or even unity with the mother is
understood to start with only as a relationship between two
erotogenic zones: the mouth and the nipple. Psycho-analysis
began as a study of one person by himself alone in isolation.
This person had to split himself into two parts: the one
observing and the other to be observed. This latter, the
observed, had to be both: clearly detached from the first, the

observing part, and yet undoubtedly belonging to the same person. The dream fulfilled these conditions ideally. Another human being could also be made the object of study in exactly the same way; it made no difference because both were equally subject to determinism. How difficult a step it was to proceed to the recognition of a relationship between the two persons, the physician and the patient, as a new determinant! Transference thus was first only a nuisance, a resistance, and only very slowly emerged as the essential dynamic force in the field. Many psycho-analytical concepts have clearly retained the stamp of this self-analytic phase, others have moved on to the two-person psychology or could only be coined in this later phase, some have a number of recognizable imprints according to different stages.

At first sight: could there be a greater contrast between this and the group situation? The patients are many, the therapist sits with them in a circle, the emphasis shifts from the pronounced inequality of psycho-analysis to a much greater degree of equality of contribution: everybody and nobody is a therapist, everybody and nobody a patient. Transferences are not received by trained impartial technicians, but reacted to by other emotionally disturbed people, met by counter-transferences of considerable charge. The same is true for all other processes: there is no consideration or timing in interpretations or in any other reactions. Do we wonder that psycho-analysts shudder?

One of the assumptions we implicitly make is the basic and not the secondary character of the social nature of man, the existence of a constant stream of communication, verbal and non-verbal, conscious and unconscious, indeed of a community of experience.

Some authors find it difficult to agree that the group situation changes all processes radically, apart from the new dynamic forces and dimensions which are particularly its own. Let us therefore demonstrate this in two simple examples.

(1) *Free association*, as understood in psycho-analysis is of course impossible in a group. Everybody would have to talk simultaneously. In any case, nobody could understand what the other is talking about if he were even silently engaged in free association of his own. Free association, by the way, in its pure form is a typical product of the first one-person phase and becomes modified in the model two-person situation. My first groups, probably the first anywhere to be asked to associate

freely, 'as far as possible', had had individual psycho-analytical experience. What then developed I described as 'free-floating discussion'. Soon I recognized that the group analyst is entitled to treat all the spontaneous contributions as the equivalent of free associations on the part of the group as a whole. This collective association is totally different from its equivalent in the individual situation and could not even be perceived without the introduction of a completely new frame of reference: the group as a whole or what we now call the group matrix.

(2) *The dream*, the '*via regia* to the unconscious', has also changed its values in the move from the one-person to the two-person situation to which move I draw your attention. Freud's 'Interpretation of Dreams' is essentially written from the one-person point of view. The dream has further changed in its significance for us with the shift of emphasis in psycho-analysis from unconscious content to resistance and character analysis and to the analysis of the Transference neurosis in the here and now of the therapeutic (T) situation. Classical analysis of the dream, from the manifest façade to the latent meaning, with the help of free association, is in current practice more in the nature of an occasional episode within the total context of the psychoanalytical process. The manifest content, in spite of its character of disguise and distortion of the latent dream thoughts, has gained in significance in its own right, especially as a mirror of the transference situation. Perhaps our schooled eye has also made its manifestation more transparent. Observations such as the foregoing do not, however, receive the attention they deserve in psycho-analysis. Yet it has to be underlined, the distinction between the manifest and the repressed, latent dream, and all that corresponds to it, is fundamental for Freudian psycho-analysis and if we gave it up, we should no longer talk of practising psycho-analysis. On this occasion I am concerned with the impact of the group-therapeutic or group-analytic situation upon the dream. The dream is particularly an individual creation, not meant for publication, for communication to others. The self, as Freud has shown us, refuses to accept it even as an internal, intraindividual communication. If patients recount their dreams in the setting of a therapeutic group—and with unskilled handling they tend to develop little epidemics of that, this is by and large the expression of a resistance. The analysis of this, the resistance, aspect becomes of paramount importance. The temptation for the therapist to

fall in with this resistance, to feed on dreams as it were, is considerable, with the inevitable consequence that the group will produce dreams as material for analysis and everybody is happy. Such a quasi-psycho-analytical approach makes, therefore, two mistakes: firstly, it rests on an inadequate understanding of the dynamics of the individual psycho-analytical situation and secondly transports this wrongly to the group situation. The group analyst in my approach, does not reject dreams, of course, but treats them like any other communication according to their dynamic significance. Above all, in our view every dream told in a group is the property of that group. Groups discern with fine intuition between what they call 'group dreams' and other dreams. These group dreams are sometimes communications of relevance, especially regarding current interpersonal dynamics, the conductor, or insights into shared but unconscious resistances. Other dreams are sometimes ignored by the group, sometimes taken up on the dreamer's own grounds for a little way, in any case they become soon absorbed into the group context as it develops from its matrix.

It is clear that all we have learned about the dream, if true, must still be true even if the dreamer is in group analysis; but it should be equally clear now, that dreams are influenced by the dreamer's situation, and quite especially by such deep-going ones as the therapeutic transference (T) situation in psycho-analysis or group analysis respectively and that these two situations show up for study quite different aspects of dreams, dreamers and dreaming. The same is true for psycho-analysis as a whole. All that psycho-analysis teaches us enters in principle fully into group analysis; structural, economic and dynamic aspects of unconscious mental processes, the concepts of primary and secondary processes, of basic conflict, the emphasis on insightful revision of pathogenic reactions in the therapeutic situation. The experienced group analyst will be able in direct observation to penetrate the presenting surface of the material and he will operate with interactions as yet not in the group's consciousness. In operational terms: the patients determine the subject-matter of each session, the group analyst is concerned with the translations of ucs material into cs[1] thought and with the analysis of resistances and defences. He uses selective interpretation, confrontation, etc., in this work, refraining from any

[1] Ucs and cs respectively denote unconscious and conscious processes in a systematic sense.

other influence. Above all he maintains the characteristic attitude of the psycho-analyst as to transference and counter-transference, using these phenomena solely for the purpose of analysis. For this latter task quite in particular the group analyst's own psycho-analytic training is of the greatest moment but he meets now equivalents of the phenomena known to him from the individual situation with a character all their own. The group is now his elementary frame of reference, and only renewed and intensive training and experience can enable the psycho-analyst to function adequately in a group.

What has so far been described is not more and not less than a legitimate application of psycho-analytic principles to the group. If group analysts were not more than that, it could be called group psycho-analysis, but as a method would fall short of psycho-analysis in some essential respects, as I have tried to make clear. If one believes, as I do, that the reductive analysis in terms of an infantile neurosis, infantile sexuality, early object-relations by the working through of regressive Transference levels, recollections and reconstructions of actual childhood experiences, if someone believes that these are of the essence of Freudian psycho-analysis, he must find the term psycho-analysis of or in a group misleading and would rather confine this term to a two-person situation.

Group analysis as practised and taught by me, however, is far more than merely an application of psycho-analytic principles to the group. Elements enter into it which far exceed the individual psycho-analytic proposition. To this aspect I will devote the rest of this chapter. The consistent use of psycho-analytical principles makes this form of group psychotherapy, group analysis, a blood relation of psycho-analysis. It is time now to look at the features which derive from its blood relation-ship on the other side, the mother's side, if you like, to the family of groups. It shares the properties of groups, especially of groups of its kind, size, psychotherapeutic nature, etc.

All psychotherapy can be said to depend on three sets of factors:

(1) What the therapist brings with him: his attitude, personality, experience, the nature of his interventions, inter-pretations.

(2) What the patient brings into the situation, not merely in terms of his conventional diagnosis, and:

(3) The conditions in which they meet; formality, regularity

and their counterpart, spontaneous or directed nature of communication and many, many other features influence decisively the material and the therapeutic dynamics.

I had often studied by experiment and in supervising individual psycho-analysis how any change in any detail alters all processes. The change from the individual—to a group—situation has naturally far-reaching consequences. For the correct appreciation and handling of the latter the psychotherapist's individual school seems to be less relevant than his training as a group psychotherapist. Two group psychotherapists of skill and experience can be in substantial operational agreement though their psychological persuasion in terms of individual schools may differ considerably.

The existence of the group therapeutic situation itself accounts for specific features, which the group-analytic approach studies. We speak of the importance of the communicational process, of ego training in action (intra-psychic action). Group-analytic psychotherapy has a much wider range of application than individual psycho-analysis. It acquires features of an action method, so foreign to psycho-analysis. Some psycho-analysts recognize that a number of conditions need other than psycho-analytic treatment. Where psycho-analytic treatment is disappointing, collective and action methods may prove more effective. For instance, in psycho-analysis, character resistances have to be changed into Transference resistances, in group analysis they can, through comparison and contrast, be analysed in the immediate interactional situation. There is much need for a differential indication as to method in various conditions and for different personalities.

Group analysis with its emphasis on the immediate T-situation in action lends itself to 'action research'. It may teach us less about developmental aspects of mental mechanisms, intraindividual conflict, the biological, bodily basis of the energies involved. It can teach us more about the conditions of therapeutic change, the interpersonal nature of mental mechanisms, about conscious and unconscious communication, the dynamics of groups and of the particular community to which they belong, the physiognomy of syndromes by similarity and contrast amongst other problems.

Thus the individual school of the therapist is one thing: it will colour his approach. His approach to the group is another. If we use operational terms, describing the relevant processes

TMKF – I

accurately, we can create a common ground on which to exchange experiences and a common platform, over and above the schisms of individual schools. From this vantage point we shall be in a better position to judge different theories and claims more objectively and shall be brought nearer to a scientific validation of our work.

Part III

GROUP DYNAMICS AND THE INDIVIDUAL

INTRODUCTION

PSYCHONEUROSIS AS A MULTIPERSONAL SYNDROME
AND THE CONCEPT OF AN INTERACTIONAL
NETWORK

The psycho-analysis of individual cases has traditionally been based on the assumption that the historical, genetic investigation of the psychoneuroses is at one and the same time the best or perhaps the only way for their theoretical understanding as well as their practical cure. Psycho-analysis has shown the importance of early object-relationships and how the genetic origin of all mental disturbances lies in the conflicts concerned with these early object-relationships. All later object-relationships are based on transference and are second-hand repetitions in the light of the individual's development. In psycho-analytic psychotherapy, therefore, the contemporary therapeutic situation is of importance only as a transference situation, in the strict sense of the term, between the patient and the therapist.

The orientation here adopted looks upon the original as well as the current neurotic disturbance as the common product of a number of persons who co-operate to bring it about and to maintain it.

The proper treatment and investigation of psychoneuroses and other mental disturbances must take into account this entire network of the psychopathological process. Such a *network* may include family members, work associates, friends, lovers, and others. The Network Concept, the emphasis on the 'multipersonal nature of the human problem' has slowly evolved in its principal importance in many clinical observations both in individual and group-psychotherapeutic analysis. Individual participants in this plexus can be seen as actors in the context of a play or drama. It is the play which is our particular field of investigation. Hence a much more powerful therapeutic attack may be expected from this approach, if it is true that any change in any one of the participants is interdependent on a corresponding change in others. New operational concepts are needed for this proposition.

The three papers in this section put the group situation decidedly into the centre for the study of psychodynamic processes. In a sense they form a culmination of twenty years' labour in the attempt of a theoretical formulation of a *social* psychopathology and psychotherapy on the basis of group-analytical concepts.

The first was delivered as the chairman's address to the Medical Section of the British Psychological Society in 1961. It is the latest of the three, but serves best as an introduction. It also carries on from the last section showing psycho-analysis and the development of a group-analytic approach in perspective inside psychotherapy as a whole. It is devoted to the main theme of the section: 'Individual and Community' in their bearing on mental (and other) illness and the possibilities of cure in both individual and group situations. The vested interests of society in defence against the therapeutic process are emphasized and an attempt is made to explain this resistance.

The next paper, presented in 1958 at the New York Academy of Medicine, whilst putting the issue on a broader basis, tries to illustrate these group-dynamic processes in actual operation in ongoing group-analytic psychotherapy.

The third paper strikes a similar note, using lessons learned in the discussion of the previous one in New York (mainly semantic, especially in connection with the term groupdynamics). It illustrates in some detail, what could only be indicated in the first, the reaction of the patient's network to therapeutic change in him.

Chapter XI

PSYCHOTHERAPY IN THE 'SIXTIES

Psycho-analysis has been the decisive influence in psycho-therapy during the first half of this century. This is largely due to Freud's own contribution, to what he saw, and was not the result of his method. Freud could have made this contribution as a writer, thinker, poet or biologist.

What psycho-analysis means to us far exceeds its importance as a method of psychotherapy. It has transformed our picture of man and his motives, and influenced all spheres of thinking. One can only have a feeling of sympathy with those who try even now to keep away from the impact of this work or to deny it. By contrast to others like myself, it has been a most significant experience in our lives. From the moment I first became acquainted with Freud's work in 1919 I knew that I wanted to devote my life to psycho-analysis, and I have never looked back. I wish therefore to make it clear that I am here concerned merely with psycho-analysis as a method of psychotherapy and as a theory of psychopathology. In this respect its greatest merits are the elucidation of unconscious processes, its concentration on the individual's problems in everyday life, his needs and anxieties, his happiness, hopes and despair, and the provision of a comprehensive theory based on biology.

In considering the second half of this century we are facing an altered situation. Twenty-one years have elapsed since Freud's death, and of his original collaborators only Jung, perhaps the greatest of them, is still with us.[1] Freud's work must be taken as a whole, an historical fact, complete in so far as it cannot be developed further by anyone else. We are left with a method and a theory, and the question is what can we do with them without Freud.

What is the situation today? The psycho-analytic school is a world-wide organization, but split into a great number of widely different groups, sometimes even within a single

[1] Jung died in 1961 a few months after this address was delivered.

Psycho-analytic Society. Unfortunately the training analysis, the most significant experience of the future psycho-analyst, is dependent on the personalities of the analyst, the analysand and on their interaction.

Let us face the fact that psycho-analysis has not been able to produce a method which is sufficiently precise and well defined to serve as an instrument of investigation with reliable results if correctly applied. On the contrary, if we know the analyst and his convictions, we can predict fairly accurately beforehand what he will find. Anyone who makes new discoveries may perhaps do so with the help of this method, but on the basis of his own capacity to see things afresh.

Psycho-analysis as a psychotherapeutic method is of limited value, indicated and practicable only under selected conditions. Its contributions are part of psychotherapy as a whole, and of a scientific discipline of medical psychology, and have become absorbed into these.

In this paper I will emphasize the defensiveness of society against the therapeutic process and try to explain it, as I see it. In a preliminary way I should like to illustrate just how this tells on the level of everyday life.

While incubating this paper I happened to change my hairdresser. At the second or third visit, he found out, in spite of my reluctance to talk, that I was a psychiatrist, that I was at the Maudsley Hospital and in private practice. He told me that there were at least a dozen psychiatrists who had their hair cut at the same place, which happens not to be very far from the Tavistock Clinic. He said they usually seemed 'far away', and often seemed to need treatment themselves. During this whole conversation my own replies were mostly confined to 'hmm' or 'Yes, yes' and similar noises. When he came up against my somewhat obstinate hair, he opined 'your hair needs hypnotizing, Sir!' This was considered a great joke all round. Each hairdresser and his respective client took up the thread: one heard laughter, funny remarks, and serious and mysterious sounding notions referring to hypnosis and psychiatry in general.

Next time, he returned to the subject, asking about several hospitals, all neurological in character, and the conversation turned to neurosurgery. He spoke with seriousness and respect of this discipline and its famous exponents. He then asked if I knew Dr X, to which I replied, 'Yes, he is very well known for hypnosis.' He said, 'That's right. There is a lot of difference of opinion about this. Another doctor I know says he doesn't think hypnosis is any good; it's all right for taking out a tooth, or for childbirth, but that's about all there is to it, and he doesn't recognize it as a treatment for these nervous troubles.' 'Hmmm,' I said. 'We have a psychologist, you know, he doesn't believe in any of this—he says nothing at all is proved. He doesn't think there is anything in it at all. But then we have another psychologist—he doesn't believe in anything else. He says he can't recognize any treatment except the psychological one, and this usually takes something from two to four years; he doesn't think there is any other treatment for these conditions. Then we have a very distinguished physician who comes here and he says he doesn't think anything any good. He doesn't believe in psychiatry at all. He thinks that the practitioner should do it, the general practitioner could treat these conditions best. All these specialists, many of whom are not really qualified to treat these cases, did more harm than good.' I said: 'Yes, we ourselves think, too, that the general practitioner should treat these conditions, but then sometimes he cannot do so and he needs the help of a specialist who is specially trained, as with anything else.' He understood this and continued to tell me that, on the other hand, he had recently read a book which stated that all medicine and all treatment should be based on psychology; indeed, that this was the treatment of the future.

Looking back now on more than thirty years of a life devoted to the study and treatment of the psychoneuroses, I may be permitted to ask the question: Why is our work so difficult? Why, in spite of the considerable knowledge and the profound insights we have gained during the last fifty years, are we still powerless to achieve more than comparatively minor changes and rearrangements in the inner dynamics and the mental economy of our patients? 'Whence does neurosis come—what is its ultimate, its own peculiar *raison d'être?*' asks Freud, and continues: 'After tens of years of psycho-analytic labours, we are as much in the dark about this problem as we were at the start.' We have never overlooked the somatic basis of psychiatric conditions and the neuroses in particular. Freud spoke of neuroses as severe constitutional diseases. Yet to say that the answer to our question is simply that we are up against the constitutional, that is unalterable, barrier is not enough.

The further we penetrate in our analyses, the more we find that we are dealing with problems which involve everybody, and not with diseases which have descended upon our patients and of which we are to cure them.

The quotation from Freud occurs at the end of Part IX of 'Inhibitions, Symptoms and Anxiety' (1926). Roughly ten years later—only two years before his death—he presented us with another jewel, the produce of his solitary master mind. This article, 'Analysis, Terminable and Interminable' (1937), is Freud's last answer to our question.

We will for our purposes leave aside the important discussion of the problem of duration and completeness of psycho-analytical treatment, with which Freud's paper opens. It ends on familiar ground, reaffirming the paramount importance of two themes: the wish for a penis in women and 'in men the struggle against their passive or feminine attitude towards other men'. For this latter, Adler's term 'masculine protest' is very apt, but in both sexes the central factor is a repudiation of femininity, which is conceived as castration. This seems to Freud a biological fact, not amenable to psychological influence, offering resistances to change which are unconquerable. Even if this resistance appears as a transference: 'The vital point is that it prevents any change taking place—everything remains as it was'.

Limitations of psycho-analytic therapy are set in the first place by the strength of the instincts, which by definition cannot be changed, and must be controlled. The best we can do is to help the ego tame them. Our therapeutic efforts therefore turn to the ego. The ego, weakened by repression, repeats its defensive mechanisms during analysis. *The crucial point is that the ego treats recovery itself as a danger.* 'Nothing impresses us more strongly . . . than the feeling that there is a force at work which is defending itself by all possible means against recovery and is clinging tenaciously to illness and suffering.' The decisive variations in the ego are again seen as primary and congenital. Certain characteristics of the libido itself, such as 'adhesiveness', immobility or rigidity, may offer special resistance to change. Of great importance is the behaviour of the two primal instincts, their distribution, fusion and defusion.

The death instinct theory may not be tenable if applied to the isolated organism. If we look upon it as a quasi-poetical notion, applying to the living substance, 'life', as a whole it makes good sense. Personally, I have become more and more convinced in the course of years of the truth and usefulness of the concept of a primary self-destructive force. Nothing is more certain than the ubiquity of destruction—a fact difficult to accept.

One of the greatest tasks still before us is to review all our knowledge of psychological conflict from this new angle. Guilt and need for punishment are only localized, bound manifestations of this instinct.

These are limitations in the patient. What about the difficulties in the analyst himself? (These are of particular importance here in view of what I have to say later on.) The analyst as a psychotherapist should be mentally healthy, yet it cannot be disputed that he is frequently not as free from disturbance as he should ideally be. Every training analyst must be familiar with the intensity and subtlety with which his trainee repeats his own unresolved and reactivated conflicts with his own patients in turn, not only in projective reversal of his own warded off transference neurosis, but in genuine interaction with his patient's neurosis. This is one of the key positions for the understanding of the therapeutic process and its problems and limitations. These same observations can be made in the supervision of psychotherapists in training. The therapeutic situation in which these interactions can best be observed and corrected in my experience is in group analysis.

Provided this situation (in training) is competently handled, it is a unique occasion for working through the countertransference problems of the future psycho-analyst. It should have the result, 'that the learner's own analysis will not cease to act upon him when that analysis ends, that the processes of ego-transformation will go on of their own accord and that he will bring his new insight to bear upon all his subsequent experience'.

I can well believe that this happy result is not too frequently achieved, but I doubt that, if it is not, further analysis, however often repeated, will bring it about. I suspect that the interminable analysands will produce more interminable analyses in turn.

The analyst, like his patient, may 'defend himself against recovery and cling tenaciously to illness and suffering'. Like his patient? Perhaps also through his patient! This disturbing thought occurred to me a long time ago: does the analyst defend himself by his very profession as a psycho-analyst, by analysing others? I kept it carefully to myself until, in the course of a correspondence I had with Freud, about five years before the paper under discussion appeared, he himself touched on this point. He had encouraged me to study by what means analysts themselves resist the effects of analysis on their own person. I had indeed done so, but felt no wish to publish on this subject; perhaps as you read this paper, you will think that it is just as well. However, I communicated my suspicion to Freud as a tenative answer. He did not react to this at the time, but the whole question is taken up in the last part of chapter VII of his paper. The salient point is expressed in the following sentence: 'It looks as if a number of analysts learn to make use of defensive mechanisms which enable them to evade the conclusions and requirements of analysis themselves, probably by applying them to others. They themselves remain as they are and escape the critical and corrective influence of analysis.'

Today I see this whole problem as a special case of a general state of affairs, which can only be understood and remedied if we take the processes involved beyond the context of the individual in isolation.

The analyst, like any other human being, is dependent for his vital equilibrium on a dynamic system which comprises a number of persons in varying constellations. Unless he finds his basic satisfactions and balances with them, his unsaturated valences are bound to lead to a more realistic and serious interdependence with the patient, especially in view of the latter's enormous avidity for this. The analyst then deeply needs his patients, instead of offering the intense, but transient, sublimated relationship which the transference situation demands.

In this connection it is striking to observe how dependent many analysts and psychotherapists seem to be on their patients and how little aware of this they often are. More recently some psychoanalysts, following the courageous example of Tower (1956), have drawn attention to observations on their own persons and others, to the effect that the patient stimulates oedipal phantasies and reactions in the analyst. These observations are valuable and honest attempts to deal with this aspect of the counter-transference problem. I am not sure whether Tower and others make this point, but it would appear to me that the oedipal, i.e. incestuous, nature of such reactions is provoked by the quasi-incestuous character of the psychoanalytic situation itself, with its particularly severe taboos. In the face of the patient's temptings under these circumstances, it is quite likely that any sexual appeal is liable to be linked in the unconscious mind of the analyst with unresolved oedipal or pre-oedipal strivings. Nevertheless, these analysts have often been extensively and successfully analysed. If their own analysis has not liberated them from these complexes, why has it not? Why should it do so, on being repeated?

On the whole then we find that psycho-analysis at the end of Freud's life has had to admit its very considerable limitations as a psychotherapy. Helene Deutsch, reviewing some of her cases after thirty years, registers both disappointment and relief at Freud's paper and states: 'We do not eliminate the original source of neurosis; we only help to achieve better ability to change neurotic frustrations into valid compensations.'

Psycho-analysis thus remains what it has been from the beginning: the first scientific investigation into the nature and origin of neurotic symptoms or syndromes and, under favourable conditions at the same time presents their cure. Psycho-analysis, it is clear, cannot finally solve the problem of neurosis. It must admit that this process is interminable.

At the end of Freud's life we find psycho-analysis confronted with very severe obstacles to further therapeutic progress. In fact, the limits of all psychotherapy seem to be in sight, in so far as they stem from constitutional or otherwise unalterable factors in human existence, which tell in patient and therapist alike.

Psycho-analysis is essentially a search for genetic origins. Its orientation is biological and it is part of the natural sciences. It must rest on the foundation of the physical organism. Inevitably, therefore, as it progresses in this direction, psycho-analysis must find quantitive factors, constitutionally given, at its frontiers. Freud has made this clear by stating that instinct has a dual aspect, a physical and a mental one. Its physical, material roots from which ultimately all energy is derived, are a matter for biology, and outside the domain of psycho-analysis. When he reached the frontier Freud found there was a gap on the other side—there was no biology waiting for him with which to link his new findings. However, there's the rub: what seemed a gap turned out to be a no-man's-land of vast dimensions. It transpired that what was to become basic for psycho-analysis e.g. the Oedipus and castration complexes, had their roots in this no-man's-land. The need arose to resort to speculation.

Freud built up on the most solid grounds he could find in the data of prehistoric developments and their interpretation, a line which was followed to a much greater extent by Jung. Others have tried to penetrate to ever-earlier developmental phases of the human individual—much earlier than Freud thought safe— in order to trace the evidence for these speculative assumptions. Inevitably the method employed in this search becomes more rather than less speculative and interpretative in character. Freud, in his theoretical system, has called this no-man's-land the *id*, which is the mental reservoir of unconscious drive. This enabled psycho-analysis to keep up its 'Monroe Doctrine' and to continue its work for the time being unhampered by undue worry about developments in other fields. But this splendid isolation cannot go on forever.

Meanwhile, other disciplines have not been standing still. Far from linking up smoothly with psycho-analytic theories, they proclaim them in part as untenable, in part as due for serious revision. Anthropological field research has thrown much new light on life in primitive communities, which invalidates the old theories; social psychologists tell us on good evidence that much that was called instinctive is, in fact, learned behaviour, and so forth. The emphasis shifts from the individual to the community or group. It is true that the family is a model of prime importance which recurs in all cultures, but the whole family constellation changes its character according to the culture (not the other way round). Modern zoology has arrived at the conclusion that cultural inheritance has superseded biological inheritance in its importance for the human species (Huxley). Even Darwin's law of the survival of the fittest can be shown, experimentally, to operate in terms of the group rather than the individual.

In the following I will show that the same development is taking place in psychotherapy. From the psycho-analytic side much valuable work is being done in the attempt to link psycho-analytic findings with these modern developments. Much of this is centred in the us a. An example amongst many is Grinker's work in psychosomatics, and, in this country, the work of John Bowlby, who makes use of the fascinating findings in ethology. These workers feel that they must be open-minded about psycho-analytic theory, and be ready to modify or discard it wherever it is not the most useful to do justice to the facts. These attempts are in accordance with Freud's spirit, that is to say, with a scientific attitude, provided care is taken lest valuable insights, such as can perhaps only be gained on the grounds of psycho-analysis itself, are eliminated in the process.

Freud assumed without question that what psycho-analysis cannot do, no other method can do. Historically, he had every right to feel this way, in view of the overwhelming importance of his own contribution. Today it would seem to be necessary to make a distinction between the analytic and the psychotherapeutic function of the psycho-analyst, and not to identify the two.

This can best be demonstrated on the model of the transference situation. The psycho-analyst, as we know, submits the transference neurosis like anything else to the psycho-analytic procedure. He wishes to destroy or dissolve it by reducing it to its original historic meaning in the infantile situation. He recognizes transference both as a positive communication concerning the infantile situation, and as a defence against such reductive genetic elucidation. This analytic process has a therapeutic effect which is optimal in the transference neuroses. Nevertheless, this therapeutic effect is a by-product only. Psycho-analysis gives priority to analysis; psychotherapy to the therapeutic processes and their study.

Psychotherapy can be radical and intensive when the therapeutic process, the therapeutic encounter, is put into the centre. There is evidence that the therapeutic result is more dependent on personal qualifications on the part of both patient and therapist than is the latter's particular school. It would seem necessary, therefore, to concentrate on the experiences and processes that all can observe in their work with patients. We must express this experience in terms that can be shared by all, and formulate theories which lend themselves to scientific investigation.

Inside psycho-analysis therapeutic considerations have led to considerably more flexibility of method, according to the nature of the patient and his condition. This has been practised by many psychotherapists and some psycho-analysts for a long time, and is an example of what should be considered psychoanalytic psychotherapy. It is, of course, essential to give a clear theoretical account of such modifications in terms of the psychoanalytic situation and its parameters, rather than to make them intuitively and in a haphazard fashion. In my opinion all such variations should be defined in terms of the psychotherapeutic

(T) situation, of which the psycho-analytic situation is one model.

While we are not concerned on this occasion with developments in psychotherapy on a broad front in any detail, it may at this point be recorded that much progress is being made in various fields.

Within the last ten years psychotherapists have become more alive to problems, have become more daring, pioneering and experimental. Quite apart from action methods and a new appreciation of non-verbal communication, quite new (and very old) media of psychotherapy are being applied and studied—such as drama, dancing, music and many other methods of expression and communication; the growing influence of yoga and Zen Buddhism should be mentioned. Of the greatest social value would seem to be the new interest in studying and using the enormously powerful influences operating in communities, societies, teams and small groups, all of which can be used for therapeutic purposes on the basis of growing theoretical understanding on group-analytic grounds.

These experiences seem at first sight far from the sphere of the individual psychotherapist, especially the psychoanalyst. Freud took a different attitude in *Civilization and its Discontents* (1930). He argues that one may be justified in considering whole epochs of civilization, perhaps whole communities as neurotic (as Burrow had maintained), and continues: 'Following on the analytical dissection of such neuroses one might arrive at therapeutic propositions, which could claim a high practical interest' (my translation). Later, Freud warns us to be careful not to transfer concepts, from the sphere in which they originated and developed, into another. This is very much my point of view, but it is difficult to prevent analysts and others from doing just this: to transfer psycho-analytical concepts into the group situation. In the end, Freud states that, in spite of all these difficulties, one may expect that 'one day somebody will dare to undertake the pathology of cultural communities'. Well, we are in the middle of this process.

Personally, I find group psychotherapy particularly valuable, not only as a therapeutic method, but as a method of investigation into the therapeutic process and its impediments. Group analysis is not so much concerned with the question of how people have become what they are than with the question: What changes them or prevents them from changing?

Why and how do they resist change, in spite of misery and suffering? By what means, with the help of what energies, do they do this? This, of course, is the salient question for all therapy and also all education. Strangely enough, the acknowledgement of the forces of self-destruction and their agencies helps us and makes us therapeutically far more powerful.

The main progressive trends in psychotherapy flow together in a recognizable direction.

It is characteristic of all modern development to emphasize the experience which is made in the therapeutic situation itself. This is the essence of the 'here and now' of existential psychotherapy, which at long last hopes to come into its own. It would lead me too far here to go into the problems this raises, especially for the psychoanalyst. Quite briefly and inexactly my view is: (1) that every good psychotherapist is or should be an existentialist in his actual contact with his patient; (2) that every existential analyst uses or should use the psychoanalytic method and procedure; (3) that psycho-analytic theory is biological in orientation, whereas existentialism is not. From this spring two dangers: (*a*) for the psycho-analyst: that it restricts him—perhaps inevitably—in his therapeutic range; (*b*) for the existentialist: that he throws out the baby with the bath water.

The significance of the emotional experience in the treatment situation has not been overlooked by Freud and the early analysts. How could it be, as all therapy, all change must of necessity be taking place in the present. Even at the cathartic stage it was clear that recollection alone is inefficient unless accompanied by emotional re-experience. Yet, characteristically, the essence of this was described in physiological terms of the isolated organism and called 'abreaction'. Equally characteristically, therapeutic effects based on unconscious emotional experiences, exchanges and discharges, however powerful, were not regarded as valid, unless they led eventually to conscious awareness and insight. 'Where id was, ego shall be' as Freud was able—much later—to formulate. The concept of the transference neurosis and its analysis, so central for psychoanalytic therapy, is the very essence of the past coming into the 'here and now' of the treatment situation.

The work of Ferenczi and Rank, Karen Horney, Schultz Henke's Neoanalysis, Rado, the Washington School, Frieda Fromm-Reichmann, Erich Fromm, in spite of their differences, and notwithstanding the fact that some of them remained close to Freud's psycho-analysis, whereas others did not, have all in common this trend of putting the experience or re-experience in the therapeutic situation into the centre of their attention.

In recent times, Jules Masserman's work on dynamic psychiatry is perhaps the most comprehensive presentation of a psychopathology and psychotherapy on these, one might say, post-Freudian lines.

The tendency in all these neo- or post-Freudian developments is, however, to consider the present as more important than the past, in contrast to psycho-analysis.

In this country, Melanie Klein's work has helped to increase the range and depth of communication in the transference situation through its emphasis on object-relations and unconscious phantasy. The basic model is that of transference and counter-transference: two individual systems react upon each other each according to its own independent interpretation of the situation, based on the separate mental economy and psychodynamics of each.

Quite another aspect opens up when one takes this relationship as the basis for orientation and operation. Close and unprejudiced observation shows that this is not only possible but necessary. In the individual field, H. Stack Sullivan reoriented the whole of psychiatry in consequence of his interpersonal theory. The mutuality of this experience, the encounter between therapist and patient and the more active participation of the therapist are stressed.

My own work with groups has been guided by similar considerations. What is true for two persons is also true for three persons or any number: as soon as they get into contact and communication they form a new unified field of interactional processes. The process of intercommunication, whether verbal or otherwise, and its theory, thus acquire a central position for all psychotherapy. Group psychotherapy thus becomes possible and even necessary.

Once formulated, these views can be relatively easily understood intellectually, but their real acceptance in the concrete situation is difficult, as they threaten firmly-established positions. The change is one of attitude, and tells in the individual situation just as much as in the group situation.

To make my own view very clear at this point: for the full understanding of the individual's psychoneurosis, its history, the past remains of fundamental importance. Psycho-analysis is the method of choice for the exploration and reconstruction of this childhood neurosis. Psycho-analysis is a method of genetic research into biological origins. The transference neurosis should therefore be rightly considered as a repetition which is to be submitted to reductive analysis. By contrast, the relationship and interaction in the ongoing psychotherapeutic situation are of paramount importance for the therapeutic process and its study.

In addition: in so far as even in the original (childhood) situation, relationship and interaction may turn out to be of decisive importance, the past can come to life again under conditions which allow for change. Psychotherapy of a radical kind therefore becomes possible under many conditions which would not allow psycho-analytical genetic investigation.

We have already mentioned that this emphasis on interpersonal transactional processes, on the group, is borne out by developments in biology itself. Instinct and ego in their constitutional aspects prove malleable to the influences which are transmitted from one generation to the other. J. R. Carballo, of Madrid, in a recent article (1960) communicates pertinent observations and formulations from which the following are taken:

He speaks of the influence which is transmitted, impalpably and powerfully, from generation to generation. Even in the life of bacteria, so-called adaptive enzymes are transmitted from one generation to the next, without there being any question of heredity. Experiments by Liddell and Blauvelt concerning mammals, birds and reptiles, show that actions performed by the mother on the new-born are of decisive importance not only for the young animals' future social conduct but for the proper development of breathing, circulation, oxygenation of the blood, muscular strength and activity. 'The young animal that has missed those first acts of motherly care in their natural sequence will later on be a biologically deficient animal, a poor looking thing, more susceptible to infections than others, and furthermore unsocial and even neurotic. . . . An untimely death is a frequent consequence, as in the children lacking affective protection whom Spitz studied.' It can be shown that even the 'constitution' of Yorkshire pigs, for example, is only to 60 per cent the outcome of Mendelian factors, and depends for the rest on the influence of man's psyche as expressed through the care, feeding and the first formative moulding. Living beings, most of all man, are born with incomplete adaptive structures. These are completed in a transactional reality, the nature of which is transmitted from generation to generation. What in psycho-analytical language is an object relation from the point of view of the child, is seen in ethology from the mother's standpoint as an imprint. Carballo sees in transference 'nothing but the reactivation of the primary object-'relation'. This is correct if we take the term transference in its broad meaning. Inside the psycho-analytic situation, the transference/counter-transference relationship represents this social interactional reality.

We see therefore that cultural factors enter even into the study of constitution itself, that ego and superego are socially conditioned and quite certainly, that pathogenesis and cure depend essentially on the group. From all sides we are forced to the conclusion that the individual's emancipation from the group matrix is very incomplete. In our own field of psycho-therapy and psychopathology this leads me to the conclusion that disturbances like psychoneuroses cannot be fully under-stood from the observation of the individual alone, but must be considered in the group context to which they belong.

The original neurotic manifestation in the childhood situation is but a symptom of a total constellation, a family neurosis so to speak. The acute neurotic breakdown in the adult is not merely a repetition in a transferential setting, but a product of interactional processes in which a number of people are actively engaged. This insight—apart from its profound theoretical significance—is of very considerable practical importance for therapy.

I would like to mention a simple example of many years ago, the first, as far as I remember, in which I could make practical use of this view. My patient was one of a pair of twin brothers who, in addition, had married two sisters. They lived on a remote farm and it took him the best part of the day to come and see me. He was impotent. It is easy to imagine what complexity of interactions, identifications, etc., operated here. After two or three interviews it became clear to me that his sister-in-law, i.e. his wife's sister and his twin brother's wife, was a key figure, and I asked him to send her to me. Fortu-nately, she proved an intelligent and co-operative woman with good intuitive insight. When I saw my patient for the next and last time, his impotence had disappeared and he felt free from all disturbance. Five or six years later I by chance had occasion to hear that all had remained well ever since.

Over the years I have found that this multipersonal aspect is never absent, and that it is, in the great majority of cases, highly significant. The attempt to bring this total network of neurotic interaction into the open consciousness of all concerned, that is to say, in the same room and at the same time, often proves quite impossible in practice. More often than not it proves impossible even in thought and principle, because the complications arising can be foreseen to be overwhelming in their magnitude. Often, if not always, improvement in the patient provokes active, if largely unconscious, opposition on the part of others involved. I have given illustrations for this from ongoing psychotherapy, both in individual and group situations. This opposition on the part of other members of the network tended to disrupt the treatment situation, and sometimes succeeded. In some examples it has been possible to demonstrate that this interference occurred with the precision of clockwork *at the very moment of a decisive change in the patient under treatment.*

Systematic investigations have been beyond my scope so far, but I have hopes to carry them out still. Others have been better placed in this respect, and their investigations confirm this experience. E. Lindemann at Harvard, for instance, showed that improvement in one patient led to the falling ill of other members of his family[1] (members of the interactional network in my terminology). The pathological process concentrates on another member or members of this network and becomes manifest in them.

This is one type of group psychotherapy which has as its object the natural, primary group—not necessarily identical with the family, but more nearly, if you like, the psychological family. It is not often practicable at present, though I believe that it will prove the key to further progress in the treatment and prophylaxis of disturbances in human interrelationships.

The other form of group psychotherapy concerns groups of strangers in an analytic situation. This is, of course, immensely practicable, and its theoretical contribution may be even more important. As in the usual psychotherapeutic, and particularly psycho-analytic situation, the individual is temporarily removed from his pathogenic network. This group-analytic group

[1] Personal communication.

corresponds to a pure culture of these interactional processes in an innocuous setting, in a situation not predetermined by previous experiences, apart from those which each individual brings with him, and not determining future interpersonal relations. In this sense, perhaps, it is justified to call it an a-historic situation, which may lend itself to experimental investigation. Nowhere can these processes be so well studied, especially in their suprapersonal, transpersonal nature. It is not adequate to describe this as individuals who compose the psychical fabric of the group. One point of importance I would like to make: these processes are not the particular property of the group situation; they operate equally in life and in the individual psychotherapeutic situation. It is therefore not a matter of whether one practises what is technically called group psychotherapy or not. One is concerned with these forces just as well in the individual situation—though group observation is the optimal setting for their study.

If it is true that we are all involved in these problems and conflicts, it must also be true that we are dependent on others for our mental health. We must consider our own existence, the life we lead, in some respects as a device for keeping out of conflict at the expense of others.

The defensive aspect of the psycho-analyst's profession thus appears in yet another light. He really defends himself by analysing others, as I suspected so long ago. On the other hand, even the existentialist—this high priest of involvement—may use his patient to help him solve his own problems. There seems to be no way out. The human observer is irreplaceable. The therapist is himself the instrument of observation and treatment and psychotherapy depends on 'experience', understanding, communion, such as is only possible between two fully engaged persons. If we go to the other end of the scale we have the scientist who needs to be objective. He wishes to remain detached and in control of the situation. From the point of view of his personal motivation he tries to deny all involvement and tries to keep out altogether. If they are of the all-denying type and use this argument to question any value in our work, these scientists are not helpful to us. We must consistently show them their own involvement as expressed in their attitude.

With those scientists, however, who admit these problems into their orbit, we can co-operate and benefit from their criticisms. It must be admitted that many psychotherapists have no special knowledge of scientific method, have little information of developments outside their own field of interest and that their attitude may be equally irrational. What is needed is a truly scientific attitude which acknowledges our special difficulties and does not allow our vested interests as therapists to stand in the way of (objective) truth. This attitude is, however, as rare among psychotherapists as it is elsewhere.

Our task is to find ways and means for investigations which do justice to the complexities of our subject as well as live up to scientific criteria. In a recent article B. F. Riess[1] gives a lucid account of these problems and interesting examples of such dynamic research. I would mention here also the type of research being carried out by J. Sandler[2] and others at the Hampstead Child Therapy Centre as a good example, though it is more systematic than dynamic.

Let us return to our cardinal question: 'Why is our work so difficult?' We have found that there is a basic defence against the resolution of the neurotic problem which emanates from the active and inevitable resistance of all members of such a network towards change in any one of them.

This attitude is one which treats improvement or cure as a threat, and is well illustrated by the following examples taken from group-analytic experience.

(1) A foreign woman psychologist joined my group. She was happily married, had a child, and functioned well all round. She was not over-defensive and did her best to join in. Nevertheless, the group was very annoyed with her for having no problems and some members were driven to fury. When pressed, she said one day that she had always liked her parents, both her father and her mother. This was never forgotten and she was never forgiven. However, she continued to do well.

(2) A patient talked rather readily and much for a newcomer, and perhaps also in a slightly patronizing way. What he did say was good common sense, and psychologically appropriate; it was not 'analytic' but less defensive, if anything, than one could expect of someone who never had any psychotherapy. He said to the group, which contained a majority of

---

[1] B. F. Riess (1960), 'The challenge of research for psychotherapy'. *Amer. J. Psychother.*, 14. 395;   [2] J. Sandler (1960), 'On the concept of super-ego.' *Psychoanalytic Study of the Child*, 15, 128.

expert and veteran analysands that he had studied psychology for himself as a lay person and that it had helped him a great deal. He gave a number of experiences which confirmed this. This made the group furious, and their anger was not mitigated when he asserted that he had plenty of problems, suffered from severe phobias, etc., and though one could help oneself to a certain degree, there were other aspects over which one needed help from other persons. At this point one of his neighbours pronounced that he would like to murder him. Another voiced her irritation and hatred in no uncertain terms. The group was only slightly appeased when I could reassure them that this man had, some years ago, had a very severe breakdown lasting over two years—the sort of breakdown which some of them spent half their lives avoiding.

In both these examples there were, of course, other motives to be analysed, but what interests us here is the Gilbertian proposition that the qualification for membership in such a group seems to be that one is fundamentally disturbed, and that the idea of helping oneself, or getting well, is treated as the equivalent of high treason.

Fortunately the recognition of this multipersonal nature of the human problem at the same time brings with it new hope for its better solution. The general tendency towards the recognition of the social network has lead to new methods of investigation and treatment, particularly group analysis in its various modifications, as well as to a different orientation within the treatment of the individual patients.

In theory, more stress is laid on the cultural and social roots of human behaviour. More recently this is also emerging in orthodox psycho-analytic theory, though perhaps it would not as yet be recognized in these terms. It is not a question of a cultural *versus* a biological orientation, as these two aspects are intertwined and inseparable. As I have mentioned, modern biology itself moves in the direction of a better recognition of cultural or social inheritance.

All psychotherapy as a procedure, as a means to an end, is a concentrated revision in a specially designed situation. It may help decisively in terms of relative improvement within the context of the patient's life. Perhaps, in favourable cases, what occurs is a switch in the pathogenic network which leads to greater personal freedom of choice in the individual concerned.

We must get away from the categories of brief psychotherapy

versus extensive or long psychotherapy, and replace them by radical in contrast to symptomatic psychotherapy. Weighing up all the factors on the basis of our growing discrimination, our aim is always the same: to achieve the optimal solution under existing conditions.

It may be helpful if I sum up some of the main themes in this chapter.

(1) The work of Freud and of psycho-analysis in the broad sense, has dominated the first half of this century. Its contributions will remain of paramount importance for all future progress. The second half of this century could develop a theory of psychopathology and psychotherapy based on a comprehensive view.

(2) The basic limitations of psychotherapy are seen by Freud as being due to biological factors, deemed to be unalterable. Modern research shows that much of what appeared to be biological inheritance is in fact cultural inheritance transmitted socially. In line with this, it perceives the community as a significant unit of observation.

(3) Within psychotherapy the same tendency is expressed by the emphasis on interactional processes, whether these are observed in two- or multipersonal situations.

(4) I have stressed the existence of a network of interaction, in which everybody tries to solve the conflicts common to all in interdependence with the others. The equilibrium of the individual, i.e. mental health, would therefore be dependent on his interaction with other members of the network. This leads to the method of analytical group observation and treatment in which the forces of the total network can be studied in their entirety—either in their natural setting or re-established in a transference situation.

(5) This method also has the particular merit that therapists of different backgrounds can look together afresh at events in a shared situation and thus find a common language for the processes which all recognize as operating, no matter to which school they may belong.

(6) In this view the neurotic would only be the weakest link in a chain, a scapegoat in a sense, and any change in him would have to contend with the automatic resistance of his network. In addition to the resistances to change which Freud so clearly perceived from the biological point of view, we have therefore to contend with this collective source of resistance.

We are thus led to comprehend the defensive function of being a psychotherapist. We also understand the general and inevitable defence against our efforts.

Our work is indeed difficult, but it is intensely rewarding. All signposts—unless there is total destruction—point to such rapid development that, looking back from the year 2000, the first half of the twentieth century might well appear as remote as do the Middle Ages to us.

In this period of rapid and unprecedented change, the human individual will need the help of medical and remedial psychology more than anything else, if he is to survive and preserve his mental health. Medical psychology and psychotherapy will have to welcome and integrate all progress from wherever it may come. Fortunately there are signs that such progress is forthcoming and that integration has begun. If so, those who follow us will not fail.

Chapter XII

APPLICATION OF GROUP CONCEPTS
TO THE TREATMENT OF THE
INDIVIDUAL IN THE GROUP

In a recent article on man's place in nature, Sir Julian Huxley has stated that Charles Darwin's Law of Natural Selection holds good and can now be studied scientifically, can be seen in action. This constitutes the *biological inheritance* of man. The particular feature of the species man is the evolution of improved brains. This has led to a development which, to quote Huxley, gave man 'the capacity for conceptual (rational and imaginative) thought and for true speech, with words and symbols denoting things and ideas instead of merely sounds and gestures expressing feelings and emotional attitudes. This enabled him to do something radically new in the history of our planet—to transmit experience and awareness cumulatively, from generation to generation.' By this capacity a second mechanism of heredity, *cultural inheritance*, has been introduced and this latter has made man the latest dominant group on earth. Man is a new and unique *kind* of organism. His evolution, Huxley says, is no longer purely biological but primarily cultural.

What now evolved in human cultures: social institutions, laws, arts, sciences, educational systems, techniques, codes of morals, characterize the species man. Huxley would be inclined to speak of a psycho-social phase. Man has been able to cross the barrier into the new psycho-social domain. He is the agent of the evolutionary process on this planet. Man has thus reached a point where he is able to define his own place and role in the world and to start on a scientific exploration of his destiny. This destiny, it would now appear, is to be the instrument of further evolution on earth. 'The time is now ripe for an intensive and scientific study of psycho-social evolution and the possibilities and limitations of mankind.' 'It is our business as men to discover and to realize new and richer possibilities for life, a greater degree of fulfilment for ourselves and for the evolutionary process of which man is now the spearhead. This is our privilege, but also our grave and almost frightening responsibility.' I could think of no finer words—and they are the words of a scientist—to define our own task as group psychotherapists when we study the interaction of human beings in groups. For this work we, as psychoanalysts, can build up on the fundamental work done already and continuing to be done in the individual field of psycho-analytic study and therapy. *Psycho-analysis*—Freud—has unearthed the human *conflict* which arises exactly between this dual biological and cultural inheritance of man. This clash between inherited constitution, instinctual needs, and the cultural restrictions is, in psycho-analysis, reflected by the conflict between the Id and the Ego and Superego respectively. Psycho-analysis has thrown most light on the infantile and primitive nature of human instinctual impulse and the conflicts which arise under cultural conditions. Psycho-analysis as a therapy has increasingly recognized the importance of the relationship between the analyst and his patient, the transference situation. In group psychotherapy the group itself, as a token representation of the surrounding community and its culture, is for the first time called into the consulting room, into active co-operation within the treatment situation. The group seems, therefore, the ideal object for the study of these basic human conflicts and particularly perhaps of therapeutic operations. This could be considered as axiomatic if the conclusion—which my observations and experiences have impressed upon me to the point of no return—turned out to be established truth, namely: that no human psychopathology can ever be confined to the individual in isolation. For many years now I look at the patient in front of me as only one link in a long chain, in a whole network of interactions, which is the real locus of the process causing both disease and cure. All psychology thus would become social psychology. The group situation would become the usual therapeutic situation, individual psychotherapy be reserved for special purposes only.

The individual's neurotic conflict appears in the therapeutic-group situation in a dynamic, even dramatic form. The individual behaves in a therapeutic group as he does elsewhere, in a way characteristic for him: he re-establishes typical conflict situations. He is not conscious of this. In a therapeutic group, however, the conflicts thus re-created are brought into the open. They reveal themselves as the most relevant, unresolved, pathogenic inner conflicts which are at the root of neurotic breakdown. For this re-creation of typical conflict situations the individual member uses other members of the group, including the conductor. He endows them with properties of persons in his real life, past and present; he uses them as personifications of inner objects, fears, reaction-formations. Any programmatic procedure would interfere with this process of spontaneous re-enactment, so important for the possibility of change. This compulsive repetition is of the essence of transference. Psychoneurosis, in its new edition as transference neurosis, thus enters into the therapeutic arena as a resistance, as something through which the old mode of behaviour interferes with adequate current behaviour. In current interaction with the other members of the group the individual co-operates in the liberation from these interferences. He thus becomes engaged in work which concerns the essential character of his disturbance, contains the area of ultimate pathogenic conflict. Whose liberation? His or theirs? His *and* theirs is the answer, they are the same thing. This is true *currently and ultimately* and herein lies the potentially therapeutic character of the group.

To see to it that the group situation acquires and maintains therapeutic character is our particular task. We must create the right situation, maintain it and do the right things in it. This would be simple if we always knew what *is* the 'right' thing. Naturally I hope that my observations help a little towards this aim.

So far we have established that the situation under consideration is pregnant with therapeutic possibilities. The word 'pregnant' prompts me to use a simple analogy for our task: we find the woman pregnant, now we have to help her deliver the child and then to bring it up. However, to return from generalities: we have established certain pointers to help the therapeutic process. We can say that such a situation should:

(1) promote a free and spontaneous exchange of interaction and range of communication;

(2) allow the pathogenic conflict to be re-established within the network of the group and thus be subject to the value system held by the group (and *vice versa*, the value system will be confronted with the conflicts which it produces);

(3) combine this self-perpetuating process of revision thus inaugurated with insight and a greater degree of consciousness.

We may also take a hint from something we have said, namely that the transference neurosis in the group functions essentially as a resistance. It would seem that this admonishes us to pay special attention in our interpretation to the defensive mechanisms.

The group-analytic situation claims to be just such a therapeutic ('T') situation. As we shall see, group concepts play a central part already in its inception and formation.

In forming the group-analytic group we make some preliminary assumptions: *firstly*, that the character of any situation which we cultivate determines what goes on and its meaning. *Secondly*, an assumption, based on universal observations regarding the behaviour of human beings brought together: they react, they show interest in each other and make contact. Thus they begin to interact, communicate and form relationships. The processes just named are mutually interdependent and form a feedback system; in a way we may consider them as two triads of such a system; the first: reaction, interest, contact; the second: interaction, communication, relationship. *Thirdly*, we assume that modification of the group and of the individual are interdependent. Any change, any modification in the group, goes together with a change in the individual and *vice versa*. It follows that if we treat the group, we treat at the same time the individuals composing it, even if we do not apply ourselves to them in particular. *Fourthly*, we count on the old inevitable repetition in transference, that is to say a displacement of old reactions into the treatment situation.

Now to the specific features of the group-analytic situation and their consequences. Any one of these features is of considerable significance and any modification changes the nature of the group itself: what occurs in it, how it happens and how it can be observed. Notwithstanding their importance, I must content myself with merely recalling them here. Such factors as number, selection, seating arrangements (sitting in a circle), frequency and regularity of meetings, also of attendance (in view of stability of composition) and the duration of each session, mode of termination, all determine the character and consistency of this situation. This is important because certain features emerge as significant only on the basis of a clearly defined situation and can only be analysed on such a basis; also for scientific purposes and for the exchange of experiences.

Now, as you know, these particular groups I am concerned with here are composed of *strangers*. This is very important in view of the transference situation. With this in view we also discourage meetings outside and separate meetings with the therapist. These strangers, strangely enough, form in time the most intimate attachments and relationships. Though we call them substitutes, in so far as they emulate family configurations, the psychological family ties between them are closer than those between them and their real families. A woman who was able to ventilate and to some extent analyse in a session a current relationship of the most problematical character with a man, felt she really ought to be able to talk it over, to talk it out with the man in question, as she did here. She had to learn that such an analysis can only be done in a therapeutic situation, as she was inclined to confuse transference relationships with life. The man was a case in point.

Two members, a married man and a married woman in a group, who at times took each other as proxies for their spouses, could discuss their marital problems on a deeper level in between them than they were ever able to do with their marital partners. That people are in terms of ordinary life complete strangers to each other establishes another important feature of the T-situation, namely that whatever might happen with the group, it has no immediate consequences in the outside reality of current life.

Our practice of a free association of ideas rests on the communicational network which we mentioned and *vice versa*. This is based on the observation that every individual communication tends to be in part a response to what has been said previously and to what is going on in the group altogether. It has partly the value of an unconscious interpretation. Freud says: 'One may indeed state quite generally that everybody is continuously engaged in a psychological analysis of his fellow beings' (*Psychopathology of Everyday Life*).

Other features which are significant for the group-analytic situation must be put in a negative form. They are features to be avoided. There is *no* occupation, organization, planning, *no* directions, meetings outside, individual sessions. We have thus set a field which allows to the full for an analytic type of operation and approach.

Our answer to the question how group concepts are applied to the individual in the group has been so far: by exposing him to the particular dynamics which prevail in the conditions created by us and which act upon him and through him. If we look after the group, we implied, the individual will look after himself.

We have already said that the specific therapeutic quality of this group is embodied in the conductor. His most general function can best be gauged if we ask ourselves what difference his presence or absence makes. He has created the group and his influence remains decisive from the beginning to the end. We have every reason to assume that the therapy which goes on in the group-analytic group in particular is crucially dependent on the therapist's presence and actions. In this light some of the features of the conductor's attitude may be worth recalling: his willing acceptance of all material, including all fantasy about his own person; of the interpretation of his role on the part of the group for purposes of analysis; his refusal to act himself in any other but his role as a therapist, his refusal to contribute more than a minimum of personal, private information. His aim to be as little as possible involved as a private person and to omit introducing any of his own personal and private valuations. By contrast his insight into his own emotional involvement *as a member of the group*, and even his individual reactions in this capacity, should be fully acknowledged and, on occasion, may have to be voiced for the benefit of the group. In some situations this is vital. On the whole his attitude is based on truth, reality, and the principles of science. I do not think it will be either possible or necessary to say more here about the conductor's own attitude.

Having created this group-analytic situation, with its specific therapeutic culture, the therapist must help to foster it. In actual fact these two phases overlap. The situation is created and maintained by its actual operation. It consists and exists only in its current practice. The conductor must not only acknowledge these group processes but recognize them *in action* if he is to make his interventions in their light. While this culture encourages the active participation of all members in the ongoing process, it discourages direct action, acting out. It practises what one might call 'suspended action', a postulate essential to all analytic psychotherapy.

Perhaps at this point we might pause to consider also some unconscious aspects of the conductor's influence on the group and *vice versa*. The more I see of groups, the more I supervise groups, the more am I impressed by the overwhelming influence of the conductor—especially the beginner—on his group. Any group seems to bear the stamp of its therapist, reflecting his own conflicts and blind spots. As I shall indicate later, this should be replaced in the mature conductor by a conscious exertion of his creative functions. Short of this, what he may aspire to achieve is that he should not create a group in his own image, but that his image be a reflection of the group. Here are some short examples of the way in which conductors are reflected by the group:

1. In a group which I supervised, Dr H. reported on one member, R, his *bête noire*, his shadow, to whom he referred as his 'pseudo-assistant conductor', asking at times whether he (R) should not be taken out of the group; he provoked sex; exhibited sex; continually denied everything; lectured, monopolized the group. Later, a newcomer to the group put R in his place, thus doing the conductor's dirty work for him. R was in fact the shadow of the conductor and *when this fact was uncovered in the supervisory seminar, a total change occurred in the group*, and the observer reported that the group now for the first time worked productively as a group.

2. There was also a *bête noire*, Mr H., in Dr M's group, referred to as the 'assistant conductor'. He was blamed for inconsistency and for always looking for a bone of contention. The observer, however, reported that Mr H mirrored the therapist and it looked as if the *therapist hated part of himself in Mr H.*

3. In yet another group the therapist recognized 'the same reaction as my own in a member of the group. He is aggressive, passive really underneath, a psychopath, he annoys me'. This group member (P) is in fact a paranoid psychopath, wanting to change into a woman. The whole group of five sexual deviants provoked this same reaction in the therapist. He feels disturbed by their passivity. In fact, there are long silences and one member of the group sleeps at times. It would appear that the group's demand to be given something (magical) by the conductor provokes his reaction. When the conductor is discussed in the group for the first time, P says the group would be better without him. (This patient wanted his parents to die.) B, the conductor's shadow, however, said that he needed the conductor.

4. Another group strongly reflected the conductor's own

TMKF - K

dissatisfaction with me. It was really a continuous demand for help and effective advice which the group echoed. One of the questions the therapist asked was how to deal with X. He had just added Mr D to the group, who is again the newcomer in the role of the therapist's helper. Mr X 'makes Mr D ill' with his attacks on the therapist. Another patient, Mr P, represents Mr X's wife. He (X) has a considerable influence on Mr P but is reported to have a tremendous need to be controlled by Mr P. There is here a strong note of jealousy and underlying homosexuality. In this group at the same time three patients strongly identified with their sisters. Mr D had an obsessional fear of becoming violent, might kill people, might die, which turns out to be in identification with his sister. This strong identification with a sister was a threat to this therapist's own mental economy at that time.

We have seen in various examples that it is often *the newcomer* who comes to the rescue of the conductor. He appears particularly to be taking things up with the conductor's *bête noire* in the group. This has been the case in Dr H's group and when the unconscious involvement of the conductor had become conscious, a total change occurred in the group.

Similar was the situation in the last example.

Here is yet another example.

5. In Dr C's group, Mr T's aggressive defensive ways were pointed out to him by a newcomer without T having to be annoyed by this. The general ambivalence in this group, in particular the jealous rivalry between Mr T and Miss D, an intellectual woman teacher, clearly reflected the ambivalence conflict in the mind of the conductor.

In addition to *the shadow* and *the newcomer*, I have seen similar personifications for part aspects of the conductor in *the scapegoat, the conductor's favourite*, and *the conductor's assistant*. In these examples the conductor's assistant was sometimes a newcomer, sometimes his shadow. It is interesting to consider all these typical personifications as indicating a split off part of the therapist's self in connection with some counter-transference problem on his part. The same events can of course also be described from the point of view of the newcomer joining the group, the constellation for scapegoats, the individual characteristics of the scapegoat, or of the 'assistant therapist,' and so forth.

The conductor's direct interventions could best be characterized as a creative selection in his activities and his interpretations. While directions are avoided as far as possible, the conductor directs the group all the time. As we cannot go into details, it might be helpful if I compare his function in a broad way with that of the conductor of an orchestra, an analogy which was quite conscious in my mind when first using the term 'conductor' for the group analyst. While the conductor does not himself participate in the production of sound, his contribution is the most significant one for the performance. Personally, I approach group processes in a way akin to music.

The conductor's selective interpretations concern actions, behaviour, defences, processes, content as voiced, all within the context of the group. A remark which might not be out of place in our present context: an interpretation does not become a 'group interpretation' because it is given in the form 'we', 'all of us', 'the group this' or 'the group that'. Neither does it become an individual interpretation because it is directed to and concerned with any particular individual. What is really decisive is whether the configuration, the gestalt, is recognized in its inception and execution (timing, etc.).

In this connection we make another working hypothesis, which claims that the figure-ground process of gestalt theory holds good in the group. Every event involves the whole group, even if apparently only one or two individuals are manifestly concerned. These represent the figure, the foreground, the rest the background of the total ongoing process. As simple examples of such configurations, the following may serve:

6. Bo and Ba had been referred to in one session as 'the others'. Next time they were absent. Now the present part of the group protested: they felt 'we are like two groups in this group', and spoke of a 'poor meeting'. They also blamed T, called him 'the bad seed'. In the following session Bo is characterized as 'thinking inwardly', whereas Ba reads a newspaper. The latter, however, had smashed up his car.

This split in the group is experienced by Miss S as a split between her parents.

7. In another group, when the therapist reduced the sessions from two to one a week, the group wanted to pay for a second session. Mrs Th became afraid of losing control and jumping out of the window. During the first long interval three members got in touch with the hospital as emergencies, after having asked for individual interviews after the first session. One or

two more had also asked for this. The anxiety in the group was evident. The group's main topic: Death.

The whole group can serve as an imago, a reflection of phantasies of the group which are in everybody's mind. Individual members are used as personifications in the sense of transference figures, substitute figures, but also personifications of the whole self, parts of the self and the body image.

8. Another group (Dr K: murderous mothers) on a deep level appears to consider the group room as the mother's body and its members as if contained inside it. The group is extremely alarmed by the prospect of one of its members leaving the group, which stands for a child being born. This corresponds to their fundamental hostility towards their own children ever having been born, i.e. their mothers ever having given birth to them. The conductor, when this is pointed out to him, calls it a psychotic interpretation, but some time later he reported that he had given this group this psychotic interpretation and they seemed to accept it and throw further light upon it.

In an example we shall mention presently, Miss P looks at the whole group as her mother.

We concentrate on themes, motifs, meaning which concerns the whole group, all of the members, which seems to underly their communications. We concentrate on collective motivations. These are most easily recognized when some external event affects the group, such as the absence of the conductor through holidays, the end of the group, a new member joining, the absence of a member or the loss of a member. We observe these dynamics for our *orientation* in the first place, not necessarily to point them out to the group, as some workers do. We rather take these 'common denominators' as a background, a framework for our interpretations.

The transference neurosis, in the sense of the repetition of the neurotic pattern of behaviour in the treatment situation, clashes with the current interaction on a more mature and adequate level. This clash shows up in the group exactly at the critical point where the individual's neurosis conflicts, or seems to conflict, with the shared group situation. It may, for instance, take the form of a request for individual interview, as in the following example, which shows a significant change in an individual clearly as a part of the group process:

9. Miss P treats the group as her mother. She cannot talk

to her mother and not of her mother in the group. Others in this group, especially one of them, can talk of their mothers. At this time there was a state of tension with apparently independent explosions which had previously been more marked by acting out. The patient became panicky and was seen once individually. At the next group session she was able to talk and tell the group—her mother—off. At the same time there was a reversal of this identification operating: she herself was identified with her mother, the rest of the group represented her own self reacting against her in the image of her mother. As the group did *not* react with hostility, Miss P changed completely, so much so that the group registered surprise. She also solved a long-standing conflict and married. While this was unearthed in the supervisory seminar, it turned out that the particular patient's impasse had interacted with conflict in the therapist, a woman, which found expression both in the supervisory and the training treatment group.

Our handling of individual phenomena is thus significantly different in the group situation. To illustrate this on a more classical example, I will take that of the dream. The dream, as you know, is an important part of an individual analysis and we, following Freud, look down upon its manifest content, which seems more in the nature of camouflage and secondary elaboration, and try to penetrate into the latent meaning and latent repressed thoughts by means of free association. However, this free association of the individual, as practised in the individual psycho-analytic situation, is of course quite impossible to obtain in a group situation. On this count alone, therefore, an orthodox analytic approach to the dream would be impossible. On the other hand, dreams occurring in actual psycho-analytic practice are put to a use in two ways, not very much mentioned though important. The one is that we often must content ourselves with picking out some aspect of a dream without analysing the whole dream, and take what analytic information we can get out of it. The other property of dreams in an ongoing psycho-analytic treatment situation is that the manifest content has meaning in relation to the ongoing current transference situation. We very often use that aspect as a genuine communication for the purpose of analysis. Now this is exactly where positive use of dreams comes into the group situation. We can express it thus: that the dream as told to the group is left to the group to analyse. The dreamer often reports events in his dream which shed light on his own situation, in particular in relation to the group, on the group as a whole, on events going on in the group, his unconscious reflections on occurrences in the group. This aspect of dreaming is of value in the context of group analysis, whereas the recounting of dreams—the product of a withdrawal from human contact—becomes more significant from its aspect as resistance. This is a good example of the application of group-analytic perspective and group concepts in actual practice and the difference they make in respect to individual manifestations compared with the individual situation.

10. For instance, after a silence, X produced what he called a 'group dream'. In fact he had a dream which referred very obviously to the last session and was to some extent analysed in that sense, the group participating somewhat less than one might expect, and I had correspondingly to do a bit more. The manifest dream was that there was a circle with one chair empty. It was just a circle like this, but there was one chair which had arms and he at once went and took this chair, putting himself into the centre with the approval of Dr F and the disapproval of Y. This was the manifest content of the dream and there was some analysis of various factors. Meantime, Y said he had also had a group dream, rather surprising very obviously homosexual in relation to Dr F: namely that Dr F gave him an injection. However, on further questioning, it turned out the injection was a truth drug, so I pointed out to him that the dream was not necessarily about the group, that it might equally well apply if he found himself suddenly flung into a treatment situation with me individually, and the group did not in fact appear; further, that, although it might under-neath be homosexual, it was in fact referring to the treatment situation in which he must speak the truth. The women in the group took up the point that in X's dream they were not mentioned, which made X recall that the women had actually been represented in his dream, but in the background and not individually defined.

This was an experience in one of my groups in one of the first sessions of that group. The most relevant aspect of both dreams, however, was the beginning of rivalry between X and Y in respect of me, as expressed in X's dreams and Y's wish 'also to have a group dream'.

Important incidents occur on the intrinsic boundary of the

confined psychological space of the therapeutic group, the T-situation, such as acting out, etc. Such incidents are often long concealed, but often tangible and manifest, for instance by demands for individual attention, individual interviews. Such demands should be analysed in the group and usually need not be followed up, but occasionally it happens, more with beginners, that such interview is granted. Now I always advise and follow myself the rule of directing the analytic endeavour in such an individual session entirely to this border-line boundary area, namely to have consistently the question in mind: what is it exactly which prevents this from being said in the group? Why is it not possible? What is in the way? I have never found, if that was correctly done, that this did not lead to the uncovering of an important conflict area inside the patient's neurosis, which was at this moment dramatized as an equally momentous conflict between him and the group, or the conductor or another member. It is characteristically linked up with the most salient conflict of old and with the most vulnerable and difficult area of conflict between him and the current group situation. The case, mentioned previously, of the girl who was seen individually before she could talk about her mother in the group illustrates the point.

Such *boundary incidents* furnish beautiful illustrations of what is meant by: all meaning is referred to the group context, which is looked upon as particularly relevant.

11. For instance, in Dr W's group, a number of apparently unconnected individual incidents seemed to be due to current tensions in the group: some members were missing, one had injured his knee, another had bronchitis. It seems, incidentally, that injury or organic disease occur relatively frequently at certain periods and also during the period of waiting for (group?) therapy.

12. In another group three women became pregnant within one year, while yet in another group of the same conductor, almost everybody moved house. These events were not brought clearly into the focus of the group context.

Better understood were the following:

13. The manifest theme of discussion was jealousy and competition in married life and guilt about spouses. This was at the same time expressed by the striking interaction in symptoms, and by moves (changes in the choice of chairs) in the group. Outside the group, one patient practised promiscuity,

another passed on his own symptoms to his wife and another one's husband felt obliged to seek treatment. This is an interesting illustration of a theme being represented in multiple, interacting media: 'variations on a theme' one could say.

14. In another group such *multiple representation* was expressed in a similar way. The distinctive feature here was that a multitude of triangular patterns clearly emerged in the group at this period as follows:

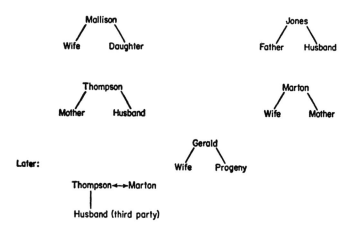

Whereas in these instances the group syndrome appears to account for these serial responses, I have often been struck in my introductory group by seeing quite unselected patients making contact, on a deep level, even over symptoms which are in themselves rare, and very much to my own surprise. Such a chain of resonance seems to be struck up, ecphorized, by one of them displaying such symptoms in a pronounced way. This happens though this is the first time these patients have ever met together and with me.

This last-named factor, *resonance*, is particularly connected with different levels of communication. The particular individual cathexes: oral, anal, narcissistic, etc., have a bearing on it, as well as certain defence mechanisms, e.g. paranoid, depressive. It is as if these different zones and strata responded readily in natural affinity to each other, right across the differences of the disguises in which they appear manifestly, thus confirming the correctness of our psychopathological concepts.

I trust that the examples mentioned, sketchy, condensed, oversimplified and deprived of much of their acumen as they are, by considerations of discretion, have shown some of the group-dynamic mechanisms in their operation.

All of them illustrate, I think, the concepts of *configuration* and *location* in the group; a collection of reactions which we have summarized under the term *mirror reactions*; and *dramatization*, apart from their more specific point.

Some reactions, if looked upon in isolation, could appear as purely individual ones. Yet some factor of which the members of the group were not conscious determined their particular reactions on a deep level at one and the same time. We were allowed to have a look into the secret mechanism by which the participants, without being aware of it, were prompted to move as they did, as if all controlled from a central switchboard. If we are to observe this, however, we must not think of individuals acting upon one another, but of the processes instead which interact in the ways indicated within the common psychic matrix. If we have not our eyes and fingers upon these nodal points of varying interactions—of *processes, not of persons*—we can neither understand the pathogenic mechanisms nor direct therapeutic operations.

The individual in life is equally determined by the various groups of which he is a part, some more, some less fundamental: his culture, his nation, his family, his clan, his time. The individual considered in isolation appears to be motivated by his personal history and the resources of his body. Psychoanalysis has gone farthest in his study. Individual features are woven into the complex psychical fabric of the group. Participation in the therapeutic group, which no descriptive effort can replace, can lead to significant and mutative experiences, which the individual should not only undergo but also understand. The all-important process of communication, with its analytic implications of an ever-growing understanding for unconscious processes and for repressed material, enables these experiences to be made as a common enterprise in mutuality.

Chapter XIII

GROUP PROCESSES AND THE INDIVIDUAL IN THE THERAPEUTIC GROUP

The disturbances, psychoneuroses in the broader sense, with which we are concerned in psychotherapy go back to experiences in childhood which have been repressed. Repression and other defence methods, which are subordinated to it, keep the repressed from becoming conscious. At the same time the tendencies against which the defence is directed are split off from the ego. This defence, albeit a function of the ego, is itself unconscious and also has its roots in the earliest months and years of development. This dissociation or splitting-off from the ego has still another significant sequel: the particle of mental life which is thus isolated assumes again the primordial, archaic, primitive character of early mental life. It is subjected to the primary process and liberated from the straitjacket of rational, reasonable thinking. Belief in omnipotence, superstition, magical thinking, which we trust to have surmounted in waking life, return into their age-old rights. It is the language of delusion and dreams, if you like, but also that of art and religion. What we meet as a symptom is the expression of elementary impulses which have succeeded in penetrating again to the ego, in a way breaking into it. The defensive war against these instinctive impulses in which the ego has been engaged, particularly under the pressure of the superego, the primitive, unconscious internalized conscience, has resulted in a compromise, namely the symptom. The instinctual impulses which are disallowed must not even now show themselves in their true nature, naked as it were, but go about under disguise and put up with all sorts of distortions. The solution of these distortions, displacements, condensations, etc., their uncovering, naturally makes up an important part of psycho-analytical work, which thus opposes a powerful part of the ego and superego. For this reason, these defending forces regularly turn as resistances against analysis and the analyst, and the observation, interpretation and dissolution of these resistances becomes at least as important a part of psycho-analytical treatment as the uncovering of the unconscious itself. Naturally, all symptoms root in the matrix of the personality and its development, so that every analysis has in fact the total personality as its object.

We have therefore to deal with conflicts which are unconscious. Without such a concept of an unconscious we cannot understand them, nor can we get hold of them without a method which permits us to make the unconscious conscious. We have said, however, that these conflicts are old, that they are the internalized results of painful, traumatic, undigested and unintegrated childhood experiences and constellations. There would be no hope for us therapeutically but for three circumstances which come to our rescue, and which are of the greatest significance.

(1) Such conflicts only occupy us if they are still active in current life.

(2) They arose in relationship to other people, originally family members or their substitutes, in interaction with them. Even now, when they become active again, this is still true.

(3) Just as the most essential and basic conflicts are compulsorily repeated in life, so they are, in pure culture, under the conditions of the analytic situation (the transference situation).

At this point we cannot enter further into the way in which psycho-analytical treatment makes use of and deals with these circumstances. This we must, up to a degree, presume to be known, as we turn towards group psychotherapy, armed with the knowledge and experiences which we have gained as psycho-analysts.

Group analysis, however, is far more than merely an application of psycho-analytical principles within the group. Its particular therapeutic possibilities, which are quite considerable, are due to the fact that we work in a group situation. As we turn now to group-analytic psychotherapy let us start from the second of the aforementioned fundamental conditions as regards our therapeutic efforts, namely, that the actual pathogenic conflict again involves—as did the original one—a number of persons.

It is my belief that in the outbreak of the actual neurotic disturbance of the individual, which after all is the real object of our treatment, a whole circle of people are again actively involved, people who are very intimately connected with one another and, moreover, this is a *regular* occurrence. It is true that they know very little of their interaction in this respect, and that they do not wish to know about it either. I am inclined to ascribe to these observations a greater and more fundamental significance than does psycho-analysis, having as its object of study one- and two-personal dimensions. I have become more and more convinced that the patient whom we see is himself only one symptom of a disturbance which concerns a whole network of circumstances and persons. It is this network of interacting circumstances and persons which is the real operational field for effective and radical therapy. Perhaps it would be more correct to say this will be so in the future. This would be group therapy in a natural group with the persons primarily involved in the conflict themselves as members of the therapeutic group. Under present circumstances, it is very difficult to put such a multipersonal therapy into operation. It would be necessary for this work that it could be shared by a team of therapists who would have to be trained in both psycho-analysis and group analysis. So far my efforts here in London have not been more than occasional sketchy experiments; they have, nevertheless, given impressive testimony for the forceful and sometimes explosive strength of such a method of approach. I will give here some examples.

(1) The man concerned, A, had been an in-patient before being sent to us. Separation from his wife was imminent. We encouraged his wife A1 to come for treatment as well, and decided to treat the couple in one common shared situation. The therapist consulted me with a difficulty. It had become apparent that the couple repeated their conflict in the treatment situation by pulling him in opposite directions. I advised the therapist to interpret this behaviour to the couple. Only a day or two later I was called to the telephone by a practitioner, PB, who insisted on speaking to me personally. He turned out to be neither the patient's nor the patient's wife's doctor, but the doctor of the wife's sister, B, and seemed rather upset. It was obviously this sister—his own patient—who had stirred the whole matter up. He said that the wife's general practitioner, PA1, had been rather astonished that his patient, Mrs A1, had been taken on for treatment at a psychiatric clinic. How could she be asked to be treated in one room with such a man as this (her husband)? Although the practitioner (PB) accepted my explanations and quietened down, he nevertheless asked my approval that his patient B's sister A1 should be sent elsewhere for treatment. Thus the therapeutic situation with my registrar had been broken up, which corresponded to A1's resolve to make an end to the marriage. The therapist, when I told him about this conversation, confirmed that the sister played a considerable part in the conflict, and was not surprised at her reaction.

We have, by the way, in a number of instances been quite successful with the joint analytic psychotherapy of such couples, and have also twice had groups of four such couples which seemed to go a long way towards resolving their troubles; but for this type of treatment to be indicated, it seems to be a precondition that the couple concerned are seriously willing to preserve their marriage. Of course a group such as a marital couple is a very simple example of what I have in mind.

What I want to demonstrate here is the subtle but intensive reaction by the whole of the network; the therapist with his technical difficulty, the couple under treatment, the wife's doctor, and the wife's sister and her doctor. All of them, as if by arrangement, became actively involved in the treatment situation. Treatment would have to take this total multi-personal network of disturbance as its object.[1]

(2) A man had not been working for many years and was unable to go out alone. His symptoms began at the time of his marriage, although there was ample evidence of childhood neurosis (enuresis, nail-biting), sexual problems (manifest castration fears in connection with intercourse and fear of causing pregnancy, coitus interruptus), and somatic symptoms. In individual treatment, to put it into his therapist's terms, he had improved so much that he could now allow his wife to go out to work. A little later, when he continued his treatment with another registrar, he improved further but just at that time a reaction on the part of his wife became noticeable. It was decided that the wife should be taken on by another registrar of the unit. He reported that the wife's reaction was indeed strong, that she had developed an anxiety state with panics. She had insight into the fact that she could not bear the husband's increasing relative independence from her. She was a 'mother' to him, was so happy while he was helpless, and

---

[1] Cf. Main, T. F. (1957). 'The Ailment', *Brit. J. Med. Psychol.*, 30, 129, for a beautiful study of such interaction.

wanted him ill again. In other words, she could not bear the improvement brought about by her husband's treatment. You see that in this case we have a different situation, the more conventional one, in which a couple is treated by two different therapists. Presently a more difficult situation arose; the wife presented some unexpected features of a paranoid type of jealousy, suspecting her husband of infidelity. (Her mother's death was indirectly due to shock in connection with father's infidelity.) On the other side, in the husband's treatment, it emerged that he had started relations with a newly married woman in his neighbourhood. It was psychologically clear that this affair was in no way independent of his wife's jealousy. One can easily see the outlines of this network. Here is a couple plus a couple of therapists, plus another married couple intimately interconnected in the ongoing dynamic process. This situation shows another difficulty, this time arising from separate treatment.

Let us glance back for a moment to the ordinary method of individual psychotherapy as it is predominantly practised today; the husband's progress would have come to a standstill, the therapist being only dimly aware of the wife's reaction. This would remain entirely behind the scenes. We are not always in the happy position of being able to do what we did in this case, to take the wife for treatment as well, but we can see even that is not enough.

Had the husband and his wife been treated at different hospitals, the wife's therapist would not have known the factual background of the wife's complaint and suspicion, nor would the husband's therapist have known of the wife's deep reactions. Fascinating technical and dynamic problems now present themselves. If we bring them together into the same room for treatment the facts must be brought out into the open. This might well explode the whole marriage. On the other hand, if this cannot be done, or must not be done, then there are obviously severe limitations to treatment.

Before presenting a further example from a group-analytic group I want to make a few comments here.

(*a*) This type of interference on the part of the multi-personal network is very characteristic and a regular occurrence. It happens always at critical points in the treatment situation, particularly so when a dynamic move towards improvement and liberation is in evidence (e.g. resolution of over-dependence).

(*b*) The group situation highlights this critical problem in a dramatic manner. In our last example the group situation makes the central issue of this whole marriage at once evident and inescapable, in that it poses the question of bringing into the open the husband's infidelity, so crucial for the pathological dependence on each other, and the wife's paranoid reaction. This is the case whether we are dealing with natural groups or group-analytic transference groups, and supports us in considering our transactions in the treatment room as significant for the patients' current lives even if we are not always aware of these concomitant implications. Our example also demonstrates beautifully that these current conflict situations are at the same time new editions of Oedipal and pre-Oedipal conflicts.

(*3*) The third example comes from a group-analytic group in which a woman, 'the daughter', was a member. This daughter showed considerable improvement until her mother entered the field and approached the therapist with the suggestion that her daughter should have psycho-analytic treatment. Two friends of the mother were under psycho-analytic treatment. The mother's interference was in turn characteristic for the daughter's preferred defence. She maintained a relationship with her mother which in recent years has been given the name of projective identification. The therapist did not refuse to see the mother, but insisted on seeing her and the daughter together, and this changed the situation. The mother withdrew and the daughter developed considerable insight into her dependence. It is interesting to note that *in the same group and at the same time* another patient who had shown considerable improvement unconsciously provoked a similar interference from outside. A psychiatrist who had at one time treated this patient, and the doctor of the patient's mother, together exerted pressure and influence that he should leave the group and be treated as an in-patient. We did not see any reason to influence the patient in this direction. When I remarked in supervision that it seemed from what I heard as if the psychiatrist and the mother were personally involved, this was borne out. Here we have two other simple examples of such a network influence. That two such incidents happen at the same time is by no means accidental, but is meaningful within the context of this group. Again this reaction on the part of ostensibly outside figures comes at the moment of improvement.

This type of group psychotherapy is of particular significance in the consideration of the importance of the natural group network for the pathogenesis and cure of the individual neurosis, but I cannot enter into it further on this occasion.

Group-analytic psychotherapy, as we usually practise it, approaches the same problems from the opposite direction. For this group it is essential that its members, perhaps seven or eight persons, should be strangers to one another. There must be no dependence on one another in actual life, so that their feelings, their attitudes and their actions (or at least tendencies to such action) can be expressed freely without any fear of consequences in external reality. As in all analytic situations gross action, such as physical attack or the taking up of sexual relationships, should be avoided. Contact between the members must also, as far as possible, be confined to the therapeutic session. Only under these conditions is it possible to maintain the request for frank disclosure and communication. Under such conditions the spontaneous ideas of the patients become the group equivalent of free association. Everything that happens, everything that is said, may be considered to have meaning in the total mental fabric of the group (collective or group association). The contributions of the individual participants also assume the function of unconscious interpretations. The group analyst at any rate has the right to look upon them in this sense, and in this way he can help the group to understand what they themselves are unconsciously saying and indicating. My observations have shown that even in quite ordinary life groups one can discern these associative components. But the very existence of real purposes, of dependencies, of the necessary caution life brings with it; in short simply everything that we rule out for our purposes, covers over and confuses these inner links.

Though verbal communication is indispensable for analytic purposes, non-verbal communications such as facial expressions, gestures, attitudes and behaviour are at least as important. Such a group is therefore, in the first instance, obliged to translate symptoms into their meaning and to transform the driving forces which lay concealed behind them into emotions, desires and tendencies, experienced in person. While doing so, the members learn a new language, a language which had previously been spoken only unconsciously. In this way the capacity for insight and communication grows. The analysis of resistances, defence reactions, and the manifold distortions, further promotes the depth and breadth of what is thought, expressed and understood (in short, everything which can be shared and communicated). The elucidation of the patients' unconscious attitudes to their symptoms, as well as to themselves, to others, and to cure, is of great significance.

It is apparent that one can use such a small group for intensive analytical treatment. The indispensable precondition for this remains the analytic attitude of the therapist, and his capacity to make the patients active participants in their own healing process. The group-analytic situation is therefore in essence a transference situation.

The phenomenon of transference is of fundamental importance for all psychotherapy. In the strict and correct sense it describes an unconscious process by which the analyst becomes the representative of properties with which the parents, siblings and other significant figures were credited in early childhood. This is often expressed in symbolic ways.

We may here recall the two other essential conditions which make therapy possible, namely, that transference is a compulsive repetition of the most relevant and unresolved conflict situations, and that we would not be concerned if these were not still active at the time in the current life of the individual. A feature of the group situation is to put emphasis on this immediate present. The importance of the 'here and now' was early recognized and expressed by me. I was then, in the absence of any other observations, of the opinion that the individual transference neurosis could not be analysed in the group situation. In the light of twenty years' experience I must withdraw this statement. True transference neuroses of the individual can clearly be recognized in the group and therefore also analysed. It is true of course that this transference neurosis does not develop in the same pure style as in individual psycho-analysis, and that it cannot be analysed and worked through in the same detail. Whether this is due to the group situation or to the fact that I am referring to weekly sessions remains to be seen. It is also true that the transference neurosis develops in a different way in view of its multipersonal distribution.

As the analysis of the transference situation and the transference neurosis forms a central part of all psycho-analytic treatment, the usage has developed in recent years to call all reactions from the analysand to the analyst transference. Equally all human feelings in the psychoanalyst in relation to the analysand are frequently designated as counter-transference. This is too general and therefore confusing. One can convince oneself of this particularly well in group analysis, where deep 'true blue' transferences which emerge compulsively and have nearly delusional character, contrast sharply with the more spontaneous reactions to actual stimulations and persons. Naturally all human relationships have at least potentially elements of transference in them. However, it is right that the analyst should understand and interpret reactions in the therapeutic situation in the spirit of the transference situation, that he does not respond to them in his own real person, whether they be friendly or hostile, loving or hating, idealizing or denigrating. This is a fundamental and elementary feature of the analytic attitude; everything that happens, without exception, is only there to be analysed.

Thanks to his training, and to his particular position in the group, it is for the therapist to represent the analytic attitude. All other members are allowed and even encouraged to react spontaneously exactly as they feel. As a consequence one is no longer dealing with patients, or cases which have a special diagnostic label, but with human beings who talk to one another about their affairs, their everyday life, their plans, their fears, their apprehensions, their worries, their pleasures, their guilt feelings, their suffering and their faith. They learn much about themselves and others which they did not know before. They act upon one another and get to know themselves and others more frankly and more truly than ever before. Increasing understanding brings with it increasing tolerance, and the possibility of a freer development of the individual. I would like to underline this. Nothing is farther from the truth than the idea that such a therapy has to do with conformity or with toeing the line. Even whether something is considered normal or not is, in my own approach, not a question of values (quite apart from the fact that it is for the group to make up its mind about this). Group analysis has not as its aim adjustment and socialization. It wishes to help human beings to find themselves and to live their own lives as well as they may be able to do. Moreover, they should do so without being inhibited, limited or disturbed by unnecessary difficulties or even, as happens only too often, by tendencies to do harm to themselves. The group analyst is no longer dependent on introspective self-observations on the part of his patients, nor need he wait until such observations are reported to him by other observers. He can himself observe the changing behaviour and reactions of his patients and make them the object for immediate analytic investigation. It is this fact of repetition under the conditions of the therapeutic situation (the 'T'-situation) which gives particular value and significance to this analytical revision. The analytic therapeutic character of the situation stems, as we have said, from the analytic attitude of the conductor.

Such an analytic therapeutic attitude is in truth an inner disposition. It has to be genuine and cannot be faked or adopted. It rests in the first place in the personality of the therapist as it has developed according to his own natural bent and experiences. The capacity of the therapist to observe what happens in the patient's mind, to comprehend it, rests on his own empathy. He can never emerge untouched as he goes through this process with his patients. At the same time he must be free enough from personal problems not to be drawn into the emotional whirlpools of his patient. If occasionally this should threaten him, we can expect that he would take heed of fine and early signals, and take counter-measures. This, by the way, is necessary in the interests of his own mental hygiene; here lies the value of the therapist's own analysis and group analysis. These are problems of counter-transference. Its influence on the therapeutic group, quite particularly from unconscious sources, is hard to overestimate. We have been studying this over a number of years at the Maudsley Hospital, at a special seminar where we follow these problems on clinical material, in connection with the training of psychotherapists.

See the preceding chapter for examples which show how the parts which patients play in a group, amongst them quite a number of typical roles, are not only conditioned by the patients' own dispositions, by their own relationships with one another and the therapist, but are also the result of unconscious projections, expectations and provocations on the part of the therapist.

The mechanisms illustrated in these examples are in particular those of *personification*, a patient *representing the unconscious part of the therapist*, of *dramatization, resonance and multiple representation*.

The patient in such a group becomes for the first time really conscious of his own behaviour and able to modify it, to unlearn and to learn afresh. To experience himself repeatedly in a new and changed role and manner becomes an experience of consequence for him; still more so as the counterreaction on the part of the group will also change. The over-coming of infantile fixations and dependence and the develop-ment of a more mature attitude thus become possible, together with real insight. Dependence on the therapist, who represents authority as conceived by the infant, is to a large extent replaced in the group by the more realistic dependence upon the group. As we know, the final solution of this dependence in individual therapy and even in psycho-analysis is a difficult problem. In group treatment the step towards society and the community during and after successful treatment is a much more natural one.

Each individual patient, if we put him into the centre of our consideration, can be caught in the attempt to repeat his own neurosis and its genesis and to force his neurotic pattern on the others. Yet at the same time these individuals between them, in their complex interactional network, produce a new dynamic field.

This existence of group psychodynamics is now increasingly recognized but too often looked upon as something totally different from, and even antagonistic to, individual dynamics. It is said, for example, that these group- or socio-dynamics are of interest to the sociologist but that their bearing on psycho-therapy is non-existent or minimal; they are external, whereas psychology is concerned with psychodynamics, i.e. intrapsychic phenomena. In my view this juxtaposition of the individual and the group rests on a misunderstanding and leads to unending and insoluble pseudo-problems.

We are concerned first of all with psychodynamics. These are rarely, if ever, confined within the boundaries of the individual but regularly include a number of interconnected persons. They are transpersonal manifestations. From the beginning my endeavour has been to do justice to the essential unity of psychodynamics, whether they are studied or observed in a one-, two- or multipersonal situation. I have attempted to base operational concepts on the phenomena and processes which can be observed and which express this identity of psychodynamics. These can best be seen within a group just because of their transgression of individual boundaries. The therapist in our group needs in any case to focus on the group context for his intervention and interpretation, otherwise he would be lost in the bewildering multitude, simultaneously on different levels, of reactions and possible interpretations. Taking these transpersonal processes as a guide, he is also prevented from being drawn into the quagmire of an individual *versus* group controversy.

It seems very hard to accept the concept of a psychic network inside which frontiers and boundaries of individual egos are continuously fluctuating, now suspended, now re-established. On this level the group is an intrapsychic one; configurations are dramatizations of inner unconscious processes; the others are personifications of split-off parts of the own ego. On a more everyday level, this same group is of course composed of definite individuals, who act upon one another or who revive old family constellations with one another in transference. It seems not easy to orient oneself here. The group analyst should be able to enter into all these wavelengths, if not at the same moment, at least in quick oscillation. It is only in this way that he can really follow the group, understand what is happening, and judge whether his intervention is necessary or possible.

The group-analytic orientation is mainly a matter for the analyst, and is personified in him. I will, therefore, sum up some of the principles from his point of view. In the first place he creates and maintains the group-analytic situation as I have described it. He leaves the choice of themes to the group, gives full rein and validity to phantasy, including his own person. In this respect he is completely receptive; he follows the patient and his attitude is that of the psycho-analyst. In the interpretation and analytic elucidation of resistances and defensive mechanisms he is far more active. He promotes spontaneous communication and insight through his comments, confrontations and interpretations, and through this exerts a catalytic influence. In the transference he must be prepared to tolerate a considerable measure of dependence upon him, especially in early stages. But, step by step, he weans the group so that dependence becomes replaced by greater independence of thought and action. Thus the need to be loved and to be led, and the belief in authority, is gradually replaced by the authority of the group which after all reflects the values which are 'normal' in the particular culture. But all valuations are subject to analysis, regardless of whether they are considered normal or not.

The therapist has a creative task. In a sense he is continually active, and at times markedly so. That we stress the group as a whole for the orientation of the therapist must not confuse us. This form of psychotherapy is, in the last resort, alone in the service of the individual human being and the freer development of his individuality.

Part IV

GROUP ANALYSIS IN OPERATION

INTRODUCTION

It happens that much of my earlier experiences and experiments were conducted under military conditions, in conjunction with the introduction of group psychotherapy into the psychiatric services of the British Army. What had been a co-operative effort during the war lost its unity afterwards and I have attempted to record at least the gist of these experiences in *Introduction to Group-Analytic Psychotherapy*, referring to them as the 'Northfield Experiment'. This name which was at the time used both colloquially and in publications, for instance by H. Bridger in his contribution to a symposium on Northfield 'The Northfield Experiment' (Bulletin of the Menninger Clinic, May 1946).

As far as I am concerned, this refers to work done during 1943, 1944, and 1945 at the Military Hospital and Psychiatric Training Centre at Northfield, Birmingham (in peacetime known as Hollymore Hospital) and had no connection with an earlier 'Northfield Experiment' which lasted five weeks and of which I heard, if I remember correctly, only late in 1944. It should be kept in mind that group psychotherapy could not have been a part of this earlier work, if only because of the shortness of time. In order to avoid the confusion which has arisen I shall now and in future avoid the term Northfield Experiment, or designate it 'The Second Northfield Experiment'.

The heads of the Army Psychiatric Services initiated this work and supported it throughout. Credit for this is due first and foremost to the inspired leadership of J. R. Rees and the organisatory contribution of the late G. R. Hargreaves, always receptive to ideas and creative in execution.

Apart from the relevance of these experiences in the case of another war—which we all pray will never come—they are *mutatis mutandis* equally applicable in times of peace. The papers here included are selected from this point of view. They will be of special interest to the psychiatrist in a mental hospital who wishes to embark on group psychotherapy without having the benefit of prior special training, still difficult to obtain. This is a topical problem.

Based on a paper read to the British Psycho-Analytical Society in 1945 Chapter 14 takes a broad view of the application of group-analytic principles; it is field work in group psycho-therapy and is as it were an illustration of Chapter 16, while providing a practical basis for the systematic survey in Chapter 3.

The description of a ward meeting at the end of this chapter illustrates the dynamic view of a bigger meeting of about eighty persons. This was my contribution to a symposium on Northfield which appeared in the Bulletin of the Menninger Clinic (Vol. 10, No. 3, May 1946), following on a memorable visit of an American Committee consisting of Dr Leo Barte-meier, Dr Lawrence Kubie, Dr John Romano and Dr John Whitehorn, in April 1945. The contributors were Dr W. R. Bion, Mr H. Bridger, Dr S. Davidson, Dr T. F. Main, Dr M. C. Dewar and Dr S. H. Foulkes. Dr Dewar's and Dr Davidson's technical and clinical papers are good samples of the type of group psychotherapy then practised at the hospital.

Apart from group psychotherapy this work, in conjunction with that of Bion and Rickman, was pioneering the important conception of 'the hospital as a therapeutic community' (see also Chapter 16).

Chapter 15 is based on parts of a memorandum for the Army Medical Services (AMD 11) and is chiefly concerned with method and technical principles, leading from simple to more ambitious techniques, and is deliberately encouraging.

Chapter XIV

GROUP-ANALYSIS IN A MILITARY
NEUROSIS CENTRE

This is an account of the way in which Group Analysis was
developed during the Second World War within the framework of a Military Hospital, Northfield.

The principles of group analytic psychotherapy were extended
so as to serve as a basis for a group therapeutic approach in a
broad sense and to a great variety of groups.

Eventually the whole hospital was understood to be a therapeutic group or community.

The soldiers were inmates of a military neurosis centre,
whose period of stay was as a rule limited to a maximum of
three months. They shared the ward under the same psychiatrist and also had in common all the other features of hospital
and army life as a whole. Under these conditions the closed
group was used more often. Individual interviews were combined with the group method, as many practical points, such
as the question of disposal, had to be discussed individually.
Free association became modified to what might be called a
free floating discussion. Hospital affairs, army problems, any
matters affecting the group as a whole, became more prominent.
As the question of the character of the man, his morals, his
co-operation, or his attitude to further service, became of
paramount importance, the emphasis of observation shifted
from content to behaviour and attitude in the group and
towards the group. The group meetings became more group
centred, treatment of a group rather than in a group. This
phase coincided with a hospital atmosphere which was not
always helpful for psychotherapy. The conductor found himself

sometimes siding with the patients in respect of some of their criticisms. This did not do the slightest harm provided he himself was honest and his attitude fundamentally positive. Naturally, with lessening conflict in his own adaptation to army life, such criticisms appeared to arise less frequently and could be dealt with even more easily.

Two or three weeks after admission patients were transferred from the hospital wing to the training wing. The Training Wing, although belonging to the hospital, was sharply divided from it, even by its khaki as opposed to the blue uniforms of the Hospital Wing. It was equally divided in its spirit and orientation. The move from Hospital to Training Wing, symbolizing a return to army life and soon to Duty, was therefore a rather sudden jump.

This could be exploited therapeutically by accepting the situation as a reality to be faced, and the reality of army life in particular. The soldier who had been sent to hospital just because he could not adapt himself to this army life, found himself confronted with an edition of it, which had some of the unfavourable and few of the good features of life in a Unit. Nevertheless, in the net result, group treatment had a particularly marked effect just on the improvement of morale towards the group itself, towards the Ward, the Hospital and the Army. All this is mentioned here because it forms a striking contrast to a phase to be described presently, when the hospital had become a most helpful therapeutic milieu. At the earlier stage all that was possible for the therapist was to create a good atmosphere within his own sphere of influence, on the ward. Few realized the importance of this. It fitted with a competitive spirit between individual psychiatrists as to their therapeutic results and the standard of morale of their patients. Group treatment and an equivalent approach to individual treatment, weighted on the side of positive co-operation and community sense, won this competition hands down on all counts, even statistically. The main new features characterizing this stage were:

Treatment group centred, conductor following the lead of the group rather than leading it, object of treatment more the group as a whole. Emphasis shifted to present problems affecting the group as a whole. While the common background of personal difficulties came more to the fore, individual differences appeared as variations of the same theme. The total personality and behaviour in and towards the group claimed more attention than individual symptoms and their meaning. The group's therapeutic function towards its members became more manifest.

A significant experience was that this shift of emphasis, at the expense of 'depth' in the usual sense, did not affect therapeutic results adversely and the group seemed to have found the therapeutic optimum under existing circumstances.

A new stage in the development coincided with some other psychiatrists beginning to take an interest in group treatment. This method, hitherto tolerated, was now encouraged and the first steps were taken to synchronize the hospital's therapeutic aims, as well as to co-ordinate the work of the psychiatrists with hospital policy. This had to be in a constant state of flux in accordance with ever-changing circumstances and claims. It was therefore necessary for practical and didactic purposes to formulate simple and clear directions for group treatment. These had to allow for the fact that not all therapists were very experienced in psychiatry or psychotherapy, still less in psychoanalysis. Furthermore, guiding principles had to be sufficiently general to allow for the widest range of individual differences which would, in any case, determine each psychiatrist's approach to the group. The first step was to help the psychiatrist to overcome his own difficulties and to encourage him to face groups. Once exposed to the dynamic forces within the group, psychiatrists became increasingly aware that it was true, that they were facing the same problems as the group and that they were members of the group. The emphasis was laid still further on the group as a whole. The main aim was to prevent the conductor from hampering the spontaneous expression and activity of the group. Thus he had to learn to tolerate anxieties and tensions within himself, to resist the temptation to play the role of the authoritative leader but rather to submit all problems to the group and facing them fairly and squarely with them. The more he succeeded in this, the more he was rewarded by the growing emotional maturity of his patients, their increasing capacity to tackle problems and conflicts by their own efforts, their growing sense of self-reliance, confidence, responsibility and independence. The psychiatrist in his turn learned that the best leader is the one who is sparing with interference, keeping in the background and who can most easily be missed. The effect of all this on the psychiatrists would make a fascinating chapter. Light was thrown on the psychiatrist's own emotional contribution in maintaining an unsound, infantile, neurotic, doctor-patient relationship. Group treatment in this form put this basic problem into the centre of therapy, much to the benefit of patient and psychiatrist alike.

The outstanding feature of this stage, therefore, was that treatment was not merely in a group or of a group but by the group and, of course, for the group.

Meanwhile a large-scale transformation of the hospital had taken place, with the idea of letting it grow into a self-responsible, self-governing community. No effort was spared to sense the patients' needs, to unearth their spontaneously felt desires and urges, to create opportunities for all conceivable activities whether for work, artistic interest, sports or entertainments, in and outside the confines of the hospital. While the patients were given every encouragement to express their wishes and helped to articulate them, coercion was neither used nor needed. The initiative had always to come from the patients and the onus of responsibility in the execution of matters, large or small, rested on them. The importance of all this from a therapeutic point of view was that the patient was at every step brought face to face with a social situation, to which he had to give his characteristic response. The degree of his adaptation could thus be observed and influenced. Thus the relationship of the therapeutic group in the narrower sense towards the hospital changed, the smaller unit becoming more definitely oriented towards the larger community of the hospital. The exact way in which the small group changed and re-oriented itself towards the new conditions in the hospital was one of the most interesting points to observe. This showed how the individual person's mind is conditioned by the community in which it exists. Under these conditions, a group approach could be developed in a variety of new forms and new dimensions could be added to it.

There were spontaneous group formations. Patients could be seen in the social setting of their selected activities. This might be a fluid and loosely knit, casual community resulting from doing the same type of work or being in the same hut together, or it might be a more organized body, working together as a team at the same project. Such a team could be drawn from the patients of different psychiatrists, or it could be formed deliberately from one's own patients. In turn such a team might or might not meet in the same composition in therapeutic session.

Very interesting and promising features developed in such groups as were deliberately chosen to go through the whole of their time in hospital together as a closed group. They had their beds together in the ward, shared group sessions and worked together on the same project, preferably one related to the hospital itself. For instance, one group did all the work for the stage, from cleaning to designing and making the properties. They did all the technical work in connection with the performances, including lighting arrangements, etc. Others would constitute the hospital band, or produce the hospital newspaper, from collecting the material, reporting hospital events, writing articles and editing, to printing and selling it. A group was formed to receive new patients and introduce them to the hospital, conducting them round and giving them all help and information they wanted. Others ran the club or had special functions in their own ward.

There was a great variety of therapeutic groups of all descriptions, selected according to a variety of points of view, as well as quite unselected ones. There were also a number of experiments with spontaneous acting, individually and in groups. Groups were confronted with each other. For instance, the newspaper group at one time would act their own daily office meeting for a special purpose, but also all sorts of impromptu themes which they liked. While solving their own problems in connection with the newspaper itself, they often discussed one difficulty or another which they found with 'the patients', their readers. It was proposed that they might invite one of my groups to watch their performance, so that they could approach them directly. This led to a lively discussion between the two groups with far-reaching effects on both of them as well as the relationship between the paper and the hospital.

Often patients were seen from the very first in groups of about eight together, individual treatment being used only to settle special problems, a method which I personally used by preference and found very expedient. Many patients improved so much under this management that not only individual treatment but even psychotherapeutic group sessions tended to dry up or became subsidiary to the work project, ward activities or the social activities of the hospital. The effect of all this on the psychiatrists' group was very interesting too.

Many interesting observations could be made on the importance of assignment and selection, but in this respect we never reached a stage which would enable us to make systematic use of them. After all, we were not an experimental station or a research unit, but a military hospital working under high pressure and the practical needs of the day had to be met. But the stage of the war made certain interesting selections for us. For instance, at the time of the 1944 landings, groups formed of acute battle casualties were flown straight over from France. Group observation easily selected them into two main categories: those who were to return inside a week or two to fighting duties and those whose condition ruled this out. The latter needed far longer treatment and shaped for modified employment or discharge. Again there were the groups of returning prisoners of war, who were studied both in pure culture and mixed with others who were not prisoners of war. In my opinion the latter was on the whole preferable. In this type of task the group approach showed its amazing superiority in finer diagnostic and prognostic assessment and in bringing out the salient problems shared by the group, quite apart from its therapeutic effects.

At a yet later stage equally interesting observations of *disintegration* could be made. The war was now over, the staff was depleted by demobilization. The hospital policy had changed semi-officially to one of rehabilitation for civil life. Everything was affected. The old division between khaki and blue uniforms had changed its meaning completely. A certain note of apathy had descended upon both staff and patients. The hospital life had become stale and incoherent, the activity side somewhat departmental and institutionalized. What was to be done? I had the good luck, on my own request, to be transferred to the activity department. It became quite clear that levers had to be used to bring about an effect on the hospital spirit as a whole. *The situation suggested the remedy.* Groups had to be formed whose task was directly related to the hospital itself and who, from their function, were forced into contact and co-operation with others. I was reminded of the words Freud wrote as a motto to his *Interpretation of Dreams*: 'Flectere si nequeo superos, Acheronta movebo'. In principle as well as in detail, this new approach opened fascinating vistas. One had to find one's way into the hearts of groups, or remnants of them, and bring them to life again. One had to be very active in this before one could be spared and the individual group once more would live and grow and move under its own steam. I needed help. I founded one group called the Co-ordination Group who with new-found enthusiasm soon became a most active factor in the life of the hospital. Their influence was felt within a week or two throughout the hospital, from the C.O. to the last patient, orderly or office girl. New life blossomed from the ruins, brains trusts and quizzes between psychiatrists and patients, and similar events resulted, producing once more healthy and positive contact and co-operation. These experiences were among the most interesting I had yet had.

Returning to the psychotherapeutic group in the narrower sense it, too, had found a new meaning again. It became the best occasion for working out all these experiences and for reflecting upon them. Quite informally, I termed it the 'reflective' group, as distinct from the 'functional' or activity group. Once more, but on a higher plane, it had found its particular place: that of imparting insight, intellectual and emotional, into the more profound and individual, personal and at the same time more general and universal significance of all this turmoil of life around and inside itself.

It will be seen that in the development described, the following shifts of emphasis emerged:

From individual centred to leaving the lead to the group.

From leader centred to group centred.

From talking to acting and doing.

From the still artificial setting of a group session to selected activities and to groups in life function.

From content centred to behaviour in action.

From the controlled and directed to the spontaneous.

From the past to the present situation.

In order to avoid misconceptions as to the role of the conductor, I am bound to say that, in spite of all the emphasis on his receding into the background, he is in fact a most active agent and his influence remains the decisive factor in a therapeutic group. While it is easy to become a leader—in the popular misconception of the term—it is much more difficult to wean the group from having to be led, thus paving the way for their own independence. With both methods one can have success and it is in the last resort a political decision or a question of 'Weltanschauung' which one prefers. One way lies Fascism, the other a true democracy. Moreover, in the latter form, the truly democratic one, the group method pays in fact the highest tribute to the individual.

Chapter XV

ADAPTATIONS TO MILITARY CONDITIONS

Fortunately, the group approach is so flexible that it can be adapted to almost any circumstances. Everyone, deemed otherwise to have the qualifications to treat psychiatric patients, can learn to handle and treat men in a group and if he is courageous enough to expose himself, including his own personal reactions and shortcomings, genuinely to the searching test of a group situation, he will have no difficulty in starting. As he goes along he will become not only a better group therapist, but a better psychiatrist and a better human being as well.

Merely handling patients in groups in the way described introduces a number of potent factors helpful to treatment. A great step forward is already achieved if the patient's interest is awakened, whatever the subject of his interest may be. Furthermore, he is active—another important factor. For difficulties in social adaptation and disturbed interpersonal relationships, which are essential factors in a neurosis, it is the method of choice—the only one in fact which can approach these matters directly on the spot. The men under observation are bound to reveal much of their personal and interpersonal reactions which can be followed up in individual interviews.

Observing his patients in a quasi-real life social situation, the psychiatrist will find that he gets to know them much better than in the artificial setting of the individual psychiatric interview. He will have presented to him in a living way the material on which diagnosis and prognosis must be based. He will see what symptoms and complaints really mean, how they affect the patient's behaviour and how the latter is setting out to overcome his difficulties, here and now, in the group in the hospital and in life itself. Unexpected light will be thrown for good or bad, on the patient's attitude, morale, co-operation, and on his powers of resilience and compensation.

When the group therapy begins a set of factors springs to

life which is peculiar to the group itself. The dynamics of the group as such are being newly created as well as being brought to light—a totally new object for observation and for treatment presents itself—a new organism as it were quite distinct from the individuals composing it. Seen in this light, the group is in itself an element, the smallest entity, a unit of observation, out of which the composite unit of the hospital is built. The currents and cross currents permeating the hospital—and in a further sense, the Army of which it forms a part—are reflected in this small group and can be influenced from it. If and when the therapist is able to appreciate and master these group-dynamics and use them as levers to influence also the individuals of which the group is composed, he has become a group therapist in the true sense. If he can penetrate the surface and take the unconscious dynamics into account as well, and bring them to light and active interplay, he is a group-analyst. Since the psychiatrist in a hospital is concerned with the treatment of individuals he must to some extent engage in a more individually-centred group therapy. He should, nevertheless, observe these group phenomena carefully—if only as a background—and direct his attention at least in part to their handling, that is, to the handling of the group as a whole.

People do not like to alter their ways or any aspect of themselves. They cherish prejudices, theories and convictions, which have been firmly rooted and strongly guarded in their minds since they were ingrained into them by the most potent figures in their childhood. Neurotics in particular are anxious lest anything should touch them and avoid instinctively, like the plague, anything which could make any difference to their condition. The more then the group is spoon fed and the less it needs to think and do for itself, the better it likes it. To get them actively engaged and in a state of spontaneous participation is uphill work indeed. If, however, one succeeds in doing so the other side of the picture comes to the fore. It is remarkable how much keenness and ingenuity the same group will display, and how much unexpected talent, intelligence, interest, experience, rich emotional life, humour and even wisdom or genius can be found in every group. It is then that the therapist's measure will be taken, that he must prove his worth, that he will be found out for what he really is for good or bad. He will be taxed and exposed mercilessly and there will be no chance of escape. It will be discovered then whether he has a genuine right to stand in front of other people and claim to guide them to a better way of dealing with their problems and difficulties. If he passes this test he can proudly say to himself: 'I am a human being'. He will find no difficulty in being truly modest and in feeling genuinely: 'Here we are, together, facing reality and the basic problems of human existence. I am one of you, not more and not less.'

This is the fundamental position of group therapy. No wonder that it raises anxieties in the therapist himself. If, however, he has overcome in himself the claim to perfection, if he is not afraid to be found wanting, imperfect and ignorant, he can allow himself to be honest and sincere and stand firm on the grounds of reality. In doing so he exerts by his own example a valuable and powerful therapeutic influence.

It will be noted that our attention has become focused on the group therapist himself as one of the basic ingredients of the group. He will ask himself no longer: 'What do I do with the group? How do I start them? How do I treat this or that situation? but: 'What (in me) prevents this group from starting, makes them silent, impedes their interest and free exchange? What are the barriers and are they in me? Am I prepared to face the problems which this group may bring up? To do myself what I ask of them, namely to face anything, come what may, fairly and squarely, with no other orientation at my disposal than is at theirs, and, if necessary, without any orientation at all?' The therapist must ask himself these and similar questions before he embarks upon group treatment of the freer style and he must continue to ask them while he goes along. But he can count upon the fact, once he has made the jump, that the group will carry him along as well and enable him to give more satisfactory answers. When he feels ready to adopt this freer type of approach he should embark upon it in an adventurous and experimental spirit ready to follow the lead of the group. Thus will he also best develop his own style.

He can approach this in steps and stages. He may start with the A.B.C.A. discussion stage, then gradually allow more liberty in the choice of theme until perhaps later he does not need any set subject at all and can rely on the spontaneity of the group, including his own. Instead of merely observing the personal factors in the group he may put them up for discussion. Thus, from stating: 'X says a, Y says b. What is to be said in favour of a or b and who has any other opinion?' He proceeds to stating: X says a, Y says b. Why does X say a, and what in Y makes him say b?' Similarly he may draw parallels between similar or contradictory attitudes in the same person or in different members of the group. In short, the subject under discussion loses in importance and the participants in the discussion come to the fore.

The therapist may make a different approach to the same end by posing the problem to the group in this way—'We come together to deal with your difficulties. What do we want to know and why? Let us discuss it.' From the start the themes which arise are chosen, preferably by the group itself, with reference to the patients' problems and thus the personal factor is topical *per se*. Interactions between individual members can be observed and deliberately used for therapeutic ends, or special situations planned and created to achieve certain results.

It is, of course, possible to conduct psychotherapeutic groups from a totally different angle. In the past, hypnosis in groups has been practised with great success. One can encourage a strong transference relationship actively or let it develop spontaneously, which is more efficient. One can use one's authority to treat groups actively, by persuasion, suggestion, explanation, re-education. For such purposes a selection of groups according to leading symptomatology, e.g. stammerers, enuretics, or, alternatively according to similar problems, say marital, fear of V.D. is useful.

If the principle of the analytic approach is used, the group is given to understand that they should bring forth anything they wish and that they need not stick to any one point brought up but should continue expressing anything which comes to their minds. They can be given certain initial explanations of how this helps their condition, but in general they can be left to discover by themselves, in the course of time, that this is a part, even the essential part of their treatment.

The therapist brings forth the spontaneous activity of the group and encourages the exchange of information and opinion with its many therapeutic potentialities. He takes part, and, in so far as necessary, acts as a co-ordinator and interpreter. He is a member, as well as an observer, of the group, and his function is multidimensional. For example, he has to weigh up how far a topic should be followed up in the interest of (*a*) the individual concerned and (*b*) the group and, following our rule of 'the group first', may have to relegate further enquiry to an individual interview. On the whole, however, the therapist tends to recede more and more into the background rather than directing the group. He observes the dynamics of the group and the interpersonal relations between its members, while steering it delicately towards a therapeutic end.

One of the inestimable advantages of this whole approach is that the group is brought up against its own difficulties, resistances, opposition. It cannot fail to realize that they are self-manufactured, and under rising pressure of tension—it cannot in the long run avoid tackling them. The avowed purpose of the group is to get well and fit. As we know, this is not, as a rule, in truth the foremost desire of the neurotic patient in hospital. He likes to be able to say 'I am suffering from this and that. I can't help it. I've tried hard. Now you, doctor, come and cure me.' He does the same in a group. It is therefore essential that, slowly but surely, the onus of responsibility is brought back to the patient, where it belongs in reality. If he cannot comply with the request to speak his mind freely the difficulties must be his own. If a group dries up, they show their own lack of interest, of urge to co-operate in their cure. They are confronted with their own resistances. This can be pointed out to them. The task of bringing resistances and other defences into the open, making them manifest and conscious is as integral a part of group-analysis under civilian conditions as it is of an individual analysis. In military psychiatry this is not quite so. One has to achieve the best result possible within a shortish time and has to sacrifice more far reaching therapeutic aims. The therapist, under these conditions, may have to make tactical concessions in order to keep the group interested, co-operative and receptive. As a rule of thumb one may say that the analysis of such negative attitudes should not take up more than one out of every four sessions and is not worth undertaking at all unless the group has still a good period of its stay in hospital before it. The same is approximately true for the analysis or interpretation of material on a symbolic level, although this varies far more with the composition and understanding of the particular group. It is a different matter if the group, as sometimes happens, approaches matters on such levels of its own accord. One need not be afraid of going too deep in this respect as the group shows generally a far better appreciation of symbolic material than the individual, but the therapeutic value of analysing such material must not be exaggerated. Similarly, insight should not be overrated in its importance. Insight is a good thing where it can be had and when it falls into one's lap like a ripe fruit. But therapeutic effect is not in direct proportion to the insight achieved.

To conduct a group on the lines outlined above, makes great demands on the therapist's patience, balance and judgment. It is a fine art and at the same time a far more interesting procedure from a scientific point of view than any other form of group therapy. It has, also, compensations in the nature of its therapeutic results with the added advantage that genuine progress in a limited field tends to make itself felt in other fields not touched upon, as the immunity achieved in a small area of the body alters the relationships as a whole.

From what has been said it will be clear that one cannot condense the technique into a set of rules. But since experiences in group analysis are the syntax of all other forms of group therapy, any form of group therapy worthy of the name rests basically on these principles. Some empirical hints may therefore be found useful.

Selection. Much remains to be learnt about the principles by which a group should be selected. These principles can only be learnt in a hospital where a number of specialists who are undertaking group therapy have their patients allocated to them in groups rather than individually. Under such conditions one can begin to make a more scientifically planned assignment, not only of patients to specialists, but also of patients to each other.

It is sound practice to take unselected patients to form the group and then to reject certain of them if they are found to be unsuitable. Alternatively a group may be formed from those patients who are in need of more intensive treatment, are reasonably co-operative, intelligent and good at expressing themselves, and are likely to stay in hospital not less than four to six weeks. By and large the most important point to watch is that the diversity within the group is not too great particularly in such characteristics as age, intelligence and expected disposal. In blending a group one proceeds like a good cook. If the group contains a number of rather shut-in, shy and anxious people, the therapist may think it well to place one or two forthcoming and dynamic personalities with them. A few psychoses or near psychotic individuals often do well in a group of more inhibited neurotics. A good group can carry some hangers-on or depressed patients. In ways such as these one makes the best out of the material one has and in conducting the group sessions one makes allowances for the particular character of the raw materials of which the group is compounded.

In general, groups will be 'open'. That is to say the participants leave the group at different times and are replaced by newcomers. The group remains, its members change. For the therapeutic group in itself such a flow, as long as there is sufficient overlapping, is not unfavourable. It does not of course fit so easily into a fixed course or 'programme' of therapy. The 'closed' group in its extreme form passes through the hospital from A to Z intact with its membership undamaged.

The principle of the 'closed' group fits in best with 'a work group' undertaking a 'project'. If we call such a working group a 'team' to distinguish it from a therapeutic group, we can have the following possibilities in a psychiatric hospital.

(i) A team may be composed of patients of different therapists.

(ii) A team may be a deliberately chosen entity under one therapist. Some of its members may receive individual psychotherapy only, while others may be members of different therapeutic groups.

(iii) A team may be identical with a therapeutic group.

Type (i) suffers from the drawback that the group reactions are not therapeutically observed, concerted and exploited, but happen blindly. Type (ii) is better in this respect. Type (iii) permits of two variations: (*a*) the team project may be incidental and supplementary to the therapeutic group; or (*b*) the therapeutic group may be supplementary to the team project. The latter is the ideal form for such cases that are not in need of intensive treatment or where time does not permit this to be undertaken. The patterns (*a*) and (*b*) are, of course, not immutable and the emphasis can be shifted according to circumstances from one pattern to the other in the same group at different stages.

To exploit this type of team 'work project' to the full, an elaborate and flexible occupational therapy organization working in close co-operation with the psychiatrist in the provision of these 'selected activities' is an essential part of the hospital. Where no such organization exists there should be no difficulty in finding suitable tasks in any hospital, even one that lacks particular tools and equipment. The more a project makes sense in reality as a socially useful piece of work the more valuable it is therapeutically. It should grow naturally from the prevailing needs, conditions and situation of the hospital.

Numbers. Groups can be of different sizes. A ward is a group—three or four people are a group. A team can vary between something like four to five up to ten. But we find that a therapeutic group, in the more restricted sense, is too small when below seven and too large when above ten. The optimum number is eight.

Time. For a group therapy session an hour seems the satisfactory minimum, and one and a half hours about the optimum. Sometimes a session can go on for hours but it does not appear to serve much purpose either for the therapist or the group to extend it for more than two hours. The more the therapist approaches an analytical technique the more he will probably find it the best to stick to a fixed period for consecutive sessions with the same group. For a less analytic approach the length of the session can be varied according to circumstances. As regards the frequency of sessions, we find that once or twice a week is quite adequate. Regularity and, if possible, fixed times are more important than frequency. Rather one session a week regularly at a fixed time than three in one week to be followed by none or only one in the next.

Therapist's Handling. The right attitude in the therapist himself is the main condition of the successful handling of a group. Each therapist should feel free to approach it in an experimental spirit to find out the style most suited to his own personality.

In early sessions the main aim is to get the new group functioning *as a group*. At this stage he will be more active and talk more than in later sessions. In general this is equally true for the beginning of each actual session. It is a good rule to let the patients go on, whenever they show inclination to do so, and not to help them too readily even out of prolonged silences. More often than not the conductor will hinder the group rather than further it when he tries actively to help. He should observe whether members participate all round remembering that some participate very well even though they talk little. He should always encourage exchanges within the group.

Whenever anyone else speaks it should be considered preferable to the conductor himself. He should broaden the group before deepening it. Sometimes half the group may be quite heated while the other half is bored. The conductor may suddenly stop the active half and draw the others out. Resistances and opposition should be aired as one goes along. When a group becomes definitely stagnant and apathetic one may have to tackle the resistance actively and treat it as a main topic, even for a whole session or two.

There is what one might call a group strategy and group tactics. It is often necessary temporarily to act against all strategical principles in order to get a tactical advantage. As long as a group and its members do well one should be content and not try to improve on it—there are always more than enough things of interest to watch. This is a simple rule but not often appreciated. The effect in group treatment, as in individual treatment, does not come about in proportion to high dramatic tensions and breathtaking disclosures; on the contrary, apparently insignificant details may be of great portent. Very much more goes on behind the scenes and is said between the lines than becomes manifest in the group session. This is where individual treatment can supplement the group.

Finally I will describe one kind of group which may serve as a good standard type. This should be widely applicable and allows for a wide range of modification. From the outset the patients were seen together in a group of about eight or ten. They were introduced into the hospital, ward, etc., and generally put into the picture. A first psychiatric approach was made by asking them in turn about their complaints, recent history and relevant experiences, ideas of treatment and cure. If it has not been done before, this is a good stage at which to introduce a questionnaire to them, if one works with this method. This might take one or two sessions, in between which a personal interview can be fitted. The need for such an interview will have become apparent probably in a proportion of the cases. One or two may have turned out to be unsuitable for group treatment, or for this particular group—they can be replaced by others. The group should now share the same sleeping quarters with beds in close proximity and, if possible, without others in between them. As soon as possible they should be prepared to discuss and agree on a common project of work. Then they should be introduced to the staff of the department which will help them to obtain facilities for the project they have chosen. They discuss details with this department, starting work straight away planning the work themselves. The project must be flexible enough to allow for the bias of the individuals concerned, in so far as they take an active enough interest to voice any. For instance, one group of patients put the concert hall stage in order, repairing, redecorating, designing scenery and generally improving it. Another group built three cold frames, two for tomatoes and a third for growing mushrooms experimentally. Some members built the brick foundations, others made the glazed tops and so on. This group was seen by the therapist at work as well as in a group therapy session once a week. In addition they had an 'open hour' for individual interviews, when they could come to the therapist without appointment if they chose. Apart from this the therapist saw them daily on the morning round, and weekly at the general ward meeting, the A.B.C.A. discussion (weekly discussions on current affairs) and the weekly meeting of 'all my patients together'. In all other activities of the hospital they participated individually. Contact with the therapist was in this way very close and the group session soon developed an atmosphere of personal intimacy at least equivalent to that of the individual interview. Any individual interview became a matter of special importance, as it should be. If no desire for it was expressed from the patients' side and no need arose from the therapist's the patients were seen individually from time to time in turns. Often they did not know what to talk about, had no complaints and the therapist had just a short conversation with them, sometimes in connection with the group and their role in it.

There is no reason to think that the genuine improvement of the patients' social capacity will not bear fruit elsewhere, even though the group itself is disbanded when its members leave the hospital. The group should be given ample warning of its impending dissolution so that its members may be able to prepare themselves for the separation and bring out their reactions to it while they are still together. Everything should be handled in the open as much as possible so that they can trust the therapist and each other and not feel tricked in any way. This point is of great importance if the therapeutic result is to be reliable. If simultaneous discharge from hospital for all members of a group is administratively practicable there are many advantages in handling a group, or team, as a fully closed one.

Naturally, staff, sisters, orderlies should be having group sessions as well. In each ward the psychiatrist should have a meeting with all his staff, once a week in order to help them function as a unit; and the sister, apart from attending the general meetings should attend occasional therapeutic group meetings. This is a great help in bringing both sister or other staff and patients together.

A Ward Meeting. A psychiatrist may wish to convey various matters to all his patients together, or to a whole ward. In such a situation he will talk differently than when talking to one patient alone. If encouraged, they will talk back and also to each other.

One of the first things the therapist will notice is the general atmosphere. His patients may appear obediently or curiously expectant, bored and apathetic, good humoured or tense with anxiety, adversity and hostility. The conductor will become aware of their predominant attitude towards himself. He will sense, for instance, whether and in what way his presence influences the picture. This may be due to the sort of person he is, what he may or may not do, what he has to say and how he says or does it. He will be observed by the group, scrutinized and summed up, quickly and precisely, as by common consent, yet by intangible ways of perception and communication.

Meanwhile his own observation of the group becomes more detailed also. The patients are not a uniform body. Sometimes they are in good agreement, sometimes sharply split and clashing over an issue only to march in perfect unison a few minutes later. They may be with him, or against him. Many of them stand out from the main body, and gradually all of them acquire individual characteristics. Some are absent altogether and others keep out of range choosing their seats behind the therapist: some sit aside in isolation; some are at ease while others are tense and preoccupied. Some are attentive while others talk, and here and there is a man persistently unconcerned about what is going on, while another is restless and fidgety. A man sitting in a corner, suddenly, as if awaking from sleep or out of a dream, makes a sarcastic remark or voices violent opposition or shoots off at a tangent; another, who had not spoken yet and remained undefined, unexpectedly sums up a whole discussion humorously, follows this up by one or two constructive proposals and alters the whole situation.

The psychiatrist listens and mentally registers. His 'patients' have become alive, acting in a reality which he can share with them, under his own eyes. He need no longer rely on their own accounts and descriptions, based on self-observation and intro-spection, with all their fallacies, but can see for himself how they behave, feel and react, where they fail or are hampered by their disturbances. If he is in a position to check this against other observations, he can convince himself of the significance and reliability of this display. He is then fully justified in attaching importance even to the smallest detail observed. Frequently a patient shows up quite new facets, which the psychiatrist can follow up with further observation and enquiry.

Thus a first contact is established. It is a mutual contact. The therapist need not be afraid of this searching test, unless he could be credited with bad intentions. All he need be is honest. Pretence and acting would not go far. Nor is there need for them for the group psychotherapist is not concerned with making a good impression, with being liked or disliked. By this first mutual contact a community of feeling has been experienced by the patients among themselves, as well as in relation to the therapist, and in addition embracing the whole little community, therapist and patients together. The impor-tance of this cannot be overrated. While in itself a potent therapeutic agent, in particular against a background of the usual pre-existing apprehensions and misapprehensions, it is the indispensable matrix for other therapeutic steps. If the therapist is open and sensitive to this contact, meets his patients more often and regularly in this way, he can learn to play on them at will, as on an organ, and could on this basis alone lead them almost anywhere, if that were his task.

This, however, is not his task in a psychiatric hospital where the patients' difficulties are essentially of such a nature as to prevent them from standing on their own feet and grappling with their own problems. If the psychotherapist resists the temptation to be made a leader, he will be rewarded by their growing independence, spontaneity and responsibility and per-sonal insight into their social attitudes. It happens in exact proportion to the psychiatrist's art of making himself super-fluous. He can, however, resign only from something which he is strong enough to possess, and if there are doubts as to his capacity for leadership, he had better accept this function offered to him until such time as he is quite certain and secure in it. He must not hesitate to lead when the situation demands it.

The ward is the patient's temporary home and surround, his refuge from that strange and bewildering turmoil, the hospital. Here he meets with his pals with whom he is to share the ups and downs of his present life and, more or less intimately, the experiences of the past and the worries at home, his and theirs. These are people with whom he will talk on lonely walks and after 'lights out' at night. The spirit which permeates the ward, and which the psychiatrist must foster, is thus of the utmost therapeutic significance. The ward has another function: that of a bridge between the patient and the hospital. It occupies a definite place and has an active, responsible and powerful part to play in the hospital. As a member of the ward, the patient shares in this, he begins to realize that the hospital is his, is what he makes out of it, that he is the hospital.

More is needed, however. The patient needs insight; insight into his own inner conditions and life, insight into his present feelings, behaviour and reaction. Therein lie the limitations of a large meeting (30–80 men): the patient's reactions cannot be brought to light, voiced, described, realized or brought home to him by others. For this a more intimate setting is essential: the small psychotherapeutic group. It could be said that such a group has boundaries like a membrane of variable permeability. If the hospital milieu is opposed to the spirit prevailing in the group, if the osmotic pressure is high, these boundaries harden and become more selective; if the spirit inside and outside is in harmony, they may almost or completely disappear. The more the hospital as a whole becomes a therapeutic milieu, the more can it become the main function of the psychotherapeutic group to activate and prepare the patient for the impact of the hospital community upon him and in turn to work out with him the stimuli thus received. This puts the emphasis of treatment not upon past history but upon the immediate present—a desirable shift where time is short—and one of the most important aspects of this therapeutic approach in groups.

Chapter XVI

APPLICATION TO THE MENTAL
HOSPITAL IN PEACETIME

Based on a lecture given at a R M P A
Maudsley Bequest lecture course; 12th February 1962

The experience at Northfield has been a very significant one for all those who participated in it. Those who did will, I am sure, agree that the changes which went on in both patients and staff alike were nothing short of revolutionary. From morning to night and from night to morning, everything which happened was seen as relevant and used in the service of a true and quite rádical form of therapy.

The conviction that man's neuroses and their treatment change their form decisively in accordance with the community in which they arise is fundamental for a group approach. This was experimentally confirmed at Northfield. In psychotherapeutic observation both in individual or group situations, I could observe how the patients' mind, concerns, attitudes and even symptoms, changed according to the dynamics of the hospital as a whole.

It is, however, necessary for this observation to be made that one does not submit material to pre-formed interpretations with a fallacious and fateful distinction between superficial and deep in psychotherapy.

Human beings at all times are members of a great variety of groups, whether this be in the family, at work, at sport, in social life or in institutions, army, factories, prisons, hospitals and, of course, mental hospitals. For this reason our experiences are relevant for all these situations universally, but the conditions for their study must arise from the situation in which you work. They have each time to be hand-made again. The sort of disturbance which we have to consider is not confined to an individual in isolation but to a whole network of interdependent persons and their interactions.

The basic network genetically is, of course, the family group. Later all sorts of groups can become the ground of operation for such a disturbance including the group or groups in which the patient finds himself in the hospital itself. As we know, by way of displacement and transference, the individual tends to or is even forced to repeat his basic behaviour and his basic conflict situation in each contemporary group. The psychotherapeutic group, in the narrow sense, the group particularly constructed for the purposes of explicit psychotherapy could even be characterized as one which gives the patient the maximum chance, the optimal conditions for disclosing and becoming aware of the conflict situations which are characteristic for him.

Under prevailing conditions in mental hospitals there is great scope for the analysis of any disturbance in the operational group, in the situation in which it arises spontaneously, be it in a formal or informal group setting.

All relevant representatives of such a network are seen as the object of therapy. This orientation is firstly in the mind of the psychiatrist and he need never assemble the participants for the purposes of treatment. As soon as he wishes to avail himself of their actual interaction *in flagrante,* however, it will become necessary to have the individuals meet at the same time and in the same room. Their open or concealed interactions and interrelationships can then be ventilated and analysed with their own active participation.

If you follow a disturbance which arouses your attention into its ramifications, you might then find that you have a number of interacting people, of patients and staff mixed up with each other. You can bring the relevant persons—three or four or five of them—together and have an analytic group investigation with them. This will be most enlightening and significant, and powerful also therapeutically. You may alternatively confine yourselves to using your observations in concurrent individual or group psychotherapy and keep your patients and staff apart for the purposes of explicit ventilation. In the long run, the analysis of the staff seems more important than that of the patients.

A group assumes a character of its own superceding the individuals composing this network. In their interaction they create something new which in turn is conditioning them. In so far as the group itself and its functioning are the object of treatment, we have to look upon this new entity and address ourselves to it. In so far as in therapy ultimately the individual is our true object, we must look upon these group dynamics only for our own orientation but address ourselves to the individuals. In one case we treat really the group for its own sake, in the other the individual inside the group with the help of the group.

Individuals thus find themselves by sharing and in the contrast of differential responses. They are not learning to march in step or be uniform and lose their identity. On the contrary, with therapeutic progress, as the individual becomes more integrated and secure, he shows greater respect and consideration for the group without feeling threatened by it and the more mature group can afford to encourage individuality.

In the following, I should like to illustrate the type of psychotherapeutic intervention in the operational group which I have outlined, in two examples. I may be pardoned if these are taken from old experiences at Northfield. They are used merely as models to show how the dynamics which I am talking about operate under hospital conditions.

Let us take first a very simple example. The report of this was written by a sergeant, in civilian life an artist, who was in charge of the painting classes in the hospital and who had great skill in bringing out the patients' spontaneous efforts in painting. I had taken occasion to visit this class once a week for a while—the following report of one such meeting was written at the time by Sergeant Bradbury.

'Present: Major Foulkes, Sergeant Bradbury and fourteen patients. Discussed the series by Private M, an ex-prisoner-of-war and two drawings by Guardsman B. The group, though much larger than the previous week, were slow to respond to the drawings, and the paintings that M showed caused little excitement. Even the most depressed of M's works were accepted with little interest though everyone agreed upon the drabness of the colouring in each case and nobody suggested the pictures could be cheerful despite a cheerful element in each. Private G, realistic and usually reserved, made a long, cynical and determined statement on the unresurrected dead which appeared in one of M's drawings. None of the group opposed or seconded G's opinions but though he appeared to be serious enough himself, the group was inclined to be amused. Drawings by Guardsman B provoked an outspoken discussion on English women, their lack of loyalty in this War and personal attitudes to foreign countries. Staff Sergeant S, direct sufferer in this respect, gave heated replies to one or two who defended English women. Usually Staff Sergeant is quiet and agreeable but he was exceptionally difficult today. Practically everyone took part in the discussion excepting B himself. The group was not interrupted and ran on to tea-time, that is two hours. Deviation caused by Major F's remark 'You don't think much of English women' after the subject had cropped up on one of the paintings.'

This is the sort of group activity you might find going on in a mental hospital.

Now what did I do? What happened to make this session into a valid psychotherapeutic, or at least potentially psychotherapeutic experience?

There was a hut in which these soldiers met for their drawings and paintings. The first thing that I did was to go there. The effect of this was that these people assembled once a week round the table in the presence of Sergeant Bradbury and myself and looked at each other's work and spoke to each other, all of them. They were made to understand that they should make any comments they liked arising from the paintings or the conversation. In this way, a situation was created which was different from what it would have been without me. Without this, the whole thing would never have taken place.

My only remark which was relevant enough for the Sergeant to note, my only contribution was to say: 'You are not then very keen on English women?' But you see in this group this provoked a lively discussion on a very important theme, on a highly cathexed theme, namely faithlessness and all insecurities connected with worries about their wives at home. The sergeant called it a deviation as it arose merely as a by-product from these spontaneous paintings.

Another feature I want to underline is that this theme arose from this group of people and was not in any way taken further than the manifest meaning and content it already had.

What is the structure of this group in group-analytic terms?

(*a*) It is organized but very loosely and supervised by an expert (the art teacher).

(*b*) It is not selected for therapy.

(*c*) It has an 'occupation' (painting).

(*d*) The psychiatrist goes to the group and participates informally once a week.

(*e*) The individuals are brought together and look at each other's work.

(*f*) They are encouraged to talk, comment about each other's work, in fact interpret it consciously and unconsciously.

(g) They are encouraged to go further and talk not only to each other but about each other and to 'deviate' as much as they like.

It is really indispensable to have always a clear picture of any group situation in which you wish to operate in terms such as these.

By comparison, in a purely psychotherapeutic group these people would have been selected in a different way, there would have been fewer of them, they would have been called to the psychiatrist, they would have had no paintings to start from but the material on which their conversation would centre would be provided by their own spontaneous communications.

Now for another example which shows the therapist in a more active vein. In this case, instead of painting, the men were engaged in a group activity, an activity which itself was borne by the whole group but with changing membership.

We are dealing with a small group of musicians who constituted the hospital band. The band had been failing badly of late and I was interested to explore what this disturbance meant in terms of the hospital, in terms of the band's own members, in short what was the configuration or location of this disturbance.

I went out one Sunday morning to find sitting round a fire in some hut the pianist, the trumpeter, the violinist and the drummer, practising. They were the members of the old band but there were two newcomers—another pianist and a clarinetist.

I made my contact with them and enjoyed listening to their music when it became soon apparent that the two pianists did not get on at all with each other. They were blaming each other for playing in two different keys. (This by the way is a beautiful example of a displacement of a conflict into a different medium of expression in group terms; an equivalent of what one would find in individual analysis as an intrapsychic process. This is just one example of what I mean by equivalents of such processes in the group matrix.) One of them whom we will call 'the psychopath' because that was his psychiatric label had been the pianist and leader of the previous band. He was a professional musician and in civilian life a member of a dance band. He unceasingly expressed criticism and disapproval of the other pianist who was an ex-prisoner-of-war, a brave man who was not easily discouraged. The psychopath criticized him for having no sense of rhythm and in fact, no idea of playing. He went on repeating 'It is not my business as I am going out on Tuesday (out of the hospital that is) but . . .'

The new pianist had most patiently tolerated this and withstood the provocation, but at last said: 'Well, then I am not interested.' The psychopath seemed satisfied. He went away, and returned with another pianist. Meanwhile, the drummer, himself a very good musician, who was a faithful pal of the psychopath chimed in and attacked the new leader. Up to this point, the tension had been rising continuously. The psychopath had already announced that he was intending to fetch a vocalist, who turned out to be his girl friend. At this time he decided to search for her and they all decided to have an interval for tea in their wards.

When walking back with the men towards the hospital I contacted the prisoner-of-war, expressed my appreciation of his performance and encouraged him. After the interval I said to them that I did not see how it could have a good effect on their co-operation if their new pianist was discouraged and belittled in front of the others. It was quite likely that the old leader, being a professional, was more efficient at his piano, but this would be of little help in view of his leaving the hospital on Tuesday. In fact, it was better for him to leave the new band alone. Eventually the psychopath left the room shrugging his shoulders, and I had occasion to offer them all help in finding new talent among the hospital population.

I will jump here some proposals I made which had the effect, apart from helping them, of linking them up with other groups in the hospital. There was a rising spirit of agreement with me except for the drummer who remained ambivalent.

Meantime, the ATS girl, the vocalist, defended the psychopath, her friend, and said he was really a very nice chap if one knew him. They also said there were plenty of able musicians in the hospital but they were all afraid to come forward because they feared that if they did well in the band they might lose their chance of being discharged from the army. I reassured them on this point. (In fact, the policy at this stage of the war was predominantly to rehabilitate people for civilian life and only those who were likely to be fit enough to participate in the Japanese War were to be retained. In addition a large number of our patients were ex-prisoners-of-war. This may explain why their only idea at this stage was to be discharged and that

I could accept this as legitimate and reassure them on this point.)

The band settled down to practice and the POW pianist was reinstated. It started performing during the same week: it found no difficulty in recruiting new members. After a further week or two, the band was one of the highlights of the hospital. No 'social' was conceivable without it, and there was one nearly every night. It also settled its problems of suitable accommodation for practising and the like. They played very well indeed. A few weeks later the band, now composed of five different members again, was unaware that I had ever had anything to do with its existence.

The apprehension shown by the members of this band spoke volumes about what was going on in the hospital. While our idea was to make them better for civilian life, they were afraid of showing any improvement for fear they might be retained in the army.

My intervention in this case was a truly analytic one but again taking only the immediate concerns into consideration. The disturbances of this group were in a clear interaction with the larger group of the hospital. The hospital had a disturbance which amongst other things showed itself as a symptom in that it could not produce a good band. The band had a disturbance which reflected the major issues amongst the hospital population but there was also a conflict of a more subtle kind concerning its leadership, passing on leadership of the group to another musician, jealousies about the girl friend, etc., and on yet another level, the purely individual level, this disturbance reflected truly and faithfully the psychopath's lifelong personal problem. A little later I found him at a loose end somewhere in the courtyard. We made our peace and had a long conversation in which I explained to him all that had happened and the reasons for my actions.

He turned out to be an intelligent and amiable fellow who understood very well. He confided in me that all his life he was up against the same kind of difficulty and could not get on for any length of time with his fellows. He pondered for a while and then said 'Is that why I cannot get on with them? I think I understand now'—or words to that effect and thanked me. He had apparently found an insight to one of his life's problems. This was the last treatment he received before he embarked on his new civilian life.

In this example you see something which is very characteristic in the light of a group-analytic view. A fundamental
disturbance in the hospital is revealed of which the failure to
produce a band is only a symptom. There is a typical group
disturbance in the band itself and the psychopath demonstrates
how the individual's conflict is activated and involved in such a
disturbance.

These are examples of a psychotherapeutic approach applying
group-analytic principles. If you wish to run more specifically
psychotherapeutic groups, they should arise from the problems
which emerge as indicated. They should be seen in the context
of the whole situation in which you find them and if you confine
yourself entirely or largely to the manifest topic, the manifest
disturbance, you can rest assured that the therapy is not superficial; quite on the contrary, it is in the highest degree efficient
and relevant.

For these purposes it is useful to confine oneself to groups
which are called together on the basis of a common situation or
common problem. This makes selection and the conducting of
the group easier. It makes the group more meaningful and
allows it to come to a more natural and satisfactory conclusion
in a limited period of time. The therapeutic gain can be quite
considerable.

This type of approach applies mainly to out-patient conditions. The composition of the group may be of a mixed type of
neurotic patients and include some amenable psychotic conditions but preferably not depressives if the depression is marked
or acute.

The formal diagnosis is less important than motivation and
that members are well matched in relation to such items as
education, intelligence, age, marital status. Seven or eight
patients are the best number and they should sit round in a
circle. I find regular attendance charts very useful and would
prefer the therapist to make notes, if any, after the session.
Patients soon begin to talk as human beings about their concerns, moving from symptom to problem. As communication
grows, so does understanding, tolerance and relevance. An
analytic process goes on, even though unconsciously, through
the interaction of various forms of communication, through
symptomatic expression and defence in the light of which insight develops on the basis of similarity and contrast with others.

The attitude of the therapist is decisive, his function catalytic, clarifying, interpretative—especially in regard to defences and resistances. The therapist must understand and accept transference to his own person, as well as to the whole situation. He should maintain an optimal degree of tension, acting like a thermostat in relation to the emotional temperature of the therapeutic situation. The group configuration is important for the therapist's orientation, but in his interventions and interpretations he must not forget that it is the individual who counts. Improved communication is a good general aim.

In your own interpretations always remain concrete in the actual situation, start from the surface, the presenting symptom, behaviour or meaning. The range of the therapeutic situation should be clearly defined and consistent and conditions must be equal for all members. A therapeutic situation which is operationally well defined has fairly clear-cut boundaries. These must be carefully watched as incidents in that area, for example acting-out or physical illness, and their handling are of special importance.

In weighing up the different group activities and forms in which group therapy and group psychotherapy can be practised in a mental hospital, let us not forget that in the main we rely on the restorative and healing power of nature, that our first principle must be *nil nocere*, not to do harm. If we can further the therapeutic process so much the better. Mere participation in a group which achieves something, preferably fulfills a real purpose, and which is appreciated has great positive integrative values. Security and self-confidence grow as difficulties in personal relationships are overcome. For this to happen it is necessary, however, that the group has a good morale, that its members are friendly and tolerant. If they are torn by disruptive emotions, by undue competitiveness, envy and jealousy or hatred, then analytic intervention is indicated. It is as well to remember that the analytic approach in itself is a more disturbing one. It does not gloss over difficulties, but on the contrary is out to reveal them. After making such difficulties in the first place more striking and more disturbing, this will serve a very good therapeutic purpose and will in the long run help the hospital to become a better instrument for therapy.

Northfield thus became the first prototype of a therapeutic community understood as such.

After the war many mental hospitals made use of these new

experiences by way of what has come to be called therapeutic community, the organization of hospitals, group management and group psychotherapy. A similar development took place in the US A. Jerome D. Frank in his book *Persuasion and Healing* [1] expressed these developments very concisely:

'Ever since World War II, mental hospitals have been undergoing a quiet but massive revolution from essentially custodial institutions to active treatment centres, involving progressive breakdown of the barrier between the mental hospital and the community and a redefinition of roles of patients and treatment staff within the hospital walls. These changes are closely related to a change in the psychiatric image of the mental patient.'

A systematic account of such observations was given by A. Stanton and M. Schwartz in their book *The Mental Hospital*.

In Britain Netherne Hospital, Warlingham Park, the Cassel Hospital and Ingrebourne Centre amongst others who took up this new concept. The concept of the therapeutic community was utilized in a pioneering effort to deal with psychopathic individuals at Belmont (now Henderson) Hospital by Maxwell Jones who also used psychodramatic methods. It is not claimed that these developments were due to group analysis, and the example set at Northfield, alone. Developments have certainly been stimulated by the experiences of the War Office Selection Boards (so-called leaderless groups) and of the Civil Rehabilitation Units. The latter in turn owed much to the Northfield experience and rehabilitation officers had occasion to take part at Northfield Hospital in the group activities as part of their regular training. Above all credit is due to Joshua Bierer and his pioneer work which he started before the war at Runwell Hospital which however was not on group-analytic grounds.

A beautiful account of such a development, much more systematic and more consciously group-analytic in spirit, is given by David H. Clark (*Lancet*, Vol. I, 1958, April 19, 1958). He calls this 'administrative therapy' and describes how the principles were carried through by him as Medical Superintendent of Fulbourne Hospital near Cambridge. His approach stands out as a thoroughly practical and concrete application on the lines laid down in the third report of the World Health

[1] Oxford University Press, 1961 (p. 197).

Organization's expert committee on mental health (Geneva, 1953). Clark defines 'administrative therapy' as 'the manipulation, modification and constant scrutiny of the relationships spreading out from the administrator with the aim to control their effect on the patients'. As to the patient's life the first move is the abolition of restraint, seclusion, locked doors and over-sedation. Wards have definite functions and a full work therapy programme is organized which 'must include a proper system of rewards and payment'. Next steps are the development of self-government 'experience in communal life—group therapy, discussion groups, play reading, hospital magazines and mixed units'. Concerning the staff and its organization one is up against deeply ingrained 'whole series of custodial and often punitive reflexes which are not easily abandoned' and rigid status barriers between the different categories of staff. In most hospitals there is a 'rigid hierarchical system with orders passed down from above and a severe blockage on the flow of opinion upwards'. Faced with this the administrative therapist 'cannot just plunge in naïvely with the idea of making everybody democratic'. Very wisely Clark decided that the emphasis should be on communication. This is very much in line with group-analytic principles and with our experience at Northfield. As to the medical organization, problems arising for constructive leadership are equally understandingly handled. Neither does Clark omit the task of dealing with the hospital management committee and the public, including the co-operation of the local press.

As to community leadership he states: 'If any human organization is to work well, it should have confidence in itself, it should have a policy and it should have good morale.' The establishment of the right atmosphere of the hospital is considered the most important task of all. To achieve this the administrator needs 'openness, consistency, respect for everyone's human dignity and a welcome for everyone's contribution'.

Apart from wholesale developments such as these, of at least equal significance for the revolution taking place is the difference in the way psychiatrists look at their task. Of this a good example is given by Dr D. V. Martin and Dr E. F. Carr in a paper on 'Group Psychotherapy in a Mental Hospital'.[1] They introduced a therapeutic in-patient group at a neurosis unit at Claybury Hospital. The situation they found was that fifty

[1] Unpublished communication.

female patients needed psychotherapy but the doctor time available was quite inadequate. Ages ranged from 18 to 78 with some chronic patients having been in the unit already up to two years. Diagnoses included 'neuroses of all types, depressions of all types, early schizophrenia and organic psychosis'. It is characteristic that these two authors now looked at the group dynamic situation and noted that the mixed nature of the community aroused anxiety, tensions between the old and young, resentment among those who had no specific treatment against those who had, and hopelessness. There was no constructive way of dealing with these feelings, and conditions tended towards 'institutionalization'.

Changes introduced were on two lines: weekly ward meetings attended by patients were encouraged to make constructive suggestions as to the running of their units and secondly a therapeutic group was started for twelve of the patients which met daily for one hour on alternate days with one of the doctors in turn, and in the intervening days for discussion of their paintings as well as an 'alternate group session' (without therapist). There was a rapid improvement in the psychological climate of the unit but they also noticed the emergence of 'anti-therapeutic factors'. Their group-analytic assessment revealed that the 'unit was split into two camps: the therapeutic group with its conductors in one, and the rest of the community in the other'. This split affected both the relations between the staff and the patients and those between the group and the community at large. There was even a paranoid fear 'that there might be a leakage into the hospital surroundings community'. This experience taught the authors what might have been predicted and is a good example of a failure to take sufficiently into account the total situation in which such treatment takes place. The unit was reorganized—in the light of this split—into two separate administrative halves, twenty beds for those who had group treatment and thirty beds for non-group patients. They also divided the two doctors' time equally between the two therapeutic groups. Their experience also shows that it would have been better for each doctor to have one group as his own, which they later introduced. Another problem arose through the only ward sister attending both groups. The sister had lost some of her traditional functions in connection with discipline, allocating ward duties and as intermediary between patients and doctor. With this she lost some of her position as a person in authority: 'she finds herself living in the ward instead of supervising it from an office and listening to the troubles of friends rather than to the complaints of patients'. In addition the sister was 'subjected to considerable hostilities from some of her colleagues who view with traditional mistrust the innovations made. They are jealous of her special position, have fantasies of complete anarchy in her ward and imply grave suspicions of her relationships with the doctors concerned. They may make the sister over-anxious about the success of the unit and especially about her responsibility for it. She is apt therefore to be angry with the patients for not trying hard enough to get well and with the doctors for not giving enough help.'

This interesting report was here gone into at some length as it illustrates well the type of problem encountered in this change of atmosphere and attitude in the mental hospital.

David Maddison ('Blue Print for a Model Psychiatric Hospital', *The Medical Journal of Australia*, January 9, 1960) has presented these new ideas to Australian physicians in an original manner by way of a fantasy, as if he was introducing them to a mental hospital in the year 1999. Maddison also views family and group therapy as a base line for future psychiatric treatment and gives a well thought out and detailed image of mental hospital treatment inside a community which is by now in itself 'therapeutic'. A group which Maddison himself conducted at the Maudsley Hospital and which he reported will be noted later (see p. 263).

Chapter XVII

A PATIENT'S GROUP EXPERIENCES IN A SURGICAL UNIT

INTRODUCTORY COMMENTS TO MRS KILMENY FOULKES' PAPER

The following contribution is offered here for three reasons. First for its objective value from the point of view of similar units, surgical or otherwise, and perhaps of in-patient conditions generally. The unit described was run consciously on group lines.

Secondly it is of interest as a study in group psychology, showing how group-analytical concepts apply in a particular group situation. Furthermore, this is the experience of such a situation from the *patient's* point of view.

The third reason is a personal one, but important to myself: the writer and observer was my late wife. It should perhaps be said that her death four years after this time had nothing to do with this particular operation which was a full success and from which she made a complete recovery. She herself was too modest to submit these notes for publication. They are presented now in honour of her memory and as a token of my enduring gratitude for her intense interest in my work and her loving participation in it. In applying these concepts and orientation to her very personal experience as a member of this particular group she shows the deep sense with which she had made them her own.

S.H.F.

GROUP FORMATION AND GROUP REACTION IN A SURGICAL UNIT

A PERSONAL EXPERIENCE

BY KILMENY FOULKES

COMPOSITION

Our common point of departure was that we were all patients in a special unit. The majority were operation cases with a uniform stay of ten days: two before and eight after operation. Others were there for observation and treatment. We were a mixed assortment of varying backgrounds, comprising several different nationalities. We numbered just under thirty, all women with the exception of one man. Ages ranged from 14 to around 60.

THE LEADER

This, the raw material of the group or groups, was strongly leader centred on one man: the surgeon. We had all been seen by him previously at the clinic and all arrived with a strong positive transference. His background presence dominated our life. The arrival of a new patient in our midst would invariably be followed sooner or later by a restatement of our admiration for his skill, his humanity and his spirit of dedication to his chosen task. From him sprang the group approach which characterized his Unit. A lady from Devonshire felt compelled to explain her presence in our midst. 'He does not approve of private rooms. He believes in the therapeutic value of being with other people.' Another patient, reluctant to agree to operation, had been told by way of inducement that she would meet all kinds of interesting people in the Unit. On departure she said with feeling: 'It has been a real pleasure to get to know you all. I feel as if we had known each other for years.' Those with previous hospital experience tried to analyse what gave this unit its unique quality. We agreed that from his attitude to us derived our attitude to each other. We felt responsible to him for our own good interpersonal relationships. Commenting that he could never get a word out of our very shy young member, he said he hoped we could get her to talk and tell us what she was feeling. He gave us the greatest freedom in our daily lives and there was a striking absence of the usual hospital discipline and regimentation. He never made a formal ward round but came upon us suddenly, unannounced, liking to see what we were doing with ourselves. Over our days hung the question, usually voiced as the day wore on: 'Would he come?' And when it became clear that he would not come that day, we tried to be glad that he had spared himself.

THE UNIT

The Unit consisted of:

Two surgical wards of six beds each, capable of being divided into cubicles by curtains. The use of these was not without its significance.

One eight-bed ward, mainly treatment and observation cases, but sometimes accommodating an overflow of operation cases.

One three-bed ward, normally used for men patients, but at this time occupied by women.

All but the latter opened on to a large glassed-in balcony, which was our common rendezvous.

There were also a few single rooms for those in special treatment. After three days' solitary confinement they were free to join the balcony group, where they received a special welcome.

The two six-bed surgical wards, to one of which I belonged, formed closely integrated groups. All were there for the same purpose; all had the same length of stay. Although we made up a typical 'open' group, with its constant changes of personnel, it had many of the qualities of a 'closed' group, with its identity of purpose and experience and its limited but intensive participation. Morale was high. It is, nevertheless, significant that when, towards the end of my stay, we were built down to four, with a view to reorganization and an intake of men into the three-bed ward, a striking disintegration set in with greater tendency to critical discussion of the temporarily absent member.

The treatment and observation ward found integration impossible. They had the widest age span. The length of stay varied from chronic bed cases of a year's standing to those admitted for a routine three-day test. These latter proved the most intransigent elements of all and the most vocal as to their boredom. They never became assimilated.

The three-bed ward proved to be a singularly unhappy composition. They were operation cases, striking for their high incidence of post-anaesthetic sickness and 'feeling miserable'. Their morale was poor and they sought out the balcony group to escape from their suffering sisters, while we of the good morale (there had not been a single case of sickness in *our* ward) did our best to cheer them up on the balcony or went out of our way to visit them in their beds.

The balcony was a long room with tables and many easy chairs. Here all ambulant cases forgathered. Four radiators stood under the long windows. Though it would have been warmer (it was November) for us to form four separate groups, each round a radiator, a nuclear group would form round one radiator and anyone entering was greeted with 'come and join the circle', until a large ring of people was focused on one radiator. Here the members of the misfit wards had a chance to find themselves members of a true 'open' group. It was a loosely knit group, characterized by its spirit of tolerance, an escape from the more exacting ward group. It approximated more nearly to a normal 'social' group. The ward groups were striking for the frank and outspoken nature of their talk.

Nevertheless, in both the ward and balcony groups the absence of sub-groups was remarkable. 'Pairing', it is true, did take place between those admitted and operated on the same date. Theirs was an understandable affinity. They had much in common, but they were never group disruptive.

Of those who drifted in and out of the Balcony Group, there were certain isolates. Above all, there was *Betty*, who caused us much uneasiness. She was 14 years of age, grossly over-weight and mentally retarded. We felt guilty. We were not as nice to her as we might have been. She was a constant topic of discussion in our ward group. She had a desperate need to 'belong' and attached herself to one like a little dog. She was the most under-privileged amongst us, but as she was on a diet, we could not salve our consciences by offering her of our abundance. There was nothing for it but to give of ourselves. Her remarks, too, could be disconcerting, for in her simplicity she sometimes voiced what we suppressed. One day the lady from Devonshire, playing her daily game of patience, offered to teach Betty to play. Betty was delighted at this attention but soon got up from her chair exclaiming 'I don't call that a game. You can't play a game by yourself.'

Very different were the two fourteen-year-old public school girls. Their social poise was remarkable, they made excellent contact with each and all and faced their ordeal with courage. Their patience with Betty put many of us adults to shame. But age disparity made it impossible for them to 'belong' in the fullest sense and in their presence the Balcony Group reverted more than ever to being a social microcosm.

Finally, there was 'the man'. Our first was a lively and amusing Scot. When he joined the Balcony Group, he arrived like a bombshell, disturbing the ordered pattern of balcony life. With a 'Who wants a game of Rummy?' he at once gathered round him a laughing crowd. At the sound of his voice they came leaping from their beds, while others crept away to theirs. He split the Balcony Group into two. He was followed by a quieter, more intellectual type of man who came and went amongst us on the balcony almost unnoticed, so little change did he make in the pattern of balcony life.

This, then, was our dynamic potential. All the rest, doctors, nurses, ward maids, were peripheral. They moved amongst us, doing their jobs, and we did what they asked of us, but they in no sense formed part of our group. They were not of us. Even Sister held no terrors for us. They all passed before our eyes, the raw material of casual and generally friendly comment, which seldom went further than reiterating how nice they all were. Frank or critical comment was turned upon ourselves.

ATTITUDES AND THEMES IN A SIX-BED WARD

It is the six-bed surgical ward of which I propose to speak. Ten days is not long in which to experience a group of shifting composition. But though personalities change, the unchanging pattern of each one's sojourn gives cohesion, so that arrivals and departures cause the minimum of disturbance. Yesterday's admission becomes tomorrow's operation case; today's operation case becomes tomorrow's convalescent. Fellow members of the Ward Group become primarily figures in your own journey. In them you see yourself, past, present and future. Personality is an enrichment, the material which can mitigate boredom or provide distraction from anxiety.

The Start

I arrived on the scene at tea-time. When I had said good-bye to my clothes, and with them part of myself, my defence against the outside world, Nurse drew back the curtains of my cubicle and left me to face my new surroundings, adding 'You don't have to stay in bed, you know. You can go anywhere you like.' Being tea-time, all were in their beds, where all meals were taken. On my right I found my fellow new admission, my 'pair' to whom I was to feel so near as time went on. On my left was Mabel the acknowledged 'leader' of the Ward Group who at once introduced the other members of the Group: she and Mary, the young married woman opposite her, had been operated on two days before and were already allowed up. Opposite me was a Polish lady, the next day's operation case. She was to prove our problem member. Next her was the oldest inhabitant, due out in a few days' time. Her place was taken by the lady from Devonshire. We newcomers then introduced ourselves. We even learned from the 'leader' that the previous occupant of my bed had been five months' pregnant. This aroused great interest in my 'pair', who then told us that she too was pregnant. She had been very worried about being operated at such a time and declared herself much reassured by this information. After tea, Mabel took us round the other wards and introduced us to the Balcony Group. We were impressed by how much she knew about everyone, although she herself was only in her fourth day. That night the surgeon made a round. He explained to us newcomers 'We ask you to come in two days early so that we may get to know you and so that you can get to know us.' He waved his hand in a manner that made it clear that 'us' embraced patients, not only staff. Tomorrow we would be 'us'.

The Ward Leader

That we got off to a good start we undoubtedly owed to the qualities of our ward 'leader'. She was a woman experienced in interpersonal relationships. In her absence we agreed how nice she was, how kind. We admired the entertainment she provided for us by her skilled conversational gambits in dealing with members of the periphery. Her daily exchanges with our depressive wardmaid were pronounced worthy of ITMA.[1] We

---

[1] 'It's That Man Again', a famous Radio feature (BBC) at the time.

all said how we would miss her when she had gone. She went, and we remarked how pleasantly quiet it was. She really had been very tiring, too talkative. How nice Mary the little quiet one had been, Mabel's 'pair', who left on the same day. She had unassumingly done so many of the chores: getting the early morning tea, the mid-morning and after-lunch coffee, doing the flowers night and morning. And we were sure she had not always felt too grand. Look how often she had popped back into bed, curled up and gone to sleep. How we missed her. The following day I received a long letter from the departed leader, with many individual messages for each member of the ward. I read it out. It aroused not a flicker of interest.

The Operation Case

There was one haunting element in our lives with which we had to come to grips: the day's operation case. We met her on our first morning when at breakfast time Nurse drew the curtains round her bed, shrouding her in mystery. We asked a few tentative questions of the old hands. But on her return, there were no curtains to mask the inescapable. She sat there, rigid and silent in our midst, our friend of yesterday, peaceful yet infinitely disturbing. Betty voiced our unspoken fears. 'Coo, looks like a stiff, don't she?' She was once more a member of the group, absent yet present. It was our duty to watch for signs of returning consciousness, to speak to her and tell her it was all over now, to receive her back. But in the meantime, there she was: the picture of each one of us. Later we reassured her: 'You looked quite lovely. Really you did, like a Titian with your auburn hair and your pale face.' Even experience, though, did not totally dispel this uneasiness. When visiting time came round, she was again discreetly shrouded from the eyes of ordinary people. Only we were called upon to face our ghostly member. A member of the three-bed ward came on to the balcony in desperation: she could not stay in her ward with 'two of them'. A more cynical observation case from the eight-bed ward remarked that she was reminded of Walter Pater's remark when watching the middle-aged playing hockey: 'Let's go. It doesn't seem quite kind to look at them.'

Attitudes to Fear and Anxiety

In its attitude to fear and apprehension *before* operation, the group was infinitely tolerant and sympathetic. To reassure before the event was a primary duty of the group. Expressions of shame and apologies for tears and lack of control were brushed aside as quite uncalled for. But once the milestone had been passed, the group had scant sympathy for the complainer. All were in the same boat. Allowances need no longer be made for the anxiety of inexperience. Each could see for herself that everything passes, tomorrow would be different. Our Polish member caused increasing irritation by her minute analyses of her feelings, her fear that, unlike the rest of us, all was not well with her. As a concession to her foreign background, we painstakingly explained to her the ideal of the 'stiff upper lip'. It could safely be left with the experts to detect any cause for anxiety. This had no effect whatever. When next the surgeon came, she spoke to him of her anxieties. We waited, intent, to see how he would deal with our problem member. He was patient, reassuring. Then he offered her to see the psychiatrist. She refused. From then on she forfeited our sympathy. The next day he did not come, nor the day after, nor the third day. We were convinced she was causing him to withdraw from us. Hostility towards her was unbounded. Disintegration had already set in with our becoming a four-bed ward. We missed no opportunity to discuss all her shortcomings when she was absent. With his not coming, humanity deserted the group.

Pattern of a Day

Apart from the ordeal by operation which all must surmount, the biggest problem of the group was the defeat of boredom. The day began when the lights went up at 5 a.m. Fortified by tea and a bath, we were back in bed again with a good two hours' wait for eight o'clock breakfast. Talk at such a time was inevitably a little desultory. The night's dreams were recounted, but nothing was attempted by way of interpretation. One member told how instead of the expected operation she found to her amazement that the surgeon had tattooed her all over. A free floating conversation would take place during which we enlarged our knowledge of each other. Hospitalization loosens taboos. Due perhaps to the fact that one lady was a beauty specialist by profession, personal appearance was a frequent subject of discussion. Comment at this early hour was frank but friendly. No one wished to be provocative at such an early hour. Hair styles were criticized and experiments made in re-styling. Similar experiments were made with make-up.

The arrival on the scene of the ward maids led to our daily experiment in conversational skill. We arranged which one of us should make the opening gambit. Afterwards we appraised the results. Only our first leader could hold us spellbound for the duration of the whole session, carrying the entire brunt of the conversation, providing us with first-class entertainment. Others petered out dismally in their efforts and the next member of the group had to take up the challenge.

The arrival of breakfast provided us with the first good grumble of the day, after which we all felt more group minded. After breakfast the first operation case went up and on the part of the others there was a general adjournment to the balcony. Whether in the ward or on the balcony, all were agreed that they just could not read. Many had looked forward to a chance to do some reading during convalescence. Someone remarked 'It's not just weakness. *That* passes very soon. I've always enjoyed reading in hospital before. It seems a form of escape. Here you feel as if you are missing something if you read.' For the same reason, no doubt, the earphones hung neglected on the bedheads. Balcony conversation was generally lively and tolerant, tolerant even of the long lectures to which the American treated us, breaking off only to say 'Shucks. Am I bored!' She was a three-day observation case. It was a pleasant change to try our skill at non-verbal communication with our Greek girl who spoke no word of English.

For lunch the ward group reassembled. The operation cases were down again. All afternoon there was an uneasy movement between ward and balcony. Silences prevailed. Talk was desultory.

Visiting time was a welcome interruption. All had to be in their beds for that period, whether being visited or not. This was not resented. We took an unashamed interest in each other's visitors arriving and departing, though during the visit the unvisited would often draw their curtains slightly, remarking afterwards to their neighbours 'I thought it was nicer for you'. Often though, we told the others of our expected visitors and invited their comment afterwards. Supper followed upon visiting time and was one of the most lively periods of the day. There was fresh material to stimulate talk. We passed benevolent comment on the visitors, especially on husbands: their looks, their attentiveness. The Polish habit of hand kissing came in for much approval. Where women visitors were concerned, appearance as always, excited great interest.

After supper a slight restlessness was noticeable. It was one of the hours when He might come.

Night Nurse as Mother

With the approach of bedtime, the group's responsibility ended. We drifted gradually to bed. It was tiring to sustain for a sixteen-hour day the role which one was called upon to play in such a community. At this hour of the day we allowed ourselves to admit our convalescent state. The stiff upper lip, which we had preached by day, could be relaxed. We awaited with pleasurable anticipation the arrival of the night nurses. They were more approachable than the day nurses. They had more time for you, gave to each one a more personal attention than the day staff. We admired their fine instinct for being there when needed, anticipating every need. Acute resentment was expressed by one member of the ward when another member went to make her hot drink in the middle of the night. 'What did she want to interfere for? Nurse would have come in a minute.

And so we laid down our burdens of responsibility, each for the other; night nurse came and with her great peace. Mother had come to put us to bed.

Postscript

To sum up, for we discussed it often, there was something quite special in this particular unit. Apart from the spirit which stemmed from our surgeon, the unit of six patients seemed a happy number, capable of closely knit relationships and intensive reactions at times, but relieved by the responsibility of alternative membership of the more casual Balcony Group. Most people agreed that they had been remarkably happy there and in many ways really sorry to leave. All said they would miss the group. Someone characterized our particular group by saying that, being relatively uninterested in our common symptoms, particularly after operation, we were able to by-pass boring reiteration of case histories and get to know each other better as people. As a matter of purely personal experience, I can only add that never have I returned home in so disoriented, so trancelike ˙ a condition. It seemed as if something was fermenting, seething within my mind: so many undigested impressions. I felt as if I had glimpsed through a half-open door the way leading to better and happier inter-personal relationships with the most unlikely people. Only when I had jotted down the notes for this paper did the events of those ten days fall into place and leave me in peace.

Section II: Group Analysis in Private Practice
and at Out-Patient Clinics

Chapter XVIII

GROUP ANALYSIS IN PRIVATE
PRACTICE AND OUT-PATIENT
CLINICS

When group analysis is used as a method of psychotherapy it is
called group-analytic psychotherapy (G.A.P.). Whereas in the
foregoing we have been concerned with in-patients we are now
turning to out-patient conditions, that is to say people who
pursue their usual lives uninterruptedly whilst undergoing
treatment. This is the chief domain of this type of treatment.
When no external restrictions limit its course, e.g. in private
practice it has proved to be, in now nearly twenty-five years of
experience, an intensive and deep going form of psychotherapy.
Its effects can only be compared to prolonged individual psycho-
analytic treatment and in many cases it seems superior to this
in its therapeutic effect. It must be said, however, that under
these circumstances it tends to be a prolonged form of treatment, to be thought of in terms of several years rather than
months. In terms of economy the difference is still considerable;
assuming G.A.P. to be on a once-a-week and psycho-analysis
five times a week basis the ratio for time spent is one to five.
G.A.P. can be stepped up to two or more sessions per week
and can be combined with any number of regular individual
interviews. It seems likely that the optimum interval between
meetings would be less than a week, sessions being held two
or even three times a week. It is certain that meetings should
not be less than once weekly. Some workers advocate 'alternate'
meetings, that is without the therapist present, between ordinary meetings. I have as yet no systematic experience with
this procedure. It has certainly some advantages but raises **a**

number of serious objections especially from the point of view of the transference situation. My own experience has been predominantly with weekly groups without individual appointments unless these were indicated by particular circumstances. These with increasing experience arise only very rarely.

There is no doubt that an intensive form of psychotherapy results from a combination with individual interviews. In this case every member of the group should have such individual interviews and as far as possible conditions should be equal for all members. During the first years of experimenting with G.A.P. I practised this type of combination. Gradually I have come to the conclusion that individual treatment where necessary should precede, or better still, follow G.A.P., but that the aim should be to make concurrent individual treatment unnecessary. Within recent years I have reintroduced a form of combination in the following way: each participant has one personal interview with me in weekly turns, that is to say, meets me once in two months. This modification resulted from the fact that intensity became so great that it was not always possible to deal with individual implications sufficiently within the time available. This procedure has so far worked out very well. If an increase in the number of group sessions to two a week is possible this might well be preferable.

The number of patients might drop by one, two or three below eight, but it should not exceed that number. The group takes the form of 'slow-open' groups, individuals being introduced as vacancies occur from time to time. In the Appendix some facts and figures will be given in more detail based on two such groups which have been going on for a number of years.

These groups contain psychiatrists and other doctors who joined for training purposes. Some of them had undergone intensive psycho-analytic treatment and training. For obvious reasons I tended for a number of years to reserve membership in such training groups to this category. However, deep seated character defences tended to be shared and organized in professional channels. Mutual analysis tended to become predominant, taking the place of frank personal exposure and could easily be rationalized. Now they share groups with other professional or otherwise compatible patients who come entirely for therapeutic reasons and this works much better. The therapists expose frankly their personal problems and it is an object lesson for all when these conflicts involve them in their own relations with their own patients in turn. Not surprisingly perhaps the 'patients' in the group tend to project some categorical differences between themselves and the 'psychiatrists'. This complication lends itself to analytical solution.

Under the conditions of a hospital out-patient clinic considerable pressure of numbers and a relative shortage of staff calls for many adaptations and concessions.

The particular problems which arise under conditions such as these can briefly be put thus: too many patients, among them a high proportion of difficult ones, to be treated in too short a time by doctors relatively inexperienced in psychotherapy.

We will now illustrate the problems of out-patient psychotherapy and an attempt at this solution by a concrete example, namely, the O-P Psychotherapy Unit at the Maudsley as it operated under my direction for a period of twelve years. This will be described in this chapter in the first place in order to present orientation and principles. Some facts and figures, as far as available, are given in the Appendix.

My own experience has been first at St Bartholomew's Hospital (this has been reported in 'Introduction to Group-Analytic Psychotherapy') and for the last twelve years at the Maudsley Hospital in London.

This latter will be the basis of the present account. As the unit in question, in accordance with the functions of a teaching hospital, served not only the treatment of patients but also the training and teaching of postgraduates, it has been built up with the idea of a close integration between these two functions. In Chapter 19 the set-up of the unit will be described in some detail; in Chapter 20 teaching, study and research will be treated under separate headings.

Type of patient: Patients were referred by the general psychiatric consultants of the hospital from their out-patient clinics, mostly when prospects of spontaneous improvement were not good and the case had been unresponsive to treatment. They were mainly psychoneurotic patients who could in principle be expected to benefit from psychotherapy. There was also a sprinkling of psychotic and potentially psychotic patients. Some of these responded well to psychotherapy, others had sometimes to be admitted as in-patients before their treatment could begin. Only in a minority of referrals was there what one might call positive selection, in the sense that patients were referred with a good prognosis and good motivation for psychotherapy. In addition a goodly number of patients were referred whose condition had been serious enough for them to require a shorter or more prolonged stay in the hospital and who were about to be or had recently been discharged.

Psychotherapists available: postgraduate doctors with more or less psychiatric experience, but often little if any experience in psychotherapy. Most of them had expressed a degree of interest and a positive inclination towards psychotherapy and some were training to become psychoanalysts and were undergoing their own analysis. These latter were not necessarily better in the practice of psychotherapy of a shorter variety as they were inclined to consider such treatment as a frustrated form of psycho-analysis. On the other hand they had a much better appreciation of unconscious implications and the dynamics of the transference/countertransference situation. Experience and skill are of particular importance when difficult cases have to be treated in freer style and in shorter time.

Limitations: Our physicians served at this unit for a term of six months or exceptionally one year. Thus no sooner had they acquired some experience when they had to leave. Patients had to envisage the end of their treatment very soon or else be transferred to another doctor with all the problems this raises. For individual treatment the average time available was approximately one weekly session for, say, three to four months. Groups were also held usually at the rate of one session per week but fortunately it was often possible to carry on for a longer time because the therapists were ready to continue with their groups from personal interest after they had left the department. Thus groups had a lifetime of from one to two years or more. It was also easier for groups to carry on for another term with a new conductor than for patients in individual treatment. This particularly applied to the open type of group.

Supervision: There again less time was available than would be ideally required. It was possible to reserve one to two weekly hours for each registrar but this would include dealing with the practical administrative points and current matters of some urgency. Not more than two or three cases could be supervised regularly in any detail but in surveying the whole material there was occasion to discuss some specific points in treatment, the handling of particular situations and so on.

Supervision of Group Treatment: This was done by way of a weekly seminar in which all groups were reviewed in turn and the points discussed concerning the various groups were of interest and instructional value to all. Of this more later.

Orientation: My orientation to all this has been to accept these difficulties not as accidental complications but simply as a reflexion of the situation in which psychotherapy finds itself at the present time. In this way the task was accepted in a positive spirit. This attitude found expression in the organization of the unit. Without such positive orientation the registrars themselves could not have been expected to approach their task in a positive frame of mind in turn. This, however, is necessary in my opinion if psychotherapy is to be successful. If the psychotherapist—confronted with such difficult conditions—cannot find a positive solution he had better not accept them; alternatively he would have two choices: either to be content with an attempt at piecemeal and symptomatic amelioration or else he must proceed cynically without any conviction that he could do any good. My idea was that it is not much good teaching and preaching therapeutic tenets, however sound they may be unless the practice upon which they are taught sets a good example. It is not satisfactory to proclaim principles but continuously have to point out that they cannot be practised here and now because of practical difficulties.

Therapeutic aims and the means by which one hoped to achieve them had to be formulated in view of the actual reality of the situation (time, experience, availability, etc.). All individual component factors of the therapeutic situation which condition the dynamics of treatment have to be compatible with each other. For instance, it would not make much sense to put the patient on a couch or to base his treatment on free association or to analyse his dreams if his next interview took place a week later and the total duration of treatment was no more than twelve or twenty hours. Nor would it make sense to embark on intensive interpretations and analysis of transference. In this connection an interesting observation was made which could lend itself to more systematic enquiry and that is that transference reactions seemed to become clearly discernible around the sixth treatment session—in our case mostly coinciding with the sixth week of treatment. In some cases transference had to be taken up or even had to be in the centre of attention from the beginning. In others the therapist was well advised to observe it but leave it alone unless it forced itself into prominence particularly as a resistance. Variations in regularity, dosage of interviews in the light of the stage of treatment particularly its ending were important items in the dynamic handling of the case. The importance of the therapist's attitude and how it was conveyed to the patient in the beginning of treatment were stressed. The termination of treatment was well prepared and ample notice given. In a sense the end was envisaged from the beginning. It cannot be over-emphasized how much the result is influenced by the expectation cultivated in the patient in words or by implication or, to put it another way, how much harm can be done by lack of awareness and skill in this respect.

Patients under psychotherapy make infinite claims and it is to some extent true that the more of these are fulfilled the more arise for quite legitimate reasons or from dependency and transference needs. If it is to be kept within reasonable dimensions in time it is important that psychotherapy is never allowed to become an institution. It is my impression in longer and even very long psychotherapy that from time to time an optimal point for ending treatment is reached. When this is missed it takes an increasingly longer time before a similar position is again reached which is favourable for the termination of treatment. It is a kind of spiral phenomenon; for instance a case may have reached a good point after six hours (weeks), again after six months; the next time may be after eighteen months or two years, after which it may be a matter of years. On the whole the tendency is for the therapist to hesitate too long with the termination of treatment and to underrate the patient's ability to manage without him.

As I have sometimes formulated, in many cases we have done a good deal if we helped the patient to translate his symptoms into his problems or, if he had presented us with problems, have analysed with him what had prevented their solution by himself or that and why he looked for answers which we could not give him. This may sound modest but we have preferred to aim at more modest goals but such as we could reasonably hope to reach under the given circumstances. Furthermore we thought it important that whatever change had been achieved should hold good after the relationship with the therapist had been given up and the patient been required to stand on his own feet again. On average we devoted the last third of the treatment to the working through of this separation from the therapist. Thus it may be stated that in spite of our limitations we aimed at treating the person rather than the symptom and we tended to focus more on central problems and attitudes than on the modification of symptoms.

It has been found useful to plan treatment with the help of a specially devised card. On this was entered firstly a dynamic formulation of the case in co-operation with the registrar who was to treat the patient and who whenever possible had seen him together with the consultant in a diagnostic interview (see Chapter 19). Then followed a formulation of the changes we felt could be achieved and the means by which we hoped to achieve them. After termination of treatment changes claimed were analysed in terms of dynamic changes in the patient and factors operating in the treatment situation and these were compared with the original assessment.

The problems and principles just outlined are of course the same for individual and group treatment. Indeed, our dynamic formulations influenced our choice for one or the other. Group treatment, however, offers special advantages. First of all, in the diagnostic introductory group the trainee can share the observations and participate in decisions based upon these afterwards. Secondly, group treatment itself as an experience brings the learning therapist into a more natural contact with his patients and influences him to be more concrete and to express himself simply. The supervision in a group situation has all the advantages of group teaching to which we shall come back in Chapter 20.

Apart from this, group psychotherapy enables the therapist to get to know more and a greater variety of patients than he would otherwise do and has the merits of a comparative psychopathology which is displayed in living interaction for him. We shall come back to some of these points in connection with the plan of the unit and the set-up (Chapter 19) and teaching (Chapter 20).

Chapter XIX

OUTLINE OF A PSYCHOTHERAPEUTIC UNIT

(OPD MAUDSLEY HOSPITAL)

In this chapter an account will be given of a model unit as developed at the Maudsley Hospital Out-Patient Psychotherapy Department under my direction. It is a model in the sense that it shows a way in which justice can be done to the claims of psychotherapy at an out-patient clinic if it is at the same time to create the best conditions for teaching and learning, clinical study and research. It is *not* a model in the sense that it should or could be transferred wholesale to other settings. Indeed, it is an intrinsic part of a group-analytic approach that rigid organization and institutionalization are avoided so as to allow maximum flexibility to ever-changing conditions. Arrangements should, as it were, be hand-made and in the closest possible contact with the realities of conditions. For this same reason this unit has been continuously changing in detail and what is given here is a schematic cross section of its working structure.

During the period under discussion the unit staff consisted of one physician (consultant psychotherapist, half-time) and two full-time registrars. In the year under review 225 patients were referred to the unit. Of these approximately 25 per cent failed to keep appointments or were rejected as unsuitable or transferred for other treatment. In 10 per cent of the total the result was very good, in 40 per cent good or moderately good and the remaining 25 per cent showed no definite evidence of improvement. Of those treated therefore $13 \cdot 3$ per cent were recovered, $53 \cdot 3$ per cent much improved or improved, 33.3 per cent showed no significant result. These patients were usually sent to the hospital by their general practitioners. Each patient was examined by one of the psychiatric consultants in charge of out-patient clinics who had referred them to us to be considered for psychotherapy. A number had previously been treated as in-patients of the hospital and were considered ready for discharge provided that they could have further out-patient treatment.

The following diagram indicates the modes and stages of psychotherapy in the unit which was on an analytic basis.

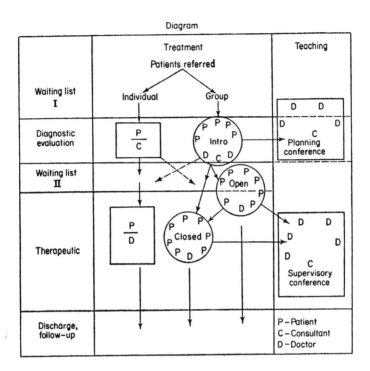

Diagram

It will be seen that treatment was broadly divided into two categories: individual and group. These are shown as two streams and linking up with the group stream teaching and supervising activities of the unit are represented in the column on the right. Supervision of individual psychotherapy is not shown in this diagram. Patients had either individual psycho-therapy or group psychotherapy but some may have had first one and then the other. Patients who had group treatment were given additional individual attention when the need arose. In a preliminary selection from the case notes approximately seven out of ten were found suitable for attending the introductory group; the others were seen individually by the consultant in the usual way. The period of waiting for this initial interview was from one to six weeks. (W.L. I)

In order to facilitate comparison the progress of patients through the unit will now be followed separately according to the two streams.

INDIVIDUAL PSYCHOTHERAPY

At the *initial interview* the consultant formed an opinion of the psychopathological structure and dynamics of the patient, of his capacity and motivation for change and formulated a provisional plan for treatment, its prospective intensity, mode of operation and target. The patient may then have had to wait from three to six months before a vacancy occurred. (W.L. II)

A treatment session took the best part of an hour. As a rule interviews took place once a week for three to six months (about ten to thirty hours). Physician and patient sat face to face. The degree of control of verbal communication, interpretation of content and relationship ('transference') were modified to suit the needs of the individual patient. The planning of such modifications took into account the way in which these various factors interact and influence one another.

The recognition of unconscious mental processes and their role in the production of the neurosis were considered important. The material for this was provided by the patients' verbal communication, behaviour and attitude towards the therapist.

It was considered important that the atmosphere was one in which judging, censoring, preaching and moralizing had no place. Much attention was given to the problem of the patient's dependence on the doctor.

GROUP PSYCHOTHERAPY

Only three groups are shown schematically on the diagram: the introductory group, an open and a closed group. The open group, in one of its incarnations was used as a preliminary (holding) group. This is indicated schematically by its extension into the space of W.L. II. It will be understood that these 'groups' represent a number of parallel groups and variations of them. The diagram shows some of the advantages of group psychotherapy: the elimination or reduction of waiting lists, the continuity or gradual transition from one stage to the next, the greater number of patients treated by a single doctor and the closeness of teaching and training opportunities. In addition group treatment has other intrinsic advantages for certain categories of psychiatric patients.

Now we will consider each section in turn, both regarding therapy and teaching.

Introductory Group: This group served many purposes but two of its functions were outstanding. Firstly, the diagnostic evaluation in the light of the patients' reactions to the perturbing situation in which they found themselves, their response to this token therapeutic approach and of the characteristics revealed in their reactions to each other. Secondly, this group presented the best possible practical introduction for those selected for group psychotherapy. From a teaching point of view it must be seen in close connection with the 'planning conference' which followed immediately afterwards and which was built up on observations made by the doctors in the introductory group.

The number of patients in this group was confined to four or five. These patients had not met each other, nor any of us, before as they took their seats in a semicircle facing the consultant and the other doctors of the unit. Such a situation is understandably tense. After some introductory remarks, however, there was considerable relaxation and the consultant began his investigations as a rule by addressing each patient in turn. He asked them not only about the complaints which brought them to the hospital but sought to throw light on their own expectations and attitudes regarding treatment. The first analytic steps in the shape of clarification, confrontation of contradictory attitudes, rectification, etc., were taken already on the occasion of this first contact. Their importance must be rated high. Spontaneity and interaction on the part of the patients was encouraged and they soon understood that they were expected to take an active part. They began to compare problems and exchange views. A patient might say with a wistful nod of his head, 'Yes, that is just the way I feel.'

Considerable resistances and objections might be raised. Two experiences were made: that these objections can be voiced without fear and that they were taken up in an analytic spirit. The introductory group meeting brought to light many of the difficulties which each patient experienced in his relations to other people which so often form the hard core of his illness.

It was remarkable to observe how these quite unselected patients could be made to interact at this one and only meeting they had with each other and how meaningful this encounter could be.

The doctors shared this experience and could observe the consultant's handling of the situation. We thus saw dynamically and often dramatically displayed just those features which affect the doctor and patient decisively when assessing therapeutic possibilities. Thus much could be accomplished in the short space of an hour at this introductory meeting. It was usually possible to recommend to each patient at the end of this hour the mode of subsequent treatment. Individual psychotherapy was recommended to about one in five of these patients while the remainder qualified for group psychotherapy.

Planning Conference: Following the introductory group meeting, the doctors met and discussed their observations and formulated more detailed plans for each of the patients seen at the introductory group. Observations were exchanged, the psychopathology as it had been observed in action was compared with that reported by the referring consultant on the basis of a more conventional examination. Observations were pooled, various interpretations discussed and prognoses considered. Each doctor shared in the decisions of the psychotherapeutic team. On the basis of shared experience we could thus discuss the patients' suitability for treatment, their differential selection for group or individual therapy, our expectations and predictions of therapeutic results. A tentative plan of treatment was formulated as well as the means whereby desirable changes might be achieved. Apart from the patients whom they treated, these doctors thus got to know the other patients as well on whom they would later hear their colleagues report at the supervisory seminar. The introductory group meeting as a whole with its particular dynamics, the physician's actions and interpretations and points of technique were considered.

The latter part of this conference was devoted to a preliminary examination of the case notes of the patients who would be invited to next week's introductory group meeting. In this way each doctor got acquainted with the details of patients whom he would see the following week and their problems and he could thus make his own formulations and check his expectations at the following week's planning conference in the light of the introductory group.

THERAPEUTIC GROUPS

These are represented in the scheme by one open and one closed group which are of course prototypes. An *open group* would admit and discharge members from time to time. It served a great variety of purposes, not always compatible in one and the same actual group. For some patients it is important to provide treatment as soon as possible. In this case treatment in the open group was preparatory only until a suitable vacancy could be found for them in a closed group. For others it provided a valuable opportunity for further diagnostic observation. It served, however, as the sole treatment group for a good proportion of its membership. It was particularly suitable for two types of patient belonging to two rather opposite ends of a scale:

(1) Patients who are less severely disturbed, though perhaps more acutely upset, can benefit from the greater variety of social adjustment demanded in such a group and can soon be discharged.

(2) The chronic patient who needs prolonged treatment, partly of a supportive kind but who can nevertheless benefit from an analytic approach. These may attend for prolonged periods. Not much emphasis was placed on regularity of attendance and patients might be tentatively discharged but return to the group later if they felt any need for this. Such a group could therefore carry a greater number of people, say fifteen, while the actual attendance might be between five and ten. Such groups could carry on indefinitely, at least in theory, with changing therapists. In practice it must be said that they came to an end from time to time. What usually happened was that a nucleus of 'regulars' developed who sooner or later became refractory towards new members. This might probably be avoided if a sufficient number of parallel groups could be run so that selection could be more careful and turnover be controlled at a convenient rate. What happened in our unit under the circumstances when the refractory stage was reached was that we refrained from adding new members and allowed the nucleus to finish their treatment as a closed group.

The Closed Group: The closed group ideally begins and ends with the same membership; as a rule, however, one or two patients have to be replaced in the beginning. This is a kind of natural sorting out and could probably be avoided where careful selection is possible. The group also loses one or two members in its course, when this is at all prolonged, for more or less external reasons. At the clinic the life of such a group was between one and two and a half years and it met at weekly intervals. My impression is that a period of nine months is a good yardstick by which to determine a group's duration—or say ten months allowing for one month's break. One such period of nine months being a minimum and three such periods perhaps the most desirable. These groups demand regular attendance from each member and they provide an intensive therapeutic experience. Individual interviews were rarely necessary during treatment. The group indicated in our diagram stands for a variety some of which will be discussed separately later.

The selection of the individuals has been discussed in its various aspects in different places in this volume. The principles of selection are not yet known with any accuracy. The main reasons for this are: (1) that there are such a great number of significant variables, and (2) that in order to carry out such selection far greater numbers of patients and staff would be required than are as yet assembled anywhere to my knowledge. As a rough estimate I think that two to three hundred currently available and otherwise suitable patients of about equal number in sex would be necessary and up to a dozen trained group psychotherapists. The scientific testing of merits and demerits of various selective factors would, even under such circumstances, be a task of many years.

Our groups are as a rule now of mixed sex, in equal proportion. Care is taken to match such factors as personality, age, religion, social status, educational level, etc. Minority conditions where they cannot be avoided should at least not be confined to any one individual in isolation. As to diagnosis we preferred heterogeneous groups with an admixture of psychotic or borderline cases but preferably not severely depressed patients.

A general principle observed was this: if the range of some of the factors mentioned was great this was compensated by more rigid insistence on uniformity in other respects. For instance, let us assume that social status and age varied considerably, then intelligence should be uniformly high; or if a group was to contain a mixture of single and married women their social status and educational level would be kept steady especially when age ranged widely.

Closed groups can also be selected according to particular problems. A few such special groups will be described in Chapter 20 as examples. If the group was composed in this way, or was otherwise concerned with a shared issue through a common situation in which the members found themselves, greater laxity was possible in other variables. Patients in some such conditions as marked sexual deviation, addiction or delinquency can benefit greatly by inclusion in such special groups when as a rule they would not fit into the usual out-patient group.

This form of group then was our usual therapeutic group. The patients are strangers to each other and are not connected in ordinary life. They were instructed not to meet outside the treatment situation, though preferably this code of behaviour would be based on an understanding of the reasons for it. This is best achieved by taking this point (as well as similar ones) up early, as soon as it arises in the group.

Quite by contrast to this we have from time to time treated small *networks* of closely related patients in small groups. Such a 'network' is as it were a cluster of psychopathological mutual mental involvement of which the patient is a part. Frequently, this may correspond to family relationships.

The Supervisory Conference: Here all groups were discussed. It took place weekly and took two and a half hours. All the doctors engaged in treatment assembled to report on their groups. Over the years there was a constant flow of distinguished visitors, both from this country and abroad, although their number had to be confined to a few at any one time. Special points of urgency which had arisen were discussed but in the main three groups on average were reported extensively on each occasion. Here again the practical work was made the occasion of instruction. Points of technique and handling were in the foreground, but psychopathological and theoretical problems were fully discussed. In this way all could share in the experiences of each individual group and could in addition compare and contrast their different approaches and above all could exchange their views in lively discussion. It was thus real group teaching in which the consultant joined. This aspect will be discussed further in Chapter 20 under Teaching. The group discussion and group analysis of the doctor-patient interaction is particularly valuable, including observations concerning behaviour in this group itself.

THE UNIT IN OPERATION

It may be useful to end this short account by considering what were the standard situations in this unit as experienced

(*a*) by a patient
(*b*) by a registrar

(*a*) The patient referred by his G.P. would be examined by a registrar in consultation with a physician, who might then send him to the out-patient psychotherapeutic unit. Here, if he were pre-selected for the 'individual stream', he would have an interview with the senior psychotherapist after an average waiting time of two to three weeks. If accepted for individual psychotherapy, he would have to wait up to six months before notification of a vacancy. Finally he would meet the doctor who was to treat him. Arrangements here varied greatly, but the average was one interview a week of forty-five minutes' duration. If his treatment could not be terminated successfully within six months, he would have to be passed on to a new doctor or complete his treatment in a suitable group.

If a patient were pre-selected for the 'group stream', he would find himself, two or three weeks after referral, in the introductory group. If, after assessment here he was found suitable for group psychotherapy, he might continue as a member of an open group, whence he passed sometimes with, but often without, a break to the most suitable closed group available for him, or he might have to wait for a suitable vacancy.

(*b*) The training experiences of the registrar were varied and intense. During his six to nine months on the unit he would undertake the treatment of about twenty individual patients. In this work he would receive weekly supervision by the consultant, in an hour set aside for him. He would conduct one or two groups, having an average number of seven patients each. He would receive guidance at a weekly supervisory conference, where he would also exchange experiences with colleagues. He would have regular opportunity for first-hand observation on the management of the introductory group by the consultant, and a chance to discuss these observations in full at the planning conference afterwards. In addition, he would have access to the total material and ample opportunity for closely observing the large majority of patients passing through this unit during his stay, an opportunity particularly difficult to realize in psychotherapy. He would have continuous opportunities for discussion, for learning from the experiences of his colleagues, and having the benefit of their criticism on his own handling of cases, and in turn, of actively participating in the critical assessment of their work. The main emphasis in treatment throughout was on interpersonal relationship.

In the next chapter some of the work which emanated from the stimulation received in this unit, in particular in so far as it has been published or at least formulated in writing, will be reviewed.

Chapter XX

TEACHING, STUDY AND RESEARCH

This chapter is concerned with the group-analytic method and approach in operation, in the first place in teaching and then for study and research purposes. The out-patient unit which formed the subject-matter of the last chapter was concerned with all these. In the course of this present chapter I wish to report on some of the fruits of our work, some of which has been published and some can at least be formulated at this stage; though it is hoped that it may still be published by the individual doctors concerned. I shall also incorporate some other work which has been more or less directly influenced by my own work and whose authors are, for the most part, members of the Group-Analytic Society (London).

TEACHING

Teaching and psychotherapy have much in common, in so far as in both a change of attitude is essential. Some authors, e.g. Dr M. L. J. Abercrombie whose work will presently be reviewed, stress the similarities almost to the point of identity. Others, e.g. Professor N. Elias, while recognizing the common matrix of the two disciplines, have been interested to highlight some of the differences. It is perhaps true to say that both disciplines move on a scale from the purely instructional end to the other end, where learning is the result of a changed attitude, which requires the overcoming of psychological emotional resistances to traditional impregnation and conditioning. The therapeutic process itself is considered by one school of thought as a learning process.

It is quite certain that in our particular field, namely the teaching of psychotherapy, the two processes are very closely interrelated. Psycho-analysis has long recognized that a most important part of the training of the future psycho-analyst is his own personal therapeutic analysis. In the field of group-analysis one comes to the same conclusion. What needs perhaps to be stressed is that this by itself is not enough. Experience as a patient is not all that the future therapist requires. Not only does he himself have to make the experience of being a therapist in the therapeutic situation, but the fullest acquaintance with the experience of other colleagues from personal observation as well as from perusal of the literature is indispensable. Method and technique can be taught, and must be learned, and a thorough theoretical framework is essential. We therefore come back to the fact that teaching psychotherapy is necessary. My experience points to a procedure in which such teaching takes place in a number of situations, graduated according to the degree in which the psychotherapeutic element, in a frankly personal application, enters into the admixture.

To put it another way, each situation, designed deliberately for its particular purpose, sets its own limitations and boundaries in this respect. These considerations apply alike to the teaching in individual and group situations.

Group teaching introduces particular additional factors, on the whole more in its favour, which in turn run closely parallel to specific factors which characterize group psychotherapy. It is perhaps not accidental that the conclusions just indicated were brought home to me in the first place by observations in conducting both therapy and teaching in groups. I should like to report here, by way of illustration, some of these observations.

When called upon to introduce a number of psychotherapists to group psychotherapy, this was done in a group situation. In a number of such groups, sooner or later, a split occurred usually about half and half, of those who demanded—explicitly or by implication—more therapy, and those who showed signs of wanting to keep away from becoming personally too much involved. The two halves moved as it were into opposite directions from the centre of the sliding scale. It was quite clear from the composition and purpose of the group that it was impossible to satisfy both tendencies, and that an integration had to be found. I did not know at the time how to achieve this. Some years later I found the same split in a purely therapeutic group in which one faction, later on termed 'the radicals', continuously criticized the other half for not committing themselves fully and unreservedly and only wanting to go far enough to enable them to control the situation as far as they themselves were concerned. On this particular occasion, after the group came to an end, the 'radicals' opted to carry on for a year with me by themselves, which I accepted. Deprived of the former members serving as projective screens, they now could locate this split as inside themselves. Interestingly enough they did not now express this conflict by new splitting in the group possibly because it only contained five members. Another demand of their radicalism had been that I myself should disclose my own attitudes more fully, and participate more personally. I accepted this condition also, but with certain reservations without which I thought actual harm might arise because after all they were quite severely disturbed patients. I said that I did not consider myself committed to answer requests for purely factual information concerning intimate details of my life, merely to satisfy their curiosity. Interestingly enough, after putting me into the centre for one or two sessions they seemed to lose all further interest in my personal concerns and reinstalled me in the usual therapeutic role. This piece of analysis, which naturally also involved and changed me, taught me that this split between radicals and the rest is partly the result of the non-participation of the conductor, in particular an expression of resentment towards this.

Since then I have learned that it recurs in a milder form in every group, and that it can be resolved by analysis. As a result of these experiences in purely therapeutic groups I was also enabled to find an answer to the corresponding conflict in teaching groups, to which I will now return in connection with the supervisory group where this problem arises constantly. I may mention here that I once had occasion to talk to some of the G.P.s who were members of one of Dr M. Balint's seminars at the Tavistock Clinic. They reflected exactly the same split, wanting to enlist my support for their idea that Dr Balint did not give them enough 'analysis'.

The Supervisory Seminar

This supervisory group seminar was conceived and conducted on the basis of the type of experience just outlined. It can be considered by its very nature to be a model for the particular problems of teaching psychotherapy. While it was devoted to supervision and to the teaching of group psychotherapy it was to some extent a therapeutic experience. That it was understood as such by the trainees is well illustrated by a paper by George Stroh which will be reviewed presently.

Here all therapeutic groups in progress were reported and discussed by therapists, observers and visitors. The advantage of learning from each other, under the consultant's guidance was generally recognized—especially as on this occasion every participant experienced himself and others in a variety of roles such as that of conductor, observer, and third person. The keynote of this conference was that the desired change of attitude in both therapist and patient was seen as interdependent. It was indeed very impressive to see how great and deep-going was the influence of the doctor's personality and approach on their group of patients. Change in him in relation to his group, particularly change on unconscious levels, would alter the course of events in the group (see Chapters 12 and 13).

Such problems of countertransference played a considerable part in our supervisory conference and were the more impressive as they in turn were brought to light and analysed by all those present.

Psychotherapy is part of a 'personal psychiatry': it cannot be learned or practised without involvement in a mutual process, comprising doctor and patient. Progress in skill and therapeutic change in the trainee go hand in hand. This supervisory seminar was not a therapeutic group; it could not be under the circumstances. We deliberately confined our discussion to the interaction between the doctor and his group of patients, including possibly the observer. On occasion we also took into account reaction within the seminar itself. This, however, is the important point: personal involvement of the registrars was brought into the open in so far—and only in so far—as it encroached upon their function in either of the two group situation in which they were currently concerned: the one in the role of therapist, with his patients, and the other as a participating member on the supervisory seminar or staff group. Problems concerning their private persons or lives were not taken up nor were they encouraged to voice them. This example may illustrate the principle: that in such a situation the boundaries regarding personal and impersonal aspects are carefully chosen and respected. The function of the group and the task of its members thus defines the field of operation and its frontiers.

In conclusion, we think that we may say that our results were satisfactory, but those with our trainees even more so.

George Stroh[1] reported on his own reactions in the role of a therapist in relation to his patients' group as they reflected in his own reports to the supervisory seminar. He noted the changes which he had undergone in his double role as a group leader and a group member. Stroh was in the habit of writing notes on his group and he showed how these reports were influenced by his own unconscious motivations and how this reflected amongst other ways in the manner in which he referred to himself. Up to the twentieth session he had referred to himself by his initials, which, at the twenty-first changed to 'therapist'. This coincided with the fact that at the twentieth session B revealed her incestuous desires for her adolescent son. There was no indication that the group was particularly anxious about this revelation. The author continues, 'the therapist however seems to have been, for he asked for an immediate discussion of the situation at the next seminar. In this his concern over his patient's incestuous thoughts became increasingly obvious. He demanded detailed instruction on how to handle the problem, and when the seminar had ended he pressed for further discussion with the supervising consultant. The consultant wondered why the therapist found it such an anxiety-producing topic. "It is strange," was the spontaneous reply, puzzling in its *naïveté*, "I haven't seen my mother for many years".' The writer himself connects this countertransference reaction with the fact that he had begun his personal analysis with a woman analyst only a few weeks earlier, and also with the changed style of self-reference mentioned above. Stroh gives further illustrations of a similar kind. He makes interesting observations on the significant manner in which these reports were written, and on his identification with the patients which, as one would expect, partly reflected his transference situation in his own individual analysis, and partly that in the supervisory group. It may be worth mentioning that taking notes for reporting is not encouraged, but nevertheless most doctors do so as a reflection of their own lack of security. I do, however, definitely advise against taking notes during the group session itself though some beginners find it difficult to abstain from doing this.

R. C. A. Hunter of McGill University, Montreal, writes under the title 'Teach or Treat' on the 'Natural History of a

[1] 'A Therapist's Reactions as Reflected in his Reporting on a Psychotherapeutic Group'. *Int. Journal of Group Psychotherapy*, Vol. 8, No. 4, 1958.

supervisory group',[1] which was conducted on the lines of the Maudsley supervisory group of which Hunter had been a member. It was based on three years' experience with supervisory groups, each limited to one year, three with first-year residents and one with psychiatric nurses. Active participation by all members was encouraged and an authoritarian atmosphere avoided. Individual transferences to the supervisor were not directly interpreted unless they impeded the progress of the group as a whole. In spite of total change in composition as to the individuals Hunter could observe definite phases which recurred regularly in each of these groups. First there was an initial period of resistance, reluctance to come forth, which was rationalized in a variety of ways, tentative questioning and altogether evidence of considerable caution. 'This period lasted from six weeks to two months and was apt to be followed by a lull. Initial orientation had taken place.'

This period was followed by a new wave of resistance with pointed criticism and fault-finding with regulations, personnel, types of patient, techniques of treatment, the programme, the rooms and so forth. 'The emphasis remained primarily on the trappings of the work rather than the work itself. The group leaders fought shy of engaging themselves in their work. Direct assurance or intervention did very little to stem the tide of these criticisms and they persisted in spite of it. If the supervisory group leader tried to deal with them on the reality level, then he soon found that new ones took their place, while he became the object of the group's hostility, if he was mild, or dependency if he was stern.'

The leader then made an interpretation pointing out persistent complaining and that this was perhaps concealing other problems. This interpretation brought out that this grumbling had indeed been a defence against uncomfortable subjective attitudes to their work, mostly an expression of a feeling of inadequacy. It further turned out that these trainees had readily accepted blame from their patient groups, and passed it on by discharging it in the supervisory groups. Hunter observes, too, that these events appear to be much more marked in this group setting than in the tutoring of an individual doctor.

Somewhat later, usually some eight months after the beginning of the supervisory group, more sophisticated arguments concerning group therapy made their appearance. The members

[1] Unpublished communication.

Therapeutic Group Analysis

behaved now as though they had matured and were ready to form and voice their own opinions. Investigation, sometimes during several hours, revealed that the group was split into those who felt that group therapy was useless and should be discontinued and those who, by contrast, claimed magical powers for this form of treatment. Actual group problems, with which each of the participants was faced in his weekly work, were avoided and their own difficulties were altogether denied. Such difficulties were instead seen to belong to the domain of research and group dynamics.

In terms of our principle of an adequate definition of the boundaries of the group according to its particular purpose, this particular supervisory group may have been allowed to shift its emphasis too much towards the discussion of its own difficulties.

Now Dr Hunter most interestingly describes the same split which has been described above. During the last two or three months of this group's life, completing the training year, the trainees made various suggestions. These included abandoning the supervisory group, discontinuing the entire group programme for ever, *changing the supervisory group into a frankly therapeutic group* (my italics). The following is quoted more fully as it illustrates so well many characteristic problems.

Frank personal difficulties in group work now occurred individually, one doctor declaring group therapy to be useless, but eventually bursting out in the supervisory group: 'I can't stand the sight of all these open mouths. It riles me to be surrounded by them.' Another doctor sought a private interview with the instructor and asked to be excused group work because of his exceedingly painful shyness. It appeared that oral-sadistic greed was projected on to the group and the group's oral dependency needs were felt to be intolerable. Special liking of the group was equally conditioned by personal unconscious motives. 'In one case the group leader approached the situation with a feeling that she would be able to obtain proof of her wisdom, kindness and generosity from the patients. She worked hard to meet the group's demands for information, guidance, favours, etc., as long as the group showed that they appreciated her. Any sign of rebellion or ingratitude was ruthlessly dealt with, however, and the group was forced to lead a compliant existence, the patients expressing their

hostility by dropping out after a month or two. It was retrospec-
tively recognized that the large turn-over of patient members
which had characterized her group was related to the leader's
basic attitude.'

In another example doctors took refuge in the group situation
from the closeness and contact in psychotherapy with individual
patients.

Dr M. L. J. Abercrombie (M. L. Johnson) has done pioneering work of the first order in the field of selection of medical
students and in teaching by free group discussions and has
examined factors which prejudiced scientific judgment and
observation. She has used the group method as an instrument
of diagnosis and teaching in scientifically controlled experimental situations. An integrated representation of her work so
far will be found in her book *The Anatomy of Judgment: An
Investigation into the Processes of Perception and Reasoning*
(Hutchinson, 1960). Dr Abercrombie is deeply conscious of
the essential kinship between these teaching techniques and the
processes operating in therapeutic groups, and she has always
generously acknowledged her indebtedness to her experiences
with group-analytic psychotherapy. Her work is an important
contribution to the scientific application of group-analytic
principles. Her 'theory of free group discussion' very lucidly
analyses the selective character of the teaching-learning process
and points out the continual interaction between information
and attitudes. Illustrating her method, using as an example a
mothers' group, Dr Abercrombie states 'the aim of free group
discussion is to establish conditions in which she can become
consciously aware of her assumptions in a situation in which it
is possible to examine them and modify them.'[1]

When all is said we have taught an attitude by practising it.
It seems that the attitude which is best for the psychotherapist
is the same as the one best for the scientist—we might call it
the analytic attitude.

STUDY

The Unit at the Maudsley Hospital (see Chapter 19) was so
organized that teaching, learning, studying and research were
all taking place as part of the on-going clinical therapeutic
function of the unit. We had therefore occasion to study many

---

[1] 'Theory of Free Group Discussion'. *Health Education Journal*, No. 3, Vol. 11,
1953.

of the problems as they occurred. Occasionally, and when our material demanded it or allowed for it, we also selected groups more specifically from the point of view of certain problems and their study. I will pass review of some of the more important ones. Most of the work reviewed here took place as part of the unit's clinical function but some work done by members of the Group-Analytic Society elsewhere will be included.

Let us start with some of the work which has been more fully recorded and is either published or awaiting publication.

In the first place there was a marital group—a group of four married couples—which was started by Dr D. C. Maddison[1] and continued by Dr W. J. Stauble. In this particular group we had one partner of the married couple, either husband or wife, referred to us as the original patient. As in their neurosis marital problems figured large and seemed to hold the key to the position we invited the other half of the couple to participate in a group discussion. We thus had four couples of whom only one of each had been referred originally as a patient. The first observation of interest was that, as we all agreed, after a few sessions it was quite impossible for anybody to make any distinction between the one who was originally a patient and the partner who had only been invited for treatment. Dr Stauble has reported on this group.[2] From the point of view of therapeutic help the impression was clearly favourable. Stauble sums his own clinical impression up as follows: '. . . that the marriages were relatively harmonious about session thirty'. He then became impressed by the fact that a dilemma arose which impeded further developments by the 'danger of disrupting the marital bonds' and now the natural pairing in this group was used defensively. This result bears out what one would expect on theoretical grounds. The most striking feature of this particular group had always been that it was a kind of hybrid between a primary group, a natural one as represented by each couple, and on the other hand a group of strangers. It was so to speak a group of four units each one being a marital pair. The fact that we used the opportunity to put the partner of the marital conflict into the same therapeutic situation proved beyond doubt that the neurosis of the individual is impossible to understand or treat fully except in conjunction with at least

[1] Now Professor of Psychiatry at Sydney University.
[2] 'Treatment of Married Couples by Group Analysis'. *Proceedings of the Third World Congress of Psychiatry Montreal*, 1961.

one representative of what I refer to as the psychological network of the disturbance: of this more later. This group therefore has the characteristics partly of a primary network group as represented by the pair and the usual analytic group which is composed of strangers who are transference objects to each other. This means that each couple naturally talk to each other and act upon each other outside the therapeutic group. In a purely analytic group composed of four men and four women such a situation would only arise if they all paired off and became married couples! The limitations therefore arise from this circumstance as well as from the fact that a common problem, in our case the marital conflict, is put into the centre. As has been pointed out elsewhere and already in my introductory book such a proposition enhances the therapeutic process and makes relatively fewer hours (in this case as few as thirty) already very powerful therapeutically but at the same time it restricts the analytic penetration. This remark refers to the whole category of groups selected on the grounds of particular problems or situations. In the group under discussion this is an additional basic factor which worked out exactly as was anticipated. The common problem itself has this effect. If, for example, we construct a group of strangers who are not in a primary relationship round the common problem: 'mothers whose children are in treatment' in a child guidance clinic, this will have the same effect, namely that the group becomes more coherent, supportive, helpful, lively but more limited in analytic range. The common theme will to some extent eliminate the opening up of other themes and canalise interactions.

This group is useful for couples who are out to preserve their marriage if they possibly can. In this case it is extremely helpful. It is not the best arrangement when the way must be kept equally open for a breaking up of marital bonds and perhaps enabling each partner to find a new life under less neurotic conditions.

Two separate groups of sexual deviants were run by the late Dr M. Rosenthall and Dr J. Guild respectively. Some of Dr Rosenthall's experiences have been reported by me on another occasion to demonstrate interesting interactions between the therapist and the deviant group. These observations were based on private reports I had from him. I have no notes of Dr Guild's experience nor do I know whether he has. It may be worth mentioning that from my recollection of his group there were very strong reactions and interactions on the part of all these psychopathic individual members and as one would expect there was a good deal of acting out. All that remains from this group is the clinical impression that given sufficient experience of the conductor and sufficient time and the right circumstances the group-analytical approach would appear to be a powerful instrument for the study and treatment of this type of individual.

Fortunately we have a published account of work Miss Ethel Perry has done at the time at the Portman Clinic. Her paper has appeared in the International Journal of Group Psychotherapy.[1] It is concerned with the treatment of aggressive juvenile delinquents in family groups. The details of this highly interesting clinical report must be read in the original. Miss Perry makes her standpoint clear when she says 'my consideration is primarily orientated towards the individual in the group even when members act in concert. I consider the psychodynamics motivating each individual contributing to the group behaviour. I look for the individual gains to be derived for participation in group activities, actions or attitudes. . . . I have kept notes of a group for only a few sessions. We keep regular individual case notes in which as well as any insight gained into the inner life, we record relationships or attitudes of individuals in the group setting whether that be of isolation or participation.' On the theoretical side Miss Perry comes to the following pertinent conclusions: Quoting the concept of the present writer of a 'social' or 'interpersonal unconscious' she states 'As I see it this social or interpersonal unconscious is the important dynamic factor determining both relationships within the group and the emergence of each individual from the common matrix of the group' and further '. . . the ontogenetic recapitulation of this process of emergence as an individual from the common matrix of the group is the story of each individual child's social development. The therapeutic family group highlights this process in a quite fascinating manner. One indeed becomes aware of a rhythm in growth whereby the individual who feels some sense of his entity merges himself with the group, the better to strengthen relationship with his peers, emerges again a more robust individual ready to experiment with new facets of himself, only again to merge his stronger ego in the group and to drive emotional roots further into it.

[1] *International Journal of Group Psychotherapy*, April 1955, Vol. V, No. 2

In such a group one sees regression such as David allowed himself in its rightful perspective as means whereby libido is freed for redistribution in progressive development. By the continual interplay of these forces of regression and progression in a world of fantasy and outer world of reality become discriminated and reconciled. Narcissism and object love balanced in the child whose potential is for healthy development.' While Miss Perry's work is a contribution to the group analysis of delinquents it is at the same time a children's group.

In this connection we must mention the work Dr Anthony did on children's and adolescent groups which he reported in our Pelican book. This work though entirely independent on Dr Anthony's part emerged from the group-analytic approach.

In this connection Dr Anthony's group on the so-called 'murderous mothers' comes to mind. This work was more directly connected with my own unit. I am not sure whether Dr Anthony moved in this work in the same direction as my original interest had been. I had been impressed by a number of mothers I had come across at that time who had *conscious* death wishes, manifest murderous impulses towards their children. These were not repressed or disguised, not expressed merely by way of obsessional impulses, but by a desire to get rid of their children, to have them out of the way, which was shared by their conscious manifest self. They admitted to have welcomed the death of their particular children. This syndrome struck me very much and I must confess that my thought was that the emergence of such an orientation into open consciousness, as an ego syntonic attitude so to speak, was an expression of the progressive demoralization of the whole of our culture since the advent of Hitler, Stalin and under the impact of two World Wars and the murder of literally millions of innocent people. We as psycho-analysts know that the relationship of a mother to her child contains a greater or lesser degree of hostility and destructiveness almost as a normal ingredient which is usually tending to be ignored. My hope was that a group of such mothers should show much of the psychopathology of this particular syndrome. I am not aware that Dr Anthony's work took quite this course. As far as I remember from hearing him report later on his group he arrived rather at a diagnostic differential classification of these types of mothers and he included in his group the better known obsessional and depressive type of disturbance. Later on Dr N.

Kreitman, under my supervision, undertook a group-analytic study of a similar group. I believe he has recently reported on this work but again from a different point of view. So far as I can recall from supervising his group the impression was of very disturbed mothers—very disturbed personality developments. The primitivity and regressive note which prevailed in Dr Kreitman's group was also expressed by the way in which the group not only represented the mother Image but seemed to represent the mother's inside, the mother's womb, the mother containing the unborn children as it were. I was struck by this through the depth and level of reaction of this group to the idea of a member intending to leave, to drop out, which seemed to be felt by these mothers as the equivalent of a traumatic act of separation in the sense of giving birth. These mothers reversed unconsciously the position: in their attitude to their own children they were exposed to the hatred and envy they had felt in the very early months of life against their own mothers. It is still to be hoped that we will hear from either Dr Anthony or Dr Kreitman a more dynamic account of their observations than they appear so far to have been able to give.

Dr J. Guild whom I mentioned above very courageously undertook the treatment of another experimental group, namely of paranoid patients. They were six in number and some of them were pronounced and active paranoid schizophrenics, others had at any rate very manifest paranoid syndromes. This goes back to my own lifelong interest in the paranoid mechanism. It is particularly striking to my mind that this is a mechanism which we understand so well and against which at the same time we are so powerless. My hope is that perhaps more light can be thrown on this configuration and constellation in a study allowing interaction with others than in purely individual observation, particularly perhaps as to the possibility of therapy. My own experiences speak in this direction from treating occasionally such patients within my ordinary group analytic groups. Here the idea was to let the fully grown paranoid syndrome interact, as it was represented by a number of individuals. The material was fascinating and the impact strong. The result was striking so far as one can tell from clinical impression derived from supervision without any direct contact with any of the patients. Whereas this group helped three out of six considerably it did not most definitely help the other three, and indeed seemed to aggravate in at least two of them their mental state. The duration was approximately two years in weekly sessions and treatment should have been allowed if circumstances had permitted to carry on for a much longer period.

For my last example of such a problem group I must again draw upon my memory as supervisor. This group was conducted by Dr R. B. Sloane, now Professor at Kingston (Ontario). I encouraged him to study the kind of veteran patients which had been hanging about in the hospital for many years and had been with many doctors in turn for shorter and longer periods of treatment including psychotherapy of one kind or another. He found a number of these on the present active list, they turned out to be predominantly women. Again I can only hope that Dr Sloane will yet find time on the basis of his notes and his own recollections to report on this group. So far he has not done so. I will describe some of the significant features. The group consisted of nine women and they were told that this was their last treatment of this sort at least in this hospital. They were informed that Dr Sloane was able to carry on for nine months with them in weekly interviews. They were then analysed with a view to ascertaining what made them persist in wanting treatment, though obviously it did not seem to help them or cure them. These women were very much of a type, had many psychopathological features in common. The basic proposition was this: they were women who throve on the frustrated love situation which they could re-establish in treatment with their doctors. Oedipal and pre-oedipal fantasy found rich reward in the therapeutic situation in which it over and over again established itself. In this respect they resembled other patients in a transference situation. They were women one might say who had been fixated in this hopeless and forlorn attachment to the unobtainable incestuous object. They re-established this blindly and compulsively. One of the most astonishing features was the countertransference situation they had been able to provoke again and again with each of their doctors in spite of their different personalities. They provided a lively illustration of the degree in which the patient's neurosis interacts with the therapist. The patient is, so to speak, a specialist in his own particular psychoneurotic way of handling the therapeutic situation. In this he is far more skilful than the doctor, especially having in mind that these doctors had been not very experienced or trained in the handling of such situations.

Dr Sloane succeeded in breaking this vicious circle once and for all and at the end of his group recommended only one patient for further treatment. This patient received further treatment with a very good result, bearing out Dr Sloane's prognostication. The particular feature in which these patients differed from the ordinary run, from the patient who can be more successfully weaned from a therapeutic relationship, was that the tabooed situation suited their neurosis too well so that in a sense their deepest longing and disappointments were masochistically fulfilled. One suspects that they have many sisters in the patients who go from one analyst or psychotherapist to the other or stick with any particular one for half a lifetime and more if allowed to do so. It is almost needless to say how important more systematic studies might prove to be ranging from psycho-analytic treatment to that of the enormous number of chronic patients in out-patient departments and in supportive clinics. These latter represent another way of trying to solve this problem, by giving in to this type of patient's need for permanent contact. It would be interesting to know whether this experimental attempt which Dr Sloane made, encouraged by myself and helped perhaps by my experience in the background, whether this really solved the problem of some of his patients so that they are now not in need of further support. Unfortunately I have not been able to follow these patients up. Another interesting aspect which this group raises is the technical and psychological one on the doctors' part which we were also not in a position to follow up and examine. This might well be done in some other place.

Network Studies

In the course of this volume I have at various points put forward the concept of a network—a multipersonal network of interaction and intercommunication—as the real locus for any neurotic disturbance. This view is a central one for my own group-analytic approach and orientation. We had occasion at various times to put such network approaches into operation though on a modest scale, that is to say we could only take into active treatment a very limited number of such a network of interaction and for a limited time. Nevertheless the various examples we were able to study showed conclusively the practical significance apart from the theoretical interest which such an approach potentially has and will, I am sure, increasingly have. It is not possible at this point to recall these observations; some of this material has been published by George Hogle and V. Cohen and in a paper by David C. Maddison (*International Journal of Group Psychotherapy*): 'The integrated therapy of family members, a case report.' This must be read in the original: it refers to the combined treatment of a mother and her daughter with the husband being observed only in the background. The results were interesting and good and illustrate well the type of this approach in its simplest form—a close family unit—which approximates this work to the sort of systematic family therapy which Ackerman and others have more recently advocated. The paper and Maddison's comments speak for themselves. I myself have more recently drawn on some experiences which shed light on the acute importance of these influences of the network—not merely the family—on the ongoing psychopathology and psychotherapy. The network influence could be demonstrated by its indirect effects, by its interference with ongoing work. These experiences can be made by everybody who treats patients, especially psychotherapeutically, without being manifestly engaged in group psychotherapy of a primary or secondary kind. The change in orientation does allow one to see these apparently external, accidental and incidental interferences and reactions in a different light and to comprehend them much more clearly as an inevitable and important part of the dynamics of any treatment situation. The systematic study of such networks, whether confined to families or in their wider aspects should teach us a good deal more about the genesis, prognosis and treatment of all conditions with which we have to deal, whether in medicine or psychiatry or the law, or education and so forth.

RESEARCH

Regarding scientific contributions we must confine ourselves to members of the Group-Analytic Society (London) or to work which is explicitly bound up with the group-analytic approach. We will however include some work which still awaits publication. Group-analytic concepts are used by many workers in this field although they appear sometimes to be unaware of this fact.

Mrs M. L. J. Abercrombie's work deserves pride of place not only because she is one of the founder-members of the Group-

Analytic Society but because of the intrinsic merits of her work which was at the time connected with teaching and selecting medical students. Mrs Abercrombie belongs to those who recognized early the importance of therapeutic group experiences for her own field of interest. Unlike many others she acknowledged this and what is more she acted upon her insight. The insight is of the interdependence of scientific with therapeutic work and of both with personal problems. This made Mrs Abercrombie realize that in order to learn more about groups as well as about herself the best plan was to join a therapeutic analytic group in her own person and she had the courage to follow this conviction.

Now after ten years or more of research Mrs Abercrombie has integrated her findings in her book *The Anatomy of Judgment: an investigation into the processes of perception and reasoning*, published by Hutchinson of London in 1960. This book must be studied in the original. We can only review it here in some of its main features in particular as they concern group experiences. The mass of information which reaches us through our sense organs is subject to a selective process. It is interpreted on the basis of past experience and used for prediction of the immediate or more distant future. This is what is meant by 'judgment'. Science is an organized body of such experience: 'It seemed that scientific ways of thinking did not automatically result from learning the facts of science and that a more radical approach to training was necessary' (page 15). Confirming the well-known findings of Gestalt psychology that our information depends on the context (total situation), Mrs Abercrombie notes that our experience is conditioned by so-called schemata which are organized according to our past experience. Such schemata which roughly one might compare to a 'complex' are built up very early in contact with the mother. Culture is thus transferred mostly non-verbally and anonymously. In this way the basic assumptions which are all-pervasive operate almost imperceptively. Mrs Abercrombie was led quite naturally to teaching through discussion in small groups. She realized that by studying the different interpretations in groups these all important schemata could be modified. This, however, would not happen without a struggle. Mrs Abercrombie formulates one of the basic truths of all group psychotherapy in stating: 'only by seeing how we resemble and differ from other people do we understand ourselves' (page 58). In such groups schemata are compared by verbal communications. The students were not aware of the older schemata they used. 'Learning in free group discussion is a process of identifying through verbalization the associations between schemata so that the new information can be dissociated from those schemata with which it is automatically associated and can be seen to be potentially relevant to many schemata instead of to a few only' (pages 79–80), and again: 'the aim was to provide in the group a medium in which the individual learned ways of behaving which would be useful to him when the group has dissolved' (page 81). While thus formulating some of the essential features of a free discussion group Mrs Abercrombie at the same time makes clear some of the fundamental dynamics of the therapeutic process as it goes on in an analytic type of group, in particular the group–analytic group. In such a free group discussion the students talk to each other facing each other, whereas the teacher is very reluctant to correct or teach didactically or interfere in any other way. Under such condi-tions the group itself forms the background upon which selection of meaning is made according to the situation and the group can therefore act as a testing ground to help to find more useful ways of behaving. The group of students functioned like a microcosm reflecting the current attitude not only of the students concerned but of the contemporary biologists who shared the same scientific culture. The students, shocked by experiencing how erroneous their judgments could be, were somewhat consoled to find that the same errors were made and for the same reasons by the experts who had written their text books. The course consisted of groups of twelve students who met for eight discussion sessions of one and a half hours each; these were recorded. Scientifically controlled comparison be-tween these students and others who had not participated in the course proved that the former did significantly better. (The same result was found in a study made at the University of Chile which will presently be reported when students who had been taught by the group–analytic method were compared to those who had not.) The tests in observation and reasoning showed a significant difference in favour of those who had taken the course as against controls. The former made fewer inferen-tial statements. Those they made were based on better evidence. They also considered alternate inferences. They were less 'set'. As to the students' behaviour it can be compared to that described above by Hunter in Canada. Mrs Abercrombie noted the fear of change, the resistance to change, which we know so well from psychotherapy and asks the pertinent question 'can behaviour be changed?' She sees a need for continual change and thinks that one of the main problems is that of belief in authority versus self-reliant responsibility. It is altogether a question of prejudices versus scientific judgment and some of the factors affecting judgment only came to light after prolonged discussion. Mrs Abercrombie is led to the following conclusion: '. . . if one is to improve one's judgment in scientific matters, habits of thought which had seemed to belong to a quite separate field of behaviour must also be changed' (e.g. whether an observer trusts people in general or not). Mrs Abercrombie in her work thus demonstrates clearly the close affinity of the teaching-learning situation with that of scientifically oriented, analytic type of psychotherapy or in particular group psychotherapy. In fact these activities seem to move on a sliding scale as pointed out in a study presently reviewed on 'Communication'. This essential identity is brought out particularly well in Mrs Abercrombie's work through her profound insight into therapeutic processes due to the fact that she set out to study the mental processes favourable for acquiring new information or resisting such acquisition and to make them conscious. In fact her technique of free group discussion approximates the analytic group characterized by free floating discussion or free association.

The difference is significant for us here to show once again how the basic condition under which a group meets determines the range of processes and depth of change which can and will take place in the group in operation. It may therefore be illuminating to look at the further steps necessary to transform this free group discussion into a fully fledged group-analytic group. In the latter no subject is given. The group itself by its own spontaneous material furnishes the stimulus for each discussion. Its freedom is furthermore enhanced by the fact that it is encouraged to bring forth anything at all which occurs with disregard to any particular context. This makes it possible to discover behind the group's productions a context which is both unconscious and concerns the members of the group as a whole. Thus interpretations are based on this continuously shifting, self-propelling and self-defining matrix. The aim in the group-analytic group is frankly personal and there is an agreement to permit unreserved interpretation and analysis of the material, as well as of interpersonal transference reactions.

A comparable report from a different field comes from the Psychiatric Clinic of the University of Chile by R. Ganzarin *et al.*[1] They found group psychotherapy to be of great value in teaching dynamic psychiatry and demonstrate this in a controlled study.

* * *

Two studies by Professor E. J. Anthony, summaries of a workshop entitled 'Age and Syndrome in Group Psychotherapy', held in New York City in 1960, are published in the Journal of the *Long Island Consultation Center*, Vol. 1, No. 2 (May 1960). The first concerns group psychotherapy with children and adolescents, entitled 'Technical Variations with Age in Group Psychotherapy'. Dr Anthony describes three separate techniques according to the age group. (1) The kindergarten child, 4–6 years: method 'small table', that is a small round play table, divided into 'territories' for each child by removable walls, and with a water trough in the centre shared by all. Each territory has playthings in a different colour. (2) The latency child method called 'small room'. (3) The adolescent which he separates into early and late. Method: 'small circle'.

In the other contribution Dr Anthony talks of psychopathological cleavages and illustrates well the concept of 'resonance' on the basis of different instinctual and defensive responses. Under the terms of 'symptom' and 'counter-symptom' he illustrates such syndromal transactions of a complementary nature. The examples illustrated concern exhibitionistic—voyeuristic complementary transactions; heterosexual—homosexual and sadistic—masochistic ones; penis pride and penis envy; manic—depressive and finally regressive and progressive types of complementary behaviour. These processes are illustrated by clinical examples. They show not only the well-known processes of opposite or complementary pairs of instinctual reactions in psychoanalysis but also how these can lend themselves to the process called by the present author *resonance* and, moreover, how this can be shown in a group-setting by the interplay of two or more participants, invoking also the process of polarization, and, in the case of the two 'alternatively

---

[1] R. Ganzarin, H. Davanzo and J. Cizaletti with the collaboration of I. Matte-Blanco and others. 'Group Psychotherapy in the Psychiatric Training of Medical Students'. *Int. Journal of Group Psychotherapy*, Vol. 7, pp. 137–53, 1958.

regressive and progressive twins' that of alternation of behaviour.

*   *   *

Mrs I. Jacobs has made studies on the change of position of members in a group-analytic group, but has not yet systematically worked them out or published them. By 'position' is meant the seats members occupy in the group session and behaviour related to this.

I should like to mention here my own observations to the effect that such a position is meaningful. It is a complex phenomenon to study. Much depends also on the different time of arrival of the different members. Those who come first determine to some extent the position of other members. A significant factor results from whether or not the conductor sticks to a fixed position. It is certainly significant that the seat next to the conductor expresses one of particular dependence or of particular protection from observation by him. I have often observed that dependent members, or those who have recently joined a group as newcomers tend to choose this position next to me, and with increasing independence in the group they become freer to move. Sometimes the seat on the conductor's left side signifies opposition, 'the wrong side'.

Another interesting observation is that of the patient who habitually sits opposite the conductor, which literally expresses *opposition* and ambivalence. There are also those who avoid by all means sitting next to the conductor. Sometimes, when late-comers leave gaps, the assembling group huddle themselves together opposite the conductor putting him into the role of a schoolmaster. This in my observation is a highly significant behaviour for deeper currents in the group.

This whole matter should be studied not only in relation to the conductor but also in relation to other members, which is more difficult. An important field to investigate is that of the general degree of change, namely whether the group strictly adheres to the same positions, and at what times changes occur more frequently and so forth.

STUDY OF COMMUNICATION IN A GROUP BY A GROUP[1]

The following study is of particular interest as a real group study. As the reader will see, it is a study of a group, by the group; though the formulation was in the end made by three or four of the members in co-operation. (As far as I can remember those mainly concerned were Dr Norbert Elias, Dr P. B. de Maré, Dr Martin James and myself.)

Members of the Commission:
            Convener: Dr S. H. Foulkes
Dr James Anthony   Dr Norbert Elias
Dr Eva Ruth Balken   Dr Ernest Hutten
Miss Margaret Bavin   Dr Martin James
Dr Erna Dalberg   Mr I. Ramzy
Dr P. B. de Maré

This preparatory Commission was made up of members who are either psycho-analytically trained or at least at home with psycho-analytic concepts. When they came together they decided to consider the problem of communication as they have found it in their various professional ways of life, which are very diverse.

At the one extreme, members are dealing with highly organized groups such as teaching classes, in which there is a definite agenda and way of proceeding, a tangible structure on which the procedure hangs. At the other extreme is Group Analysis, in which apart from a regular time and place of meeting there is a minimum of regularized procedure and no set topic or programme, an arrangement which tends to bring the personal aspects into the open.

Owing to the mixed composition of the preparatory Commission it soon became apparent that while it was possible to emphasize the differences between discipline in the organized (e.g. teaching) group (A) and the spontaneous group-analytic group (B) there was also something in common—a sense in

---

[1] Report of the Preparatory Commssion dealing with communication, particularly verbal communication, with reference to group analysis. (Prepared for the International Congress on Mental Health, London, 1948.)

which the less prominent quality from the one style of group was still present, although largely latent in the other (A^1–B^1). This recognized relationship is expressed in the following diagram:

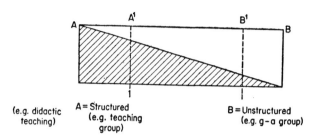

(e.g. didactic teaching)   A = Structured (e.g. teaching group)   B = Unstructured (e.g. g-a group)

It would be an interesting problem whether it is valid to think of groups generally as situated on a scale of the sort suggested by the diagram ranging from the most institution-alized to the most spontaneous—the presence of organization and framework inhibiting the spontaneity and vice versa.

The way in which this problem presents itself to us is shown by the following example. A member of this preparatory Commission, a teacher of Social Psychology, who finds these experiences of group analysis very valuable, reported that at a lecture he read out to his class an essay by one of the pupils. In this she said that with her upper middle class background, when she encountered a lower class accent, she saw the warning 'social red light'. In the discussion the student with the worst accent in the class insisted that the essayist was perfectly right because people should speak clearly. The teacher brought this example to the preparatory Commission to illustrate how his role as a 'teacher' and the role of a therapist could be called for by the same situation but would require different handling. In this case the teacher, keeping to his agenda, handled the problem differently from the therapist, who might have empha-sized the personal element in the student's contribution to the discussion.

In the group-analytic situation the personal problem is in the foreground, the institutional aspect in the background, discus-sion is free-floating. By this means group-analytic groups uncover or 'take the lid off' processes which may remain hidden in less spontaneous groups. It is a prerequisite of group analysis that the participants are agreed in bringing personal problems from their several 'private worlds', and are prepared to admit to possessing thoughts and ideas outside the range of polite conversation. The degree of candour shown varies according to the therapist and the social code prevailing in the group members, but many unexpected facets of the process of communication are seen, because of the limitation of artificial interference and the comparative exclusion of social reality considerations.

Over the whole scale of these groups, from the highly institutionalized to the largely spontaneous, communication in the group takes place predominantly at a verbal level. In choosing our topic, however, we have not overlooked the fact that in limiting ourselves to verbal communication we are making a comparatively artificial abstraction and that the language of gestures, emotional appearances, vocal tones, etc., have their own important place in the process of communication. There are, however, positive reasons that governed this choice. It is not accidental that in group analysis words are the main means of communication. Verbal communication is of a very specialized kind, not comparable to any other form of communication, and confined to the human species where it forms the basis of civilized living and scientific thinking. But words are flexible symbols, although they can conceal as much as they communicate, they are nevertheless well ordained for use in a complex milieu, such as human society, capable of strong emotional colouring. An example from group analysis will illustrate a type of communication which takes place in free-floating discussion:

A girl described her washing compulsion and incidentally mentioned that it became worse if she feels hostile towards her family. After an interval, a second member recalled (as though it bore no relation to the earlier communication) two incidents. She dreamt that she had received a telegram announcing her mother's death, and on the same day her nephew had been subject to an electric shock while in the bath. A third member recalled, after an interval in exactly the same way, that her mother, because of some nervous difficulty, could never show any affection to her children and would never allow them to make affectionate approaches to her. In this case the literal meaning of the original communication was ignored, and the theme of family hostility—an incidental part of the communication—made an impact leading to a chain of associations which are personal, intimate and normally belong to the patient's private world.

From our psycho-analytic orientation we are particularly concerned with the verbal level of communication, although we are not unaware of other levels of communication. We are aware that the problems of therapy and neurosis presuppose the need for words as symbols. In group analysis, the total situation, including the observer, is implied. The question arises whether the polar extremities of group organization, on one extreme the structured group, and at the other the unstructured group, are qualitatively different or are only differing in degree. Should we stress the differences or the similarities between the two extremes?

In writing this report, we can alternatively emphasize:

1. The history of our group and the changes which have taken place in it.
2. The conclusions we have arrived at, or
3. The material we have dealt with.

We have had to choose where, on the scale of group organization, we wished this preparatory Commission to stand. At the one extreme there was the definite feeling that personalities should not obtrude, so that we might avoid the therapeutic pole. On the other hand, in order to accumulate material we could not afford to organize an agenda. After five months we are just beginning to understand each other enough to attempt formulations, although these must be concerned less with what we have done than with what we have to do. A problem for discussion is: How far is it true that groups meeting for other purposes, for example Trade Union or religious meetings, have a similar choice to make? Another question would be: is the type of problem revealed in group analysis also present in the more structured group, but prevented by procedure from being seen? Certainly, as seen in the example quoted from the Social Psychology class, both types of situation, even at their extremes, seem to have relevance for each other.

In attempting to communicate, we take it that the communication should help to bring about a change, to exert influence, and in this sense the effect on the hearers of what is said must be considered apart from what was literally intended by the speaker. The value of the group for the elucidation of the problem of communication can be particularly seen here, for whatever the literal intention on the speaker's part, it must be accepted that what one's hearers understand one to have said, that is to say, the effect of a communication, is equally valid. A message may be understood in as many different senses as there are different members in the group. (Here naturally we include a case where the speaker's affect is at variance with the content of what he says, and the mood is communicated rather than the words.) An example of this sort of experience can be given:

Three of our preparatory Commission are members of a therapeutic group, two as therapists alternately in charge (Drs F. and M.) and the third taking part as a patient (Dr H.). Dr M. regularly makes a written report of the proceedings. In one of the reports the following appeared:

'Mrs N enlarged on an incident which had happened at 16 years of age (or 18?) when she was knocked down by a car. Immediately she had told the policeman that it was her own fault and not the driver's. She had repeated this several times, and next day the papers had headlines of her attempted suicide, when in fact there was no question of suicide. . . .

Dr F. pointed out that her insistence that it was her own fault was an attempt to retain her sense of being nevertheless in the right.'

Dr F. quoted this in the Commission's meeting as an example of misrepresentation, and stated that his recollection of what he had said was: '*Perhaps the newspaper reports were right after all*', or words to that effect. Dr H., the 'patient' and scientist, confirmed Dr F.'s version of what he had actually said. (Dr M. was not present at this meeting of the preparatory Commission.) Dr H. also mentioned, however, that Dr M.'s version reflected the *feeling of the group as regards Mrs N.*

Following this contribution the discussion at the preparatory Commission revolved round possible interpretations of the misunderstanding.

Dr F. said that, if analysing in the usual way, one could advance a number of explanations of this 'misunderstanding', as for instance the following:

1. Dr M. might be disturbed in his reception. But as he appears to report other remarks correctly, the disturbance could be localized between him and Dr F. More accurately, perhaps, it might reflect a disturbance confined solely to this particular group situation.

2. It might be a disturbance in Dr M. in relation to the *content* of the remark.

TMKF – R

3. It might be a disturbance in Dr F. in so far as he might be mistaken as to what he had actually said, and so on.

This type of analysis of a misunderstanding can of course be examined very well in group analysis, but equally well or even better in an individual situation. However, *Dr H.'s observation puts quite a different complexion on the nature of this 'misunderstanding'*. He states tnat although the report was totally wrong with reference to what Dr F. had said, it nevertheless rendered accurately the group's feeling in regard to Mrs N. It can be seen that for this fact to come to light at least a third person, in this case Dr H. is necessary. This is a good example for the new dimension which is added when at least three persons are participating in the same event ('Model of three'). In our example Dr H. voices the condensed feeling of the group, as it appears to him. The group need not necessarily agree with him, and each individual member would put his own particular complexion on to this issue. In this way the matter would appear to be far more complex, but also more rich. If the examination of such a communication between two people can be said to be two-dimensional, and that in between three people (as in the above example) to be three-dimensional, the analysis in a group situation would be multi-dimensional.

This is only one example, and a very simple one at that, to represent the type of thing we can study and follow up in the therapeutic groups which are, so to speak, our experimental situations. This example illustrates quite well two further points:

1. What aspects of communication can in our opinion best be observed and studied in a group situation, and perhaps only in a group situation.

2. How difficult it is to report this type of observation, in particular as most of the time we are confronted with far more complicated topics than the one here described.

COMMUNICATION WITHIN THE GROUP
(GENERAL CHARACTERISTICS)

1. The natural history of any group involves the development of group feeling which unites the individual members. This unity is made up in part of common experiences, a common language and an expressed common purpose. Trade, barter and sex have a similar effect but therapeutic groups have to

learn to do without these powerful aids. With the increased homogeneity of the group, communication is facilitated. By these means a common framework of reference is created and any communication within the group becomes group property. In a communication between two people, the communication has a private reference understood by the communicator and recognized by the person to whom it is communicated. Among the listeners there are varying degrees of distortion.

2. The composition of a group, however well selected or conducted, affects the rate and degree of integration. A group such as ours, drawn from so many professions, was much enriched by this very factor and curiously little disturbed, although there were some superficial preliminary difficulties experienced by members without previous contact with other disciplines.

3. It was generally recognized that examples from group-analytic experience were valuable means of communication, that communicating from experience was as effective as learning from experience. Examples are concrete, living samples of what is actually to be communicated and less prone to distortion than abstract or general arguments.

4. Disciplined or *formal group* discussion we feel is less productive or stimulating than free, shifting undirected talking. It creates an atmosphere in which problems obtain freer expression and ventilation. Individual contributions are more than interrupted monologues. Marked modifications of opinion are often observed in the course of an evening, but as would be expected, members vary greatly in their degree of intellectual plasticity. On the negative side the method allows a good many intriguing problematical fish to slip through the nets of formulation. For those concerned with exact formulation the less disciplined form of discussion was at first irksome, but even they were prepared to admit that the 'character' of a group is best liberated by this procedure. We have now decided to meet the demand for formulation by a compromise in method, the group devoting the last half-hour of the evening to summarizing what it has discussed; with these data in hand two members would then undertake the formulation submitting it to the group at the commencement of the next session. (Formulation with freedom).

5. The intended effect of a communication influences its very form.

6. The 'value' of a communication bears a direct relation to the 'standing' of the member within the group.

THE PROBLEM OF UNDERSTANDING
AND MISUNDERSTANDING

1. The problem of mutual understanding arises in every group and our own special group is no exception to this. We are thus able to observe, analyse and record our own experiences in this direction.

2. It was early realized that many misunderstandings were ultimately problems of semantics, that is, examples of verbal and grammatical misuse. It was, however, decided to accept the deficiencies latent in the actual or literal sense of a statement and to concentrate on the opposite end of communication—the effect. It was agreed that the speaker was the best witness of what he intended to say, although he may not be the best person to *express* what he intended to say. It was important always to differentiate between the intention and effect of a communication.

3. It was agreed that cases of complete understanding do occur, but are rare, but that incomplete understanding (so-called distortions) had a positive value. We are altogether impressed by the fact that both aspects of communication are equally of importance for study, that is to say how communication is disturbed as well as how it actually comes about. While it is difficult to over-estimate the degree of distortion or the great variety of meanings which may be read into even the simplest utterance, one is equally impressed by the intensity and accuracy of what is successfully conveyed and mutually understood.

4. Other distortions were called into being as communication raised simultaneous counter-communications which blocked the free reception and consideration of a communication. It was observed that the recipient of a communication while listening may already in his own mind be preparing his reply and in this way blunt or distort his ability to receive. For instance, a member mentioned that while he is listening to somebody else he has to re-translate automatically into his own terms for it to make sense. This type of observation makes us believe that the process of communication is not best described in terms of a transmitter and receiver as is usually done.

First of all we are aware that the transmitter takes into

account the receiver in preparing his remarks, and *per contra* that receiving is by no means only a passive function. This means that both people take an active part in the process. We can compare this process with the analogy of a mercury vapour lamp where there are two poles and an arc of light in between them. In this case the poles would represent the two people and the arc the communication. Whereas the two poles (the two people) are indispensable for the process to take place, the process itself is a totally different and independent phenomenon. We would go further than this formulation, which is still rather static, to say that in the case of a communication the process itself is already present in a germinal form in each of the participants.

5. Misunderstandings might arise through emotional disturbances in the recipient of the communication in relation to the speaker, the group, or the content of the remark.

6. The occurrence of misunderstanding was often a more accurate index of group experiences or trends than the literal understanding of a communication.

7. It would be more accurate to speak of *degrees of understanding* rather than 'misunderstanding'. There is always a link, however tenuous, between what is said and what is understood. 'Reaching an understanding' is an oscillatory process between the participants. Giving and taking and giving back again until a satisfactory (satisfying) degree of understanding has been reached.

THE INFLUENCE OF INTERPERSONAL RELATIONS
ON THE PROCESS OF COMMUNICATION

1. In every group we are beset all the time with the problem of considering the personalities and personal reactions of group members and the existence of interpersonal tensions. Even in purely scientific groups the swing between the therapeutic and the academic is apparent.

2. The personal factor is less to the fore where there is an immediate aim or purpose; but even in our group, well supplied with topics, the problem often arose.

3. We are particularly concerned to see if it is possible to integrate the group sufficiently to ensure co-operation in our common purpose without undue preoccupation with interpersonal and personal problems.

4. We could not help observing that basic differences of personality make-up reflect individual differences in the approach to problems with a consequent disturbance of smooth communication. It creates a further problem for every group as to whether sufficient common ground or language can be found to render full co-operation possible, while making allowances for the individual personalities involved. This is closely linked up with the problem of taking personal motives into account and bringing intimate aspects under discussion.

5. Intellectually all are agreed that in sociological studies the observer forms an integral part of the situation or field, but persons vary greatly in their sensitivity to the application of this principle in their own case. This factor in itself is a significant bar to good communication.

6. In general, the more impersonal a type of communication the more it is understood in its actual sense—the literal meaning. At the other end of the scale, where we are concerned with effect rather than sense, personalities become highly involved. This has a special bearing in relation to the communication of objective knowledge, as in teaching.

7. Complete understanding of a communication demands therefore a close appreciation of the nature of the situation leading to the communication, the personalities of the participants, the interpersonal relations and their standing within the group, together with the underlying motives, and finally the existing integration within the group. Communication is dependent upon so many variables that in trying to make an analysis one inevitably comes up against many pseudo-problems and pseudo-solutions.

Part V

A BRIEF GUIDE TO GROUP-ANALYTIC
THEORY AND PRACTICE

A BRIEF GUIDE TO GROUP-ANALYTIC
THEORY AND PRACTICE

This short outline is under the following headings: METHOD, CONDUCTOR, ORIENTATION AND PRINCIPLES, DYNAMICS, THEORY.

Numbers in brackets refer to particularly relevant chapters which should be consulted. A few concepts are explained in some more detail here, and in a few instances reference is also made to the *Introductory Book* (Heinemann, 1948): 'Intro', and to *Group Psychotherapy* (Penguin): '*GPS*'.

METHOD

This account confines itself to the standard 'group-analytic group' under the usual Out-patient conditions. The therapist and his function and technique as a conductor are treated separately.

Indication. An obvious asset of all group-psychotherapy is economy in time and expense. In the case of group-analytic psychotherapy this is combined with *greater intensity* than is that of individual methods and a closer correlation of any improvement within the treatment situation with a corresponding change in life. This is from the patient's point of view, leaving out of account the economy in doctors' time.

Group-analytic psychotherapy will rarely take less than a year, more likely two to three years of weekly sessions of an hour and a half. Sometimes more prolonged treatment is necessary, or can even be anticipated, but this should be exceptional. In these cases it is probably preferable to raise the number of sessions to two or three per week, rather than to extend the total time beyond three years. Group-analytic psychotherapy is indicated in all forms of psychoneuroses, especially in neurotic failure in success or competence, social and sexual inhibitions, anxiety states, phobias, character and personality disturbances, derealization and depersonalization syndromes. Schizophrenic conditions, when not too acute, lighter forms of depression and paranoid reactions and psycho-somatic diseases mix well with groups composed predominantly of neurotic patients, to mutual benefit. The same is true for some forms of perversions, e.g. homosexual, fetishists, trans-vestites, though on the whole these are better treated in 'special problem' groups of their own, as are delinquents, psychopaths, addicts and more acute psychotic conditions.

Generally favourable points are: good intelligence, good personality assets, motivation for a more radical approach rather than mere alleviation of symptoms, acceptance of longer duration of treatment and tolerance of temporary frustrations.

These indications are similar to those for 'psycho-analytically oriented psychotherapy', except that they are wider. Conditions treatable in 'special problem groups' are not usually suitable for individual psychotherapy. On the other hand individual treat-ment is preferable for some depressed states, severe obsessions and some forms of hysteria especially when conversion is predominant and defences strong.

On the whole it may be said that the classificatory label is less significant than the total psychodynamic profile of the patient—including the reaction of his 'network' (see *Theory*)—and that the group as a diagnostic agent (see Introductory group) is the best test situation.

The question arises of the particular selection for the *group*—rather than the individual—analytic form of treatment.

(Further, also re contra-indication and differential indication see 1, 2, 7, 8, 10.)

Selection (1, 2, 3, 8, 15)

Individual treatment need only be recommended when there are reasons precluding group treatment, when the patient is prejudiced against the group, or when psycho-analysis is indi-cated. The indications for psycho-analysis, which requires daily attendance for a number of years, are controversial (see Glover: *The Technique of Psycho-Analysis*). A patient who refuses group treatment in the absence of good reasons is usually a poor bet for psychotherapy altogether, especially of an analytic type.

Individual treatment can be combined with group psycho-therapy in various ways (1, 15). In group-analytic psycho-therapy this is usually unnecessary and it is preferred if individual treatment precedes or follows on the group (5). There are some positive indications for this. Much depends on the form and type of the group for which a selection is made (see below).

Composition

In general it is better to include patients with a variety of syndromes in the same group. The basic background should be reasonably compatible and nobody isolated in any significant respect, if this can be avoided. We prefer mixed groups as regards sex in equal numbers. Marital status: preferably either all single or all married. This seems more important in women than in men.

The 'selection' chart (Appendix) will give an idea of some of the items which need to be considered. It was found most useful.

From about twelve to fifteen candidates it is usually possible to find eight who can form a suitable group together. These are then invited and start together, having been interviewed probably once individually beforehand. If possible, it is preferable not to mix patients who had psychotherapy previously, especially if individually and of some intensity, with those who have not (1, 15).

Form of Groups

'*Open*' (for new members) useful as 'holding' groups ('living waiting list'), as long term supportive ('life line') following on short term more intensive treatment (1, 5, 15). Approach technically quite different from standard type. '*Closed*' not often realizable: starting and ending together. Most compatible with selection confined to particular problem, syndromes or situations and strictly limited duration (5, 15).

The type most commonly practicable is a group with unlimited lifetime, individual members joining and leaving on their merits ('*slow-open*'). Change in composition slow. Selection of new patients in view of existing groups. Many problems which need delicate handling arise, which can only be mentioned here, as follows. Preparing group for new members. Time factors and group reactions affecting introduction of new members. Similar considerations re members leaving. Termination of treatment. If patient wants to leave should give notice (2, 5). As to 'combined' treatment, group and individual

284 Therapeutic Group Analysis

interviews at the same period of time, this has been considered
in parts above. When practised it is important that conditions
should be alike for all. Special situations can be handled with
great flexibility, however (15). Main drawbacks: tendency to
competitive transference-situations, splitting, special relationship with conductor, tendency to diminish significance of group
situation. On the whole my experience has increasingly allowed
the group situation to be in the centre and eventually to treat
the patient fully in the group even where I thought originally
the individual situation should take over (8, 10). It is important
that the psychodynamic development should occur in one unified
therapeutic situation, wherever possible. Similar considerations
apply to 'alternate' sessions. I have had experience with these
during the war and on occasions since, but not practised them
systematically. I believe that disadvantages outweigh possible
advantages of this method and that its advocates have not the
same respect for transference phenomena and boundary incidents
(see *Theory*) as this writer.
(See also 'Intro'.)

Setting

Numbers up to eight, excluding conductor. Seven perhaps the
ideal number. Members are in no way related to each other
in their lives. No physical contact. No meeting outside the
sessions. Regular attendance required, usually for one and a half
hours, at least once weekly. Sitting in circle round small token
table on equal chairs with therapist. No eating, drinking,
smoking or other drugs, or activities. No programme or special
occupation, but uncensored, spontaneous verbal communications
encouraged (1, 2, 3, 5, 9, 15, 16, 18).
Attendance chart important (see Appendix).
Position chart for special studies (see Appendix).

Group-Analytic Situation

Given the above setting certain special features are necessary
to make the situation a therapeutic one (see 'T' situation under
Theory). These are introduced by the therapist, both explicitly
and implicitly by the way in which he handles
    (a) the patients' contributions,
    (b) their relationship to himself and towards each other.
Similar to the psycho-analyst the group analyst maintains an

'analytic attitude', but he takes the whole dynamic situation ('the group') as background for his interpretation.

Two salient features thus arise:

(*a*) patients' communications become the equivalent of 'free associations' in the group: 'free group association'.

(*b*) patients' relationships are treated as if they were transferences, i.e. accepted and subject to interpretation and analysis. The therapist himself takes these reactions up actively when they block progress. One must distinguish between true transference (repetition) 'TR', transferences in the broader sense 'tr' and reactions which are predominantly outside of these: responses to current impressions and experiences.

THERAPIST-CONDUCTOR

In group-analytic psychotherapy the therapist is called conductor preferably to leader, because he does not as a rule lead the group, but does so only in one of his multiple functions. There is also an undertone of reference to the conductor of an orchestra, as their roles can in many ways be compared, but this is of secondary importance and almost incidental.

The conductor should preferably be a trained and experienced psycho-analyst, but at any rate he must be experienced in the usual individual form of psychotherapy of an analytic type. He should if possible have undergone group-analytic experience in his own person, observed group-analysis (sitting in) and conducted two groups under supervision (1, 10, 16).

If the therapist is adequately trained as a group-analyst, it is, in our opinion, of secondary importance to what brand of individual analysis (Freudian, Neo-Freudian, Jungian or otherwise) he belongs. There are many schools, but psychotherapists vary on a scale which is independent of their theoretical or interpretative background. About the most important principles and orientation concerning him see: 1, 2, 3, 4, 6, 10, 12, 15, 16.

We shall consider the therapist-conductor under three headings: (1) What he *is*. (2) What *he represents*. (3) What he *does*.

(1) What he *is*.

The therapist's own personality is of fundamental importance. It must be in line with his position and attitude, so that he can be completely honest with the group and mutual trust can develop. He need not be perfect or in any way share the unconscious phantasy of the group of an omniscient leader or father image with magical powers. The beginner's apprehensions go often back to this. He need only be what he is, but naturally he should be adequate and competent (4, 15). As a (trainee-) patient put it to me: 'It is not what you do that is important, but what you *are.*' This being so, it is no use concealing it, but one should be conscious of one's personal equation. Quite different personalities can be equally suited to make a good group analyst. Nevertheless, this factor 'personality' should be so far as possible reduced in its importance and not magnified, and only reluctantly used and with discrimination.

(2) What he *represents.*

He is a Transference Figure, in the classical sense ('TR') mostly for individuals and in the wider sense ('tr'), mostly shared by the group. In this respect he reacts as the psychoanalyst. He represents often the 'superego' for the group, as well as an Ideal, especially as an ideal parental figure or a primordial leader image, in a sense the phallic executive of the 'mother'—group (1, 4). He personifies the group-analytic principle (13) and must altogether be aware of his own unconscious influence (in the sense of countertransferences) (12). Well known 'types' of patients often are creations of unconscious aspects of the conductor (10, 12).

(3) What he *does.*

This depends entirely on the presenting situation, and can certainly not be described in terms of 'activity' or 'passivity'. As an overall slogan one could describe it as 'discriminating activity' (5). He introduces and maintains an 'analytic attitude' (10, 12, 13, 15, 16). In the first place he must be able to listen, to receive (1) and to accept (4). The latter refers particularly to patients' transferences, aggressions, projections and so forth. With selective emphasis (5, 10) the conductor may at times actively lead the group (3, 4, 5), while he is directing it, though unobtrusively, all the time (4, 5). The better the group runs the more frequent and prolonged become the periods when no obvious directing is required. His functions include that of an analyst (1, 2, 6, 15), catalyst (merely by his presence but also when actively confronting members with material), and interpreter (4, 5, 6, 10, 12, 16). He should be aware of different levels in communication (9, GPS), never use pre-fabricated interpretations but be always concrete in actual situation and *start from the surface* (16) in interpreting. Every-thing, including the so-called depth, is always present if we have eyes to see it and know how to make it manifest and operative. There is no principal difference between 'group' and 'individual' interpretations: both are given in the group context. There is a difference in interpretations given consciously or unconsciously by members of the group or by the conductor. With all this, the good group analyst, like a good driver, will be discreet in intervention and always follow the group. Whereas he can follow the same method and principles every therapist may develop his own style, as it suits his personality and temperament. The mature analyst, knowing how important his own influence is bound to be, can permit himself to use himself consciously and creatively. Our work then becomes a creative activity, more artistic than that of a mere producer on the stage or film, or that of a sculptor or painter. Not so much, perhaps, as that of the playwright or composer, but life, as it displays itself and unfolds under our eyes is more dramatic and poetical than any play ever written. But the responsibility is great and a warning not out of place: no one should embark on this who has not the measure and control of his power firmly in his blood and system, lest he will suffer the fate of the sorcerer's apprentice.

A few personal remarks may be permitted at this point, partly looking back, partly forward awaiting future work and formulation. My own directing is unobtrusive, largely un-noticed. I am reminded of 'the indirect action' in Chekhov's plays according to Magarshack. The action is not on the stage but behind it. Similarly, I feel, is my direction behind the scene. I do not think we should always try to 'understand'. This implies to approve, forgive, sanction; it underlines inevitability. Remembering what Bertolt Brecht has taught us in connection with his 'alienation' effect, we can say that, on the contrary, *not* understanding implies: freedom of choice, the possibility to change and to act otherwise. It thus introduces the therapeutic element into the situation. In this connection I tend to leave things unresolved in mid-air, incomplete (no 'closure'). To bear this is important for the therapist of a higher order and by the same token for the scientist. It is also important in its effect upon the patient.

DYNAMICS

I. General

(*a*) In group of all sorts

Groups have their own dynamics, distinct from the sum of the individuals composing the group. This idea has been inherent in group analysis from the beginning with its emphasis on the 'group-as-a-whole'. These dynamics come into play and are relevant in the interaction of groups, or in the interaction between any group under observation and the community of which it forms a part. There is a reciprocal influence between what goes on in a group and its individual members. It is best to study this in action, and by comparative analysis of different groups. In our field work at Northfield, for instance, such observations have been made in relation to psychotherapy (hospital as a therapeutic community, etc.). Group analysis has contributed to the characterization and typification of some basic models of groups according to the most significant variables.

(*b*) In therapeutic groups (14)

Here we are concerned with psychodynamics in particular. The psychodynamics of groups in ordinary life in those arranged for therapeutic activity and in psychotherapeutic groups can be understood in terms of group-analytic concepts (3). Everything which happens is part of the psychodynamics of the therapeutic group under observation. Every event involves the total network of interrelations (5). Of particular importance in this respect are the concepts of figure/ground configurations in the group (7, 12), the dynamic location of events (3, 9) and the relationship between the individual and the group (6, 7, 9). This can be analysed in different group situations (5). There is no antagonism between individual and group psychodynamics.

II. In the Group-Analytic Group

The group-analytic situation: see Orientation & Principles.

(*a*) The group-analytic group as a structural model

All the mechanisms known from the psycho-analytic study of the dream, neurosis and defence mechanisms can be observed in the group situation. As has been pointed out in more detail in GPS and in Chapter 9 of this volume, it is essential to translate these processes on to the group as a whole as a model.

To mention relatively simple examples by way of illustration; 'splitting' operates by splits in the group, 'multiple representation' is literally manifested by different members or sub-groups, displacement can occur in that one member is attacked instead of another for quite a different reason, e.g. the scapegoat for the conductor (9). Ego, id and superego are dynamically represented in the group model, so are unconscious, preconscious and conscious processes (9).

(*b*) The group as a symbol

On different levels the group can symbolize a variety of objects or persons, e.g. the body (in a group of 'murderous mothers' under my observation it was representing the inside of the mother, the womb). It frequently, possibly universally, represents the Image of the 'Mother'—hence the term 'matrix'. On different levels: 'the others', public opinion, the world, the mind, also in structural and dynamic ways, e.g. the superego as in the chorus of the Greek drama.

(*c*) Specific processes in the group-analytic situation

Free associations of ideas in the group (1, 5, 9). This is a new principle of operation, the social equivalent of the psycho-analytic free association. The latter is originally a one-person concept, almost on a brain physiological level.

Related to this is the use of members' contributions as reactions, responses and unconscious interpretations. Inter-communication is thus seen as a group process, including unconscious communication. The multipersonal relationship replaces the two personal model of transference. Interactions in between two or more persons can be observed by others who enter only indirectly into the relationship. ('Model of Three', 'participant observer', 'transpersonal interacting processes'.)

Unconscious processes can be represented by persons (personification). Thus certain types of patients which have been described, e.g. conductor's assistant, shadow, favourite, scapegoat, etc., can be understood as behaviour which typically arises under prevailing dynamic configurations in the group and is delegated to certain members. The therapeutic process is related to the process of progressive communication (Intro, GPS) and to 'ego training in (intrapsychic) action'.

Other 'group specific factors' need only be mentioned here, such as 'mirror reaction' (1, 2, 5, 7, 9) condensor phenomena, personification (12), but something more will be said in the following about two of them: resonance and polarization.

Resonance

This term resonance is intended to denote the fact that not only is there an unconscious communication between individuals but that this unconscious communication is highly selective and specific. It is as if the individuals knew the whole of psycho-analytic psychopathology and reacted accordingly. In other words what psycho-analytic psychopathology has observed and made intelligible theoretically does hold good on an instinctive level. We all know of examples of people who unite, say in marriage or friendship or hostility, a relationship which turns out to be extraordinarily and intricately fitting, quite often in a negative sense—in the sense of clashing, on deep instinctive levels. The idea behind the concept of resonance is that an individual exposed to another individual and his communications in behaviour and words seems instinctively and unconsciously to respond to them in the same coin as it were. It may well be that the response is for instance in the nature of a reaction formation or a defence against the underlying instinctive impulse of the other person, though consciously this impulse has not been understood nor expressed manifestly. It is therefore as if a certain tone or chord struck a certain specific resonance in the other receptive individual, in the recipient.

Polarization

This is a process which can be particularly well observed in an analytic group. Essentially it consists in a splitting off of complex reactions to the same stimulus into their elements. These are then taken over and represented by different individuals, who so to speak specialize in one or other of the components and therefore assume sharply contradictory attitudes. In their concert, in their combined reaction they bring to light the total complexity of reactions to this particular stimulus. Frequently one individual is then charged with the instinctive impulsive side, say an aggressive anal-sadistic tendency, and all the impulsive reaction is delegated to this individual possibly himself identifying with this for the time being. This enables the other side, say the reaction formations and defences against this impulse, to be equally strongly expressed by others who in this way solve for the time being an ambivalence conflict. One might also put it, schematically, that one side will represent the id- and the other the ego- or superego-aspect of a certain reaction. The term polarization is intended to emphasize the fact that there is a tendency for both sides to go to extremes, to become as it were pure cultures of one or the other aspect respectively of this ambivalent attitude. The basis of such reactions is often for the time being quite unconscious, for instance takes place on the basis of resonance (see above). Such polarization may also determine the relationship between two members or more in a group for a considerable time. A young woman represented for an older woman all the latter's impulsive desires and instincts which she, the older woman, then fought against in the younger member.

THEORY

Much that is basic for the theoretical framework of group analysis has been stated in other sections, especially under the headings of Orientation, Principles and Dynamics. About principal assumptions see also 5 and 12. The essential unity of group—and individual psychodynamics is maintained (13) but psychological processes are not seen from the isolated individual's point of view.

Cultural inheritance is seen as having superseded biological inheritance in the development of the human species (11). In connection with this the concept of 'transmission' (12) is significant. There is a confluence of meanings as regards psychological phenomena, as these can be described in regard to the individual, the group in operation and the wider field, e.g. hospital and eventually the community as a whole (16).

The concept of a *network* together with that of communication is a central one (6, 7). It is assumed that the individual patient and even the nature of his disturbance is only a symptom of conflicts and tensions within his group (13). Psychopathological and psychotherapeutic processes arise from various configurations within the total dynamic field of this group (9, 15). The patient is in a sense a scapegoat, the bearer of a conflict within his network (11). There is correspondingly an almost automatic resistance on the part of the 'relatives' against change in the neurotic member undergoing treatment. This network of interrelated transpersonal processes is the true framework or unit of observation.

Group psychotherapy is an attempt to treat the total network of disturbance either at the point of origin in the root–(5) or primary group, or, through placing the disturbed individual under conditions of transference, in a group of strangers or proxy group. It is important to be clear about three concepts and their relation to each other: that of network, of matrix and of transference.

The interactional matrix in the therapeutic group is an example of a network. The individual participates in its formation and creation and at the same time re-establishes the conditions of his own primary network as experienced. This is the group equivalent of transference neurosis as observed most clearly in the psycho-analytical situation.

The Matrix is the hypothetical web of communication and relationship in a given group. It is the common shared ground which ultimately determines the meaning and significance of all events and upon which all communications and interpretations, verbal and non-verbal, rest. This concept links with that of communication (9).

Communication is a process of central importance for all psychotherapy (7). It opens the way for the operation of all other therapeutic agencies. It can be understood as a group process (20). There are different levels of communication, operating at the same time, but not equally charged (cathexed) (4). Four levels have been distinguished (9). In the therapeutic situation all phenomena are considered as communication. The therapeutic process—'from symptom to conflict'—can be understood in terms of a growing capacity for communication. Group-analytic work is most rewarding in connection with a study of *therapeutic* processes upon which a theory of psychotherapy can be constructed. It highlights on-going change rather than genetic elucidation. Individuals repeat old behaviour in the group, especially—by way of compulsion—unfinished, unresolved, internalized conflicts. These become currently manifest in the group and interfere with adequate current behaviour, in response to the existing situation. Thus the patient, in current interaction, works at his basic pathogenic conflicts. His behaviour becomes modified and open for revision by new experiences as a result of new responses and reactions and new insight, through analysis. We have spoken of 'ego training in action', of the activation of analytic and integrative processes, of corrective experiences in relation to others, to authority, the modification of ego and superego in this connection.

'*T*' *Situation*

All psychotherapy as a procedure is a concentrated revision in a specially designed and controlled situation. I have proposed to call a situation thus defined a 'T' situation. This stands for 'therapeutic', i.e. psychotherapeutic. The symbol 'T' is deliberately reminiscent of 'transference-situation', because it includes the characteristics of such a situation, yet contains other parameters, which have nothing to do with transference. This is also true for the individual psycho-analytical situation. Ideally a T-situation contains all the elements which are necessary for a radical and so far as possible, lasting change to occur in the patient, but not more than these. In characterizing it we confine ourselves to those features which make change possible, which do *not* prevail in ordinary life.

The influence of one person upon the other, the emphatic understanding by a good friend, good advice, sharing, indeed love, encouragement and success, persuasion, suggestion and auto-suggestion and so forth, as they occur in life, are powerful agencies indeed. All this can happen inside psychotherapy, but becomes an ingredient of a T-situation only when it is deliberately used for distinct purposes. Transference occurs throughout life, but what does not occur, is the use the psycho-analyst makes of it. In respect to transference we may do well to differentiate between the classical repetition of infantile, incestuous fixations and the transference in the wide sense and symbolize them as TR and tr respectively. The same is true for counter-transference (CTR and ctr respectively). If we put into the centre the way in which behaviour on the part of the patient is received, accepted and responded to by the therapist, we can say that the ga situation (in the same way as the psycho-analytic situation) is a transference situation. (T = tr.) This is a consequence of the therapist's analytic attitude, however, as for instance experienced in his refraining from judgment and valuation, personal reactions, extra therapeutic contact, physical contact, advice, his encouragement of 'abstinence', the nature of his interpretations, the whole theory of his approach, etc.

The T-situation contains quite other essential elements,

beyond the behaviour of the therapist. These concern amongst other things the way in which material is produced (e.g. verbal or active or pictorial representation) in which the relationship is treated, in short the features treated in this book under the headings of 'setting' and of 'situation', including conditions of treatment, time factors, payment, etc. We need not go into further detail on this occasion. The two main models of such a T-situation in which we are interested, viz. the psa and the ga situation, have been sufficiently described in their similarities and differences (7, 10, GPS).

One particular concept will in the following be described in some more detail, both for its intrinsic interest and as an example for the need to define the T-situation well. It is that of the 'boundary'.

Boundary (of T-situation)

Each psychotherapeutic or T-situation is determined by its parameters. These can be differently defined according to different conditions. Amongst these different conditions is of course the disturbance of the patient. What is important is the consistency. Now these parameters include the frontiers or boundary of the T-situation and vice versa these boundaries of the T-situation influence the parameters. The question is simply one of what is in and what is out of the therapeutic situation. Let us illustrate this in a simple example.

Supposing a patient misses a session; the therapist can either sit and wait until he hears from the patient or he may for instance write to him. Now as soon as he writes to him he has in certain respects enlarged the treatment situation to include correspondence, i.e. to admit communication outside the treatment room. He may merely write administratively, for instance: 'I notice that you have not attended for the last three sessions. Would you kindly let me know when you intend to come again or whether I should not count on your wishing to participate further in this treatment.' Or he may give an interpretation. For instance 'I notice that you stayed away from the group since you had a disagreement with Mrs X. and it appeared to me that this may well have touched on your own conflicts with your wife or your mother respectively. I think it would be better for you, in any case, to come and attend and put all your thoughts and feelings before the group.' Let us now assume for argument's sake that this particular patient replies in the sense that he does not think that his non-attendance had anything to do with what happened in the group. He had, in fact, to make a quick decision to change his work and had therefore to move to Birmingham. The therapist might well answer back, 'Thank you for letting me know and I wish you all good luck in Birmingham.' He has now refused to extend the therapeutic situation any further.

These are of course simple examples, merely to indicate in *one* direction what is meant by the boundary of the T-situation. It is by the way a good principle to follow to consider everything which comes into the session by whatever means as part of the therapeutic situation, unless it definitely breaks with the situation, and still treat it as 'in'. This means also that anything which does not come to the notice of the therapist within the therapeutic situation is 'out'. The only exceptions here are striking omissions which the therapist may well have to bring actively within the situation. As pointed out repeatedly in this book such incidents as happen on the boundaries, on the frontiers of the therapeutic situation appear always to be of particular significance and should be closely watched. It is also important that they are taken up with care and consistency as regards possible extensions of the therapeutic situation itself. Such extensions should not be undertaken without cogent reasons.

ORIENTATION AND PRINCIPLES

Group-analytic observations and concepts are of course relevant in any group. The particular contribution we have to make stems from the therapeutic nature of our work. This has a particular significance in so far as suffering and pain open the channels to regions of human feeling and motivation which are otherwise concealed. At the same time they activate people to submit to an analytic procedure. As we have a situation and method of approach to them these unconscious processes can be observed and studied. It does seem to hold good, that without such special motivation there is no access to these layers of mental functioning.

There are three areas particularly suited for a group-analytic approach (5). The first is the 'root group', primary group, to which any individual belongs. Originally it is the family or its equivalent, but later this network is not confined to the family. Our own work in this area has not been systematically published up to the present but some examples have been given. Recently more attention is being paid to this area often under the name of 'family therapy'. About my concept of network see *Theory*.

The second is the study of disturbances arising in selected situations in *vivo*. This has been used extensively by myself at Northfield Neurosis Centre (Introduction to Part V, 14) and some examples have been given, illustrating the principles. A common character of both these groups under discussion is that the analytic observation and treatment follow the patient into the actually operating situation (the 'operative group').

The third is the group analytic group itself, which is in the centre of this whole volume.

In all these the 'group as a whole' is considered the unit of observation (see *Dynamics* and 1, 3, 8, 10). Of special significance here are the Figure-Ground configurations in the group (7, 12) and the idea of location connected with this (3).

Here a word about the concept of 'group-situation'. Any group has well-defined features such as size, characteristics of membership, conditions of meeting, avowed purpose (see 'Occupation' (5)), degree and nature of organization, preferred boundaries, etc., which in their totality constitute the *group situation*.

The group situation is a social situation, and the medium of contact lies in the interaction of its members; its dynamics operate within the common matrix of this interpersonal situation. This network of multipersonal relationships, of great complexity, must not be identified with the transference situation which forms its counterpart in the psycho-analytic situation.

The *group-analytic situation* is a well defined example of such a group situation. All processes and interactions are observed with reference to this and its boundaries. The multipersonal but intrapsychic mental *matrix* forms the background of orientation for all our interventions and operations. The group analytic situation is further characterized by its analytic character and other aspects of a T-situation (see 12 and Theory). Therapeutic group analysis is the foundation of a truly *social psychopathology and psychiatry* (7).

Neurosis is not a disease, but arises from problems which concern everybody. All illness is seen as interpersonal and as involving the community. The therapeutic analytic group is a token community with access to the social, interpersonal unconscious. The necessary *comparative* basis of observation is made possible in this type of group. There is a differential reaction to the same stimulus (8). Light is thrown on the reasons for the defensive attitude against a truly psychotherapeutic, uncovering approach on the part of the community of 'well adjusted' normal citizens. Group analysis in operation should also prove the basis of a 'social' shareable psychotherapeutic science in that it will create a common platform above the schisms of individual schools and pave the way for scientific validation of concepts and methods.

Comparative Psychopathology

All psychopathology is essentially comparative. In the group we can study the interactional processes in between persons as well as their differential reactions to the same current material. The group is therefore an ideal setting for a comparative psychopathology in operation, in actual living reality. Moreover these differential reactions are in a dynamic state, that is to say they change, and we can therefore study when, why and how they change. Group observation can demonstrate that, how and why a disturbance of personality, e.g. a schizophrenic one, does or does not make the individual too sick for him to be tolerated even by the therapeutic group, or vice-versa for him to be able to tolerate this group, even though its culture is modified in his favour. This point is of particular importance both for the practice and clinic of group psychotherapy as well as for its theory.

In my *Introduction to Group-Analytic Psychotherapy* (Heinemann, 1948, p. 29) I said that 'the deepest reason why our patients can reinforce their normal reactions and correct their neurotic reactions in such a therapeutic group is that *collectively they constitute the very norm from which, individually, they deviate.*' It is necessary to take this statement into the present context although I have not repeated it in the present book, This statement has often been quoted, mostly in agreement, occasionally in disagreement. In either case I was sometimes under the impression that it had not been fully understood, probably because it had not been really further explained in my introductory book which I thought furnished itself a background to this statement. I still maintain after another fifteen years of experience and thinking this statement to be correct but it is perhaps not out of place to say here a few words in its defence. What our patients—the psychoneurotic, the psychosomatic, the psychotic, the delinquent or the anti-social psychopath, the eternal sufferer from bad luck, the accident prone—what all these, who are potentially our patients, have in common can broadly be defined thus: they have not outlived their childhood neurosis. They are too much bound up with oedipal or pre-oedipal psycho-sexual fixations and conflagrations. They cannot cope with reality, or their fellow beings, or their fellow beings cannot cope with them. They rebel against authority and are in infantile dependence upon such authority, etc. The question therefore arises: if they all deviate in this way from what is in any given community considered healthy or normal, how can they possibly be of use to each other therapeutically and how can it possibly be stated that the therapeutic criterion of what is normal could be largely derived from their own interaction? They would all wish to live in totally different worlds; alternatively they would have to share a deviant frame of reference, deviant standards of what is good or bad, desirable or undesirable, what is compatible with human social life or incompatible with it, and would have to agree on such a deviant orientation. Observation instead seemed to show that these deviants agree collectively in between them upon the very same basic values as are held by their own community. Perhaps this cannot be different in any given community. Whether individuals fight for or against certain tendencies, whether they are consciously opposed to certain judgments or not and however much their responses and reactions are manifestly different from each other and those of their culture, they nevertheless make these very parameters, these selfsame basic rules of co-existence their ultimate judge. This is roughly what is meant by the statement under discussion.

If this was correct it would be of the utmost interest to study deviant groups such as delinquents, criminals or psychopaths in general in pure culture and see whether they, as a group or individually, do really essentially deviate from others or not. In the latter case their deviation is only a quarrel with these values which, however, they have recognized, indeed overstress. In fact from a purely clinical point of view this differential diagnostic criterion might be more relevant than the statistic diagnostic label attached to the individual.

APPENDICES

APPENDIX A

SOME STATISTICAL DATA

In the following some statistical data will be given in so far as these are available.

It is realized that these data are quite insufficient for any conclusions to be reached. Comparison with other methods is not intended, nor any claims made for the success of group-analytic treatment. Apart from the two groups from private practice the work reported here was done by beginners in this method, mostly their very first groups conducted under supervision.

The objective assessment of change is a problem of great complexity which is as yet unsolved in psychiatry. We have given much thought to this and have been struck by the great divergence of ideas as to what would be considered improvement in the minds of either general practitioners or psychiatrists, explicitly, and even more so, implicitly. The cases referred to us were mostly such as had failed to recover spontaneously even after several years, and many had undergone various forms of psychiatric treatment including a shorter or longer period of 'psychotherapy'. From the point of obtaining favourable statistical results I estimate that 40 per cent would have to be rejected, whereas in fact we accepted for treatment 90–95 per cent of cases referred. (I might mention that some visiting colleagues who were used to the assessment of results in the usual medical way found our standards of assessment unduly meticulous.) Many patients would no doubt have benefited from longer treatment if it had been possible. Under existing conditions further extension of treatment had to be weighed up against change to another physician, quite apart from the pressure of new referrals.

Nevertheless, there is no gainsaying the importance of more adequate statistical data to be made available in the future and it is hoped that other psychiatrists working with this or similar methods will help by collecting and publishing data of this kind.

In spite of its inadequacy the material presented here is held to be of some interest. I remain impressed clinically with the potential efficacy of this method. From my own experience in private practice I am bound to say that very considerable changes do occur in a high proportion of patients and, from all accounts, on a valid and lasting basis. I am in a good position to compare my own results, including those of the most intensive individual treatment, as well as with those of other very experienced colleagues. The usefulness of this form of treatment is, for the time being, sufficiently proved by its world-wide spread.

1. SOME DATA FROM THE OUT-PATIENT DEPARTMENT AT THE MAUDSLEY HOSPITAL

Records are available of twenty-six groups conducted by registrars attached to the unit between 1951 and 1958. Of these, ten groups were 'open', sixteen 'closed' or 'slow-open'.

Fifteen groups were of mixed sex, six all-male and five all-female. (More recently all groups treated at the unit have been of mixed sex.)

Duration of groups

Under 25 sessions:	4 groups
25–50 sessions:	13 groups
51–100 sessions:	7 groups
Over 100 sessions:	2 groups
Total:	26 groups

Turnover of membership

No. of patients passing through group	No. of groups
6– 9	14 (2)*
10–13	9 (5)
14–17	1 (1)
18–20	1 (1)

* The figures in brackets are for 'open' groups; these are included in the first figure.

I am indebted to Dr L. I. M. Maclay for the following figures which she compiled from the records of three groups terminated in 1960.

Frequency of meeting—Once weekly

Average length of life of the groups—61 weeks

Number of patients treated in the three groups—24

Number who dropped out completely during period the group existed—10

Number who attended for two thirds or more of possible sessions—13

TABLE ESTIMATING OUTCOME AGAINST ATTENDANCE

Outcome	Steady Attendance	Infrequent Attendance	Ceased to Attend
Much Improved	3	1	
Improved	9		3
Not Improved	1		7

TABLE SHOWING DIAGNOSIS AGAINST OUTCOME

Diagnosis	Much Improved	Improved	Not Improved
Personality Disorder	2	5	3
Phobic		3	1
Anxiety State	2	1	
Depression		1	2
Hysterical Personality			2
Obsessional		1	
Essential Tremor		1	

Follow-Up Studies

It has not so far been possible to do any systematic follow-up studies. A recent attempt by questionnaire was on a very small scale, but it might be of interest to give some details of the answers received.

A simple questionnaire was sent to twenty patients who had been discharged from the Hospital after completing a course of group treatment. Eight patients completed the questionnaire fairly promptly, another three did so on receiving a second letter. The rest failed to reply.

Of those who replied eight stated that they felt better now than when they first came to the Hospital; one 'slightly better'; one reported no improvement and one (who had discharged herself after two sessions) reported improvement not attributed to the treatment.

Some typical replies on how the group treatment had helped the patients were as follows:

'Being made to face up to my problems helped, I think.'

'Because I could tell somebody I could really trust about my particular problem.'

'. . . to be more honest with myself . . . and more tolerant. . . . Not looking for others to sort out my troubles so much as I did. . . .'

2. SOME DATA FROM GROUPS IN PRIVATE PRACTICE

This report concerns only two groups, one of which has been going on for nearly ten years, the other for over three. The character of these groups is 'slow-open', that is to say that they are expected to have a very slow change in membership. The following may give some idea of this. (Both groups meet weekly for one and a half hours.)

Group A

Group A had been going on for nine years and four months at the time of review (399 sessions). During this time a total of thirty members passed through, fourteen men and sixteen women. Of these four men and four women were still in the group at the time of writing.

Of the twenty-two who have left the group the length of stay varied from five sessions (weeks) to 287 sessions. The average stay was eighty-five sessions or a little under two years allowing for holidays.

Sessions attended (missed sessions not included)

No. of sessions	1–5	6–20	21–50	51–100	101–150	151–200	over 200	Total
No. of members	1	5	4	7	1	2	2	22

Group B

At the time of reporting this group had met 139 times during a period of three years and three months. Fourteen members had belonged to it of whom eight were still continuing. The variation in stay (including those continuing) was from four sessions to 139 sessions. Of the six who have left the group the average number of sessions attended was 47.5.

Sessions attended (missed sessions not included)

No. of sessions	1–5	6–20	21–50	51–100	Total
No. of members	1	1	2	2	6

APPENDIX B

SOME USEFUL FORMS

A few forms which have proved useful in connection with the practice of group-analytic psychotherapy are reproduced and briefly explained here. Though not intended as a system, a combination of these forms will give much relevant information about on-going or terminated cases.

1. *Dynamic Assessment Card for Psychotherapy* (Figs. 1*a* and 1*b*)

This card has been found useful for all patients, whether individual or group psychotherapy is recommended.

Patients found suitable for individual psychotherapy would as a rule be also suitable for group treatment while some patients will be found suitable for group treatment whom one would not select for individual psychotherapy. In selecting patients for one or the other it is therefore rather a question of whether any particular reason would *exclude* group psychotherapy. If the selection is in addition for an analytic type of treatment the criteria would be almost identical for either group or individual psychotherapy apart from mere practical considerations. These are broad statements and the finer criteria of selection are not under consideration here.

Without going into more detail it will be evident from the headings what makes this assessment 'dynamic'. Special attention is given to the formulation of 'objectives of treatment', the aim being to set a limited objective which it will be possible to achieve in the given circumstances.

The section 'Outcome of Treatment' on the back of the card (see 1*b*) will, of course, be completed when psychotherapy has been concluded. It will be seen that any change claimed should be accounted for in strict relation to the initial 'problem' as stated and analysed in terms of processes and dynamics in the treatment situation itself and outside of it.

2. *Matching Patients for a Group* (Fig. 2)

The selection of patients who are suitable for group psychotherapy having been made the next step will be the matching of patients for any one group. It has been found that a pool of twelve to fifteen potential group members is needed to put together a group of eight.

TMKF – T

NAME	No.	SEX	AGE	PREVIOUS PSYCHIATRIC TREATMENT	AVAILABILITY FOR TREATMENT

SIGNIFICANT FEATURES:—	SOCIAL	EDUCATIONAL	MARITAL	OCCUPATIONAL

REFERRED ON.................................BY.................................
INTERVIEW ON.................................BY.................................
FURTHER ACTION.................................

ASSESSMENT

PROBLEM — (a) Patient's manifestations—

(b) Our formulation—

DIAGNOSIS

FACTORS RELEVANT TO TREATMENT

Patient's anticipations and attitude:

Therapeutic contact—   Intelligence—

Insight—   Verbal facility—

Special features—

CONSULTANT'S RECOMMENDATIONS

SCOPE OF TREATMENT

Individual	Group		Intensity and Duration
	Open Closed	Male Female Mixed	

OBJECTIVES OF TREATMENT

OTHER RECOMMENDATIONS

ATTENDANCE	THERAPIST
Sessions per week—	Dr..................................from..................to..................
Sessions of individual treatment—	Dr..................................from..................to..................
Sessions of group treatment—	Dr..................................from..................to..................
Weeks of treatment—	Disposal,

OUTCOME OF TREATMENT

Overall assessment—   Recovered   Much Improved   Improved   Unchanged   Worse
In terms of problems (a) and (b)—

In terms of process and dynamics—

FURTHER ACTION

COMMENTS

Edebret 1786

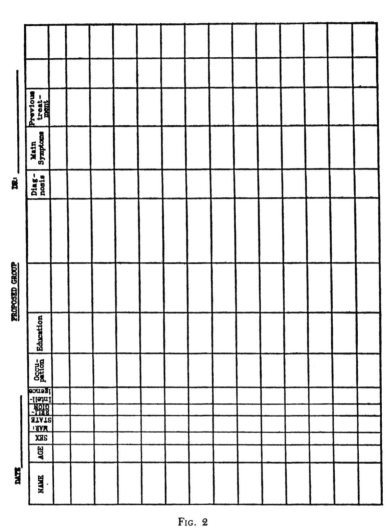

F ɪ ɢ. 2

A simple form on which the criteria for matching are set out will be found very helpful.

In a mixed group one would obviously try to have the sexes equally represented. The age span, range of educational background and standards of intelligence must be carefully considered. It is important to avoid group members who are isolated in any one of these criteria (e.g. to avoid one married member in a group of single persons, or one much younger or older than the rest). If some criteria are more carefully matched, others may be less strictly selected (e.g. a group of people of high intelligence between the ages of 20 and 30 could vary more widely in their educational background). Factors such as previous psychotherapy and main presenting symptoms should be included on such a matching chart. Any special factors can be added as required.

3. *Record of Sessions* (Fig. 3)

A system of recording attendances has proved to be useful in conveying in graphical form a great deal of essential information. It is easy to use and demands little time. The members' attendance is noted after each session. Horizontally the form records each individual patients' attendance; vertically it gives a picture of the composition of the group at any time. At the head of the form, under 'Type of Group', it is useful to record details regarding such points as sex, age span and other criteria of selection; diagnostic criteria; whether 'open', 'closed', or 'slow-open'; whether a time limit is set; frequency and duration of sessions; particular therapeutic aims. Brief notes about each patient are usefully entered on the back of the form.

Thirty weeks can be entered on one sheet. If desired, continuation sheets can be joined on.

Symbols: oblique stroke (/) signifies presence, a dash (–) signifies absence by agreement, a nought (0) unexpected absence; latecoming is noted by the symbol ∠. These symbols should be entered after each session so that the chart is always up to date and gives a complete record (it is also very difficult to reconstruct accurately from memory, once a few weeks have elapsed). The symbols have deliberately been kept to a few which have been found of real value, so as not to confuse the structure of the record. For special purposes special symbols can of course be added. The use of coloured inks also has obvious possibilities.

The sequence of patients' names is retained on continuation sheets so that seniority in the group can always be seen at a glance.

If this form of notation or some development of it should become accepted as a standard practice amongst group psychotherapists it should prove most useful for purposes of research and statistical investigations.

RECORD OF GROUP-ANALYTIC SESSIONS

No:

Place and Time of Meeting:

Type of Group:

Session No.:

Year: Day:

                        Month:

Therapist:

Attendance Quotient: No. Attended:

                        Total No.:

Patients' Names   (see back of form for details):

Symbols:

/ Present.   L Late.

− Absent by agreement.   O Absent unexpectedly.

REMARKS

Copyright by the Group-Analytic Society (London)

FIG. 3

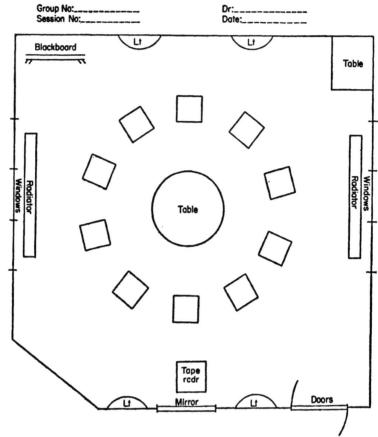

Positions occupied by therapeutic group

Group No:_____   Dr:_____
Session No:_____   Date:_____

Blackboard

Lt   Lt

Table

Windows Radiator   Radiator Windows

Table

Table

Tape
rcdr

Lt   Mirror   Lt   Doors

For empty chairs leave squares blank. For missing chairs cross out squares.
Re-draw squares for changes in position of chairs etc.

Remarks:

FIG. 4

See: S. H. Foulkes, 'Recording Group-Analytic Sessions: A Chart of Attendances and other Significant Data'. Published for the Group-Analytic Society (London) 1953.

4. *Positional Chart* (Fig. 4)
It is useful to have a simple form on which the seating positions of members are noted after each session. Interesting dynamic observations can be made on the basis of such a form.

The diagram is a drawing of the actual group room at the Maudsley Hospital. Only the chairs and table of course are standard equipment.

LIST OF PUBLICATIONS by S. H. FOULKES

BOOKS AND PAMPHLETS

1. *Psycho-Analysis and Crime.* English Studies in Criminal Science (Dept. of Criminal Science, Faculty of Law, Univ. of Cambridge). Preface by Prof. C. Burt. Publ. Canadian Bar Assoc. Toronto, 1944.
2. *Introduction to Group-Analytic Psychotherapy.* Studies in the Social Integration of Individuals and Groups. Wm. Heinemann Medical Books, 1948.
3. *Recording Group-Analytic Sessions.* A Chart of Attendances and other Significant Data. The Group-Analytic Society, London, 1953.
4. *Group Psychotherapy.* The Psycho-Analytic Approach. (Jointly with E. J. Anthony.) Pelican Psychology Series. Penguin Books, 1957.

PAPERS

5. 'Ueber die determinierende Kraft des Namens bei einem Schizophrenen.' *Intern. Zeitschr. f. Psychoanalyse*, 16, 495–501, 1930.
6. 'Zum Stand der heutigen Biologie.' Dargestellt an Kurt Goldstein: *Der Aufbau des Organismus.* Imago, 22, 210–41, 1936.
7. 'On Introjection.' *Int. J. Psycho-Anal.*, 18, 269–93, 1937.
7a. '*Ueber Introjection.*' Imago, 23, 420–46, 1937.
8. 'Some Remarks on a Chapter of Helen Keller's Book: The World I Live In.' *Psycho-Anal. Review*, 28, 512–19, 1941.
9. 'The Idea of a Change of Sex in Women.' *Int. J. Psycho-Anal.*, 24, 53–56, 1943.
10. 'Group Analysis. Studies in the Treatment of Groups on Psycho-Analytical Lines.' (Jointly with E. Lewis.) *B.J. Med. Psychol.*, 20, 175–84, 1944. (See Chapter 1.)
11. A Memorandum on Group Psychotherapy. AMD 11 B.M. 33/02/2, July 1945 (for Army use). (See Chapter 15.)
12. 'Group Analysis in a Military Neurosis Centre.' *Lancet*, March 2, 1946, pp. 303–10.
13. 'On Group Analysis'. *Int. J. Psycho-Anal.*, 27, 46–51, 1946. (See Chapter 14.)
14. 'Principles and Practice of Group Therapy.' *Bull. Menninger Clinic*, 10, 85–89, May 1946. (See Chapter 15.)
15. 'Crime Begins and Ends within the Community: It's You and Me.' *Horizon*, 14, 260–72, October 1946.
16. 'Group Therapy. A short survey and orientation, with particular reference to group analysis.' *B.J. Med. Psychol.*, 23, 199–205, 1950. (See Chapter 3.)

17. 'Remarks on Group Analytic Psychotherapy.' *Group Psychotherapy*, 4, 56–59, 1951.
18. 'Concerning Leadership in Group-Analytic Psychotherapy.' *Int. J. of Group Psychotherapy*, 1, 319–29, 1951. (See Chapter 4.)
19. 'Contribution to a Symposium on Group Therapy.' *B.J. Med. Psychol.*, 25, 229–34, 1952.
20. 'Some Similarities and Differences between Psycho-Analytic Principles and Group-Analytic Principles.' *B.J. Med. Psychol.*, 25, 229–34, 1952. (See Chapter 7.)
21. 'Group-Analytic Observation as Indicator for Psycho-Analytic Treatment.' *Int. J. Psycho-Anal.*, 35, 263–66, 1954. (See Chapter 8.)
22. 'Group-Analytic Psychotherapy. A short account.' *Acta Psychother.*, 3, 313–19, 1955.
23. 'Group-Analytic Dynamics with Special Reference to Psychoanalytic Concepts.' *Int. J. Group Psychotherapy*, 7, 40–52, 1957. (See Chapter 9.)
24. 'Comments on "Progress in Psychotherapy, 1956".' *Group Psychotherapy*, 10, 1957.
25. 'Comments on Fairbairn's Paper.' *B.J. Philos. Science*, 7, 324–29, 1957.
26. 'Out-Patient Psychotherapy. A Contribution Towards a New Approach.' (Jointly with A. Parkin.) *Int. J. Soc. Psychiatry*, 33, 44–48, 1957. (See Chapters 18 and 19.)
27. 'Discussion of Dr L. S. Kubie's paper: Some Theoretical Concepts underlying the Relationship between Individual and Group Psychotherapies.' *Int. J. Group Psychotherapy*, 8, 20–25, 1958.
28. 'Psycho-Analysis, Group Psychotherapy, Group Analysis.' *Acta Psychotherap.* 7, 119–31, 1959. (See Chapter 10.)
29. 'The Application of Group Concepts to the Treatment of the Individual in the Group.' In: *Topical Problems of Psychotherapy*, Vol. 2. Karger (Basle and New York), 1960. (See Chapter 12.)
30. 'Some Observations on Teaching Psychotherapy'. In: *Topical Problems of Psychotherapy*, Vol. 3. Karger (Basle and New York), 1960.
30a. 'Algunas Observaciones Sobre la Enseñanza de Psicoterapia.' *Revista de Psiquiaria y Psicologia Medica*, Vol. 4, No. 5, 880–82, 1960.
31. 'Theoretische und Praktische Grundlagen der Analytischen Gruppenpsychotherapie.' *Zeitschrift für Psychotherapie und Medizinische Psychologie*, 10, 229–37, 1960.
32. 'Group Processes and the Individual in the Therapeutic Group.' *Brit. J. Med. Psychol.*, 34, 23–31, 1961. (See Chapter 13.)
33. 'Psychotherapy 1961.' *Brit. J. Med. Psychol.*, 34, 91–102, 1961. (See Chapter 11.)

BIBLIOGRAPHY

ABERCROMBIE, M. L. J. *The Anatomy of Judgment*. London: Hutchinson, 1960.

ABERCROMBIE, M. L. J. 'Theory of Free Group Discussion.' *Health Education Journal*, 3, 1953.

ACKERMAN, N. W. 'Dynamic Patterns in Group Therapy.' *Psychiatry*, 7, 129, 1944.

ACKERMAN, N. W. *Some Theoretical Aspects of Group Psychotherapy*. Group Psychotherapy (A Symposium). New York: Beacon House, 1945.

ADLER, A. *The Practice and Theory of Individual Psychology*. London: Kegan Paul, 1951.

ANTHONY, E. J. 'Age and Syndrome in Group Psychotherapy.' *Journal of the Long Island Consultation Center*, Vol. 1, No. 2, May 1960.

BIERER, JOSHUA. 'The Therapeutic Community Hostel.' *International Journal of Social Psychiatry*, 7, 5–9, 1960/1.
'Psychotherapy in Mental Hospital Practice.' *Journal of Mental Science*, September 1940.
'A Self-Governed Patients' Social Club in a Public Mental Hospital.' *Journal of Mental Science*, July 1941.

BION, W. R. *Experiences in Groups and other Papers*. London: Tavistock Publications, 1961.

BION, W. R. and RICKMAN, J. 'Intra-group Tensions in Therapy.' *Lancet*, p. 678, 1943.

BOENHEIM, CURT. *The Role of Group Psychotherapy in a Mental Hospital: Goals and Problems, Training*. Columbus State Hospital, 1961.

BRIDGER, H. 'The Northfield Experiment', *Bulletin of the Menninger Clinic*, 10, May 1946.

BRODY, SYLVIA. *Patterns of Mothering*. New York: International University Press, 1956.

BURROW, T. *The Social Basis of Consciousness*. New York: Harcourt Brace, 1927.

BURROW, T. *The Biology of Human Conflict*. New York: Macmillan, 1937.

BURROW, T. *Neurosis of Man*. London: Routledge and Kegan Paul, 1949. (See also LAWRENCE and SYZ.)

CARBALLO, J. R. 'Constitution, Transference and Co-existence.' *Acta Psychotherapeutica*, 8, 400, 1960.

CLARK, D. H. 'Administrative Therapy'. *Lancet*, April 19, 1958.

CORSINI, RAYMOND J. *Methods of Group Psychotherapy.* New York: McGraw Hill, 1957.

DEUTSCH, H. 'Psychoanalytic Therapy in the Light of Follow-up' *Journal of the American Psychoanalytical Association,* 7, 445, 1959.

ELIAS, N. *Uber den Prozess der Zivilisation,* Vol. I. Prague: Academia Verlag, 1937: Vol. II. Basel: Verlag Haus zum Falken, 1939.

ERIKSON, ERIC H. *Childhood and Society.* London: Imago, 1951.

FOULKES, S. H. *Introduction to Group-Analytic Psychotherapy.* London: Heinemann, 1948.

FOULKES, S. H. and ANTHONY, E. J. *Group Psychotherapy.* London: Penguin Books Ltd., 1957.

FRANK, JEROME D. *Persuasion and Healing.* London: Hutchinson, 1960.

FREUD, S. *Group Psychology and the Analysis of the Ego.* London: Hogarth Press, 1947.

FREUD, S. *Inhibition, Symptom and Anxiety,* Standard Edition, Vol. 20. London: Hogarth Press, 1959.

New Introductory Lectures, Standard Edition, Vol. 22. London: Hogarth Press.

Civilization and its Discontents. London: Hogarth Press, 1930.

Analysis Terminable and Interminable, Collected Papers, Vol. 4, 316. London: Hogarth Press, 1950.

FRIEDMAN, J. and GASSEL, S. 'Orestes.' *Psychoanalytic Quarterly,* 20, 423–33, 1951.

'The Chorus in Sophocles' Oedipus Tyrannus.' *Psychoanalytic Quarterly,* 19, 213, 1950.

FROMM, ERICH. *The Forgotten Language.* New York: Rinehart, 1951.

GALT, W. *Phyloanalysis.* London: Kegan Paul, 1933.

GANZARIN, R. *et al.* 'Group Psychotherapy in the Psychiatric Training of Medical Students.' *International Journal of Group Psychotherapy,* 8, 1958.

GLOVER, EDWARD. *The Technique of Psycho-Analysis.* London: Baillière, Tindall & Cox, 1955.

GOLDSTEIN, KURT. *The Organism: A Holistic Approach to Biology derived from Pathological Data in Man.* New York: American Book Co., 1939.

GROTJAHN, M. *Psycho-Analysis and the Family Neurosis,* New York: Norton, 1960.

JENNINGS, HELEN H. *Leadership and Isolation.* New York: Longmans Green, 1950.

JONES, MAXWELL. *Social Psychiatry.* London: Tavistock Publications, 1952.

KADIS, ASYA L., KRASNER, JACK D., WINICK, CHARLES and FOULKES, S. H. *A Practicum of Group Psychotherapy.* New York: Hoeber Medical Division. Harper & Row, 1963.

KELNAR, J. and SUTHERLAND, J. D. 'Some Current Developments in Psychotherapy in Great Britain.' *Progress in Psychotherapy*, 1956, Ed. F. Fromm-Reichmann and J. L. Moreno. New York: Grune & Stratton, 1956.

KLAPMAN, J. W. *Group Psychotherapy.* London: Heinemann, 1946.

KLEIN, MELANIE. *Contributions to Psycho-analysis 1921–1945.* London: Hogarth Press, 1948.

LAWRENCE, D. H. 'A New Theory of Neurosis' (Review of T. Burrow's 'The Social Basis of Consciousness'). *The Bookman*, 66, 314, New York: 1927.

LIDDELL, H. S. and BLAUVELT, H. See BRODY, SYLVIA.

MACKWOOD, JOHN C. 'The Psychological Treatment of Offenders in Prison.' *British Journal of Psychology*, 40, 5–22, 1949.

MADDISON, D. C. 'Blue Print for a Model Psychiatric Hospital.' *The Medical Journal of Australia*, January 1960.

MADDISON, D. C. 'The Integrated Therapy of Family Members: a case report.' *Journal of Group Psychotherapy*, Vol. 9, 33–48, 1961.

MAGARSHAK, DAVID. *Chekov the Dramatist.* London: John Lehmann, 1952.

MAIN, T. F. 'The Ailment.' *British Journal of Medical Psychology*, 30, 129, 1957.

MAIN, T. F. 'The Hospital as a Therapeutic Institution.' *Bulletin of the Menninger Clinic*, Vol. 10, No. 3, 1946.

MARSH, L. C. *Group Psychotherapy.* London: Heinemann, 1946. (see also KLAPMAN).

MASSERMAN, J. H. *Principles of Dynamic Psychiatry.* New York: Saunders, 1946.

MORENO, J. L. *Who Shall Survive?* New York: Beacon House, 1953.

PECK, H. B. 'Group Therapy as Social Prophylaxis.' *American Journal of Orthopsychiatry*, 13, 664, 1943.

PERRY, E. 'The Treatment of Aggressive Juvenile Delinquents in "Family Group Therapy"'. *International Journal of Group Psychotherapy*, 5, 131, 1955.

POWDERMAKER, F.B. and FRANK, J. D. *Group Psychotherapy.* Cambridge, Mass.: Harvard University Press, 1953.

RIESS, B. F. 'The Challenge of Research for Psychotherapy.' *American Journal of Psychotherapy*, 14, 395, 1960.

ROSENBAUM, MAX and BERGER, MILTON (Ed.). *Group Psychotherapy and Group Function.* New York: Basic Books, 1963.

RUESCH, J. 'Nonverbal Language and Therapy.' *Psychiatry*, 18, 323–30, 1955.

RUESCH, J. and BATESON, G. *Communication: The Social Matrix of Psychiatry*. New York: Norton, 1951.

RUESCH, JURGEN and KEES, WELDON. *Nonverbal Communication*. University of California Press, 1956.

SANDLER, J. 'On the Concept of Super-ego.' *Psycho-analytic Study of the Child*, 15, 128, 1960.

SCHILDER, P. *Psychotherapy*. New York: Norton, 1938.

SCHILDER, P. 'Results and Problems of Group Psychotherapy in Severe Neurosis.' *Mental Hygiene*, 23, 97, 1939.

SCHILDER, P. 'The Analysis of Ideologies as a Psychotherapeutic Method Especially in Group Treatment', *American Journal of Psychiatry*, 93, 601, 1936.

SCHILDER, P. *The Image and Appearance of the Human Body*. New York: International Universities Press, 1950.

SCHINDLER, W. 'Family Pattern in Group Formation and Therapy', *International Journal Group Psychotherapy*, 1, 101, 1951.

SLAVSON, S. R. *An Introduction to Group Therapy*. New York: Commonwealth Fund, 1943.

Analytic Group Psychotherapy. New York: Columbia University Press, 1950.

STANTON, A. H. and SCHWARTZ, MORRIS, S. *The Mental Hospital*. London: Tavistock Publications, 1954.

SULLIVAN, H. STACK. *The Interpersonal Theory of Psychiatry*. New York: Norton, 1953.

STROH, G. 'A Therapist's Reactions as Reflected in his Reporting on a Psychotherapeutic Group.' *International Journal of Group Psychotherapy*, 8, 403, 1958.

SYZ, HANS. 'A Summary of the Work of Trigant Burrow.' *International Journal of Social Psychiatry*, 7, 283–91, 1961.

TAYLOR, F. KRAUPL. 'On Some Principles of Group Therapy'. *British Journal of Medical Psychology*, 25, 128–34, 1952.

The Analysis of Therapeutic Groups. London: Oxford University Press, 1961.

TOWER, LUCIA E. 'Countertransference.' *Journal of American Psychoanalytic Association*, 4, 224, 1956.

WENDER, L. 'Dynamics of Group Psychotherapy and its Application', *Journal of Nervous Mental Diseases*, 84, 54, 1936.

WERNICKE, C. *Grundriss der Psychiatrie*. Leipzig: Thieme, 1906.

WOLF, ALEXANDER and SCHWARTZ, EMANUEL K. *Psychoanalysis in Groups*. New York: Grune & Stratton, 1962.

Index